Joseph Maddock's Diary and Letters

# Joseph Maddock's Diary and Letters

## A Sense of the Meeting, Volume 2

Joseph Maddock

EDITED BY
M. D. Hayden

RESOURCE *Publications* • Eugene, Oregon

JOSEPH MADDOCK'S DIARY AND LETTERS
A Sense of the Meeting, Volume 2



Resource Publications
An Imprint of Wipf and Stock Publishers
199 W. 8th Ave., Suite 3
Eugene, OR 97401

www.wipfandstock.com

PAPERBACK ISBN: 979-8-3852-6999-0
HARDCOVER ISBN: 979-8-3852-7000-2
EBOOK ISBN: 979-8-3852-7001-9

VERSION NUMBER 04/15/26

"Quaker Migration to the South" used by permission of the author and editor.

To the past and present Friends of Elk Monthly Meeting in West Elkton, Ohio, who, whenever necessary, have accomplished the extraordinary.

If we look with curiosity at people who do not share our values, they become interesting rather than threatening. As I've grown older I've learnt that the world and the people in it are surprisingly interesting, and that the more you look and listen, the more interesting they become. Cultivating a questioning mind, of which conversation is the chief instrument, enriches our relationship with the world. Having a conversation with someone I may disagree with is, I have come to find, a great, life-embracing pleasure.

—Nick Cave, *The Red Hand Files*, Issue #252 / September 2023

One way to reach towards the essence of a time is to accumulate so much material detail that gradually a shape and texture become perceptible through it.

—Stephen Lovatt, *Enchanted Ground*

# Contents

# Preface

In the Preface to *A Sense of the Meeting: A History of Elk Monthly Meeting 1805–2005*, written and published as part of the Meeting's two hundredth anniversary, I explained my preference for recording history, if possible, in the voices of those who lived it.

> The best way to get "a sense" of someone is to listen to them speak. Bearing this in mind, I sought the voices in Elk Monthly Meeting—then and now—to discern a true sense of the Meeting. . . . In telling the history of West Elkton Friends, if I encountered an original voice that expressed something clearly, I resisted the impulse to summarize, preferring instead to record the voices of those who lived through and recounted events.

One of the original voices I encountered when writing the first edition of *A Sense of the Meeting* was that of Joseph Maddock in his diary, which I included then as an appendix. In subsequent years, I continued researching the history of Friends in Preble County and became more familiar with the people and events Joseph Maddock wrote about. Now I know his diary contains a wealth of information for genealogists tracing ancestors and for Quaker historians tracking the changes and the influencers of change among Friends in the nineteenth century. Joseph Maddock represents a unique moment in U.S. Quaker history: he was a *lifelong Orthodox Unprogrammed* Friend, something most contemporary Friends would find inconceivable.

I also discovered letters he exchanged with his nineteen-year-old daughter, Martha Ann, the year she attended Earlham College, 1864-1865. The diary and letters offer sometimes surprising insights into the lives of ordinary Quakers in the rural Midwest of the nineteenth century.

For instance, illness, disease, and death were ever-present in their conversations and a substantial part of their everyday lives.

Neither Joseph nor Martha Ann would qualify today as well-educated, yet they were more so than most people of the time. Neither were eloquent writers, but both were *earnest* writers. Neither wrote for an audience other than themselves and each other, so most of the time, their writing was unself-conscious (in Martha Ann's case, almost joyously so). When either Joseph or Martha Ann did become *conscious* of writing, we hear a clear shift in their voices, which briefly sound forced as they follow a "formula," or echo a style of writing/speaking used at the time in Quaker tracts or the preaching and supplication of Quaker ministers.

To preserve the voices of Joseph Maddock and his daughter, Martha Ann, two "plain-speaking" Quakers from Elk Monthly Meeting in nineteenth-century Preble County, Ohio, I have edited their writing very lightly. I corrected spelling errors and added punctuation where necessary for clarity, but, despite my years as a composition teacher, I left grammar, sentence construction, and word choice as written by Joseph and Martha Ann.

# Acknowledgments

I wish to acknowledge the work begun by Philip Johnson who served as minister at the Friends meeting in West Elkton, Ohio, from 1952–1960. When I was writing the history of Elk Monthly Meeting for the two-hundredth anniversary in 2005, Phil gave me a Xeroxed copy of some typed pages from Joseph Maddock's diary, explaining that he found them in the papers of A.T. Maddock and had always intended to publish them. It was because of Phil that I knew of the diary and, in 2004, was able to find the original handwritten copy in the files of the Preble County Historical Society. Along with it, I found the photographs of Joseph and Mary and the letters of Martha Ann Maddock.

My gratitude to the Maddock family at large whose ancestors I have come to know via Quaker meeting minutes available on Ancestry.com, Hinshaw's *Encyclopedia of American Quaker Genealogy*, and other genealogical sources, specifically Susan Shaw Tatoun who shared her Roots-Web material on the Wrightsborough Joseph Maddock.

Special thanks to Maddock descendants still living in Preble County, Ohio, who twenty years ago gave me permission to edit and publish Joseph Maddock's diary as an appendix in *A Sense of the Meeting*.

My thanks to Amanda Dowler of the Preble County Room at the District Library in Eaton, Ohio, and to Brittany Corwin, Director of History & Collections for the Preble County Historical Society (who has now digitized Joseph's diary and Matti's letters). And to Walt Mast, whose energy, enthusiasm, and dedication keeps history alive in Preble County.

# Introduction

The Joseph Maddock (1811–1889) who wrote the following diary was the great-grandson of the Joseph Maddock (1720–1794) who was a Quaker leader in North Carolina during the Revolutionary War, and later, a founder of the Quaker settlement of Wrightsborough, Georgia. That Joseph Maddock was—unusually for a Quaker—a controversial figure and the subject of many articles and chapters in books about North Carolina and Georgia history.[1] Perhaps the most well-known person to write about the Wrightsborough Joseph Maddock was President Jimmy Carter, who based his 2004 historical novel, *The Hornet's Nest*, on the experiences of his own ancestors before and during the Revolutionary War. Many characters in the novel are historical figures like Maddock, but the main character is the fictionalized Ethan Pratt, "whose family movements," Carter said, "follow those of my ancestors, from New Jersey and Pennsylvania to North Carolina and then to the Quaker settlement at Wrightsborough."[2] In 1766, Pratt, a non-Quaker, "moves with his wife, Epsey, from Philadelphia to North Carolina and then to Georgia in 1771, in the company of Quakers"[3] led by Joseph Maddock. In the paragraph below, Carter describes Joseph Maddock from Pratt's point of view early in the novel:

> The acknowledged leader of the Friends [in North Carolina] was a man named Joseph Maddock, who operated a gristmill on a creek about five miles from Ethan's home. All families in

1. For instance, see Davis, "Children of Dissent and Revolution." Also, Engstrom, "Joseph Maddock," *Dictionary of North Carolina Biography*.

2. Carter. *The Hornet's Nest*, "Author's Q & A."

3. Carter, blurb from book cover.

> the area carried their grain to Maddock's mill, knowing him to be an honest man—a rare thing for a miller—whose toll was always what he promised it to be. As did other Quakers, he posted his fees for the various services he offered and considered it a violation of truth to bargain or to modify these charges for a particular customer. Any busy farmer in the area who wanted to continue working at home could send a young boy or a slave to the mill and be sure he would get back the right amount of flour, meal, or grits, ground the way he had ordered it. Although silence often prevailed in the regular religious meetings, Maddock liked to talk, so it was natural that most farmers preferred to carry their own grain to the mill and catch up on local news.[4]

As the novel goes on, Ethan Pratt and Joseph Maddock have several conflicts, and Maddock is portrayed as arbitrary and contentious, as indeed, he appears in some historical accounts, especially those by non-Quakers.

The fact that Joseph Maddock was an outspoken Loyalist during the Revolutionary War, coupled with the Quaker attitude toward owning slaves, made him decidedly unpopular in Wrightsborough, Georgia, where life was increasingly difficult for Quakers in general and for him in particular. The last decades of his life were filled with struggle, and he lost almost everything: once a well-to-do and respected leader among Friends, Joseph Maddock died a poor man with a tarnished reputation. There is no record of his death in Wrightsborough Friends records, nor any grave identified for him, but an announcement re probate of his estate appeared in the December 10, 1796 issue of *The Augusta Chronicle and Gazette*. (For more on what happened in Wrightsborough, Georgia, see the Appendix, "Wrightsborough's Joseph Maddock and The Quaker Migration to the South.")

In 1804, Joseph's brother, Samuel Maddock, joined a forty-wagon caravan of Quaker families emigrating *en masse* from Wrightsborough, Georgia, to settle in southwestern Ohio. Traveling with Samuel were his wife, Rachel (nee Jones) Maddock; her elderly father, Francis Jones; and two of the Maddocks' grown sons: twenty-seven-year-old Nathan with his recent bride, Margaret (nee Brown); and twenty-six-year-old Francis Maddock. The forty wagons crossed the Ohio River at Cincinnati in June 1805 and made their way north to what is now Preble County,

4. Carter, 45.

Ohio. There, a few other families from Wrightsborough had settled the year before and were in the process of clearing land, planting crops, building homes, and establishing Elk Monthly Meeting of the Religious Society of Friends[5] in what is now the village of West Elkton, Gratis Township, Preble County, Ohio.

## Joseph Maddock (1811–1889) of West Elkton, Ohio

In February 1805, a few weeks before the extended Maddock family emigrated from Wrightsborough, Georgia, to southwestern Ohio, Samuel's son, Nathan Maddock, had married nineteen-year-old Margaret Brown. Sadly, she died in December 1805 and was the first person to be buried in the new Quaker cemetery in the village of West Elkton, Ohio.[6]

A few years later, in March 1810, Nathan Maddock married twenty-one-year-old Sarah Fouts, whose family had immigrated to Preble County from North Carolina and settled in a neighboring township. She was not a Quaker, so they could not be married in Elk Monthly Meeting but were instead married by a Justice of Peace. Their first child, Joseph Maddock[7]—author of this diary— was born February 10, 1811, on his parents' farm near West Elkton. In June that year, Nathan Maddock was condemned in Elk Monthly Meeting for marrying "out of unity," i.e., not according to Quaker practice. Evidently he responded properly by acknowledging his misdeed, and by the time the couple had a second child, Sarah had been accepted into membership along with her two little sons.

5. Those in the Religious Society of Friends (a/k/a Friends a/k/a Quakers) use the word "meeting" like other denominations use "church." It refers to the congregation (as in "the Meeting discerned a clear way forward") but can also refer to the gathering for worship (as in "I plan to attend Meeting this week"). A Quaker congregation may meet several times a week for worship, but it is referred to as a "monthly meeting" because it gathers once a month to consider business matters. The building where Quakers worship is called a "meetinghouse" instead of a "church."

6. Ironically, the first marriage conducted among the Quakers in Preble County was that of Nathan's brother, Francis Maddock, who married Phebe Cook in 1806.

7. Earlier Quakers used the same given names both generation-to-generation and *laterally* among families of the same generation, which makes genealogical research challenging. For instance, the diarist is referred to in Elk Monthly Meeting minutes as "Joseph Maddock, Jr." to differentiate him from his cousin, "Joseph H. Maddock," son of Francis and Phebe (nee Cook) Maddock. These two Joseph Maddocks were born in Preble County in 1811 three weeks apart, and both families were active members of Elk Monthly Meeting. Mary's father, Joseph Maddock *Stubbs*, was named after Joseph Maddock, the great-grandfather of the Joseph Maddock she married (i.e., author of this diary).

Each year for four years, Sarah Maddock had another baby: Joseph (1811), John (1812), Henry, (1813) and Rachel, born the end of December 1814. In May 1815, Sarah died, leaving her husband with four-year-old Joseph and his three younger siblings.

Two years later, in 1817, Nathan Maddock married Martha (nee Miller) Mendenhall, the widow of Elijah Mendenhall, who had three children under seven. Nathan and Martha had one child together—Samuel, born in 1818, the baby of the blended family. All four parents were part of the Wrightsborough settlers who were founding members of Elk Monthly Meeting, and all eight children grew up as members of the Meeting.

Joseph, his siblings, step- and half-siblings attended Meeting for Worship at Elk Monthly Meeting with their parents two or three times a week, and in doing so, most of them grew up with their future spouses. In Joseph's case, she was Mary Stubbs, daughter of Joseph Maddock Stubbs and Nancy Ann (nee Harvey) Stubbs, another founding family from Wrightsborough, Georgia. In 1834, when he was twenty-three and she was twenty-two, Joseph and Mary were married "under the care" of Elk Monthly Meeting, which meant that—because Friends had no hired ministers or pastors—the marriage would thereafter be nurtured and supported by the congregation.

Joseph Maddock (1811–1889)

Mary (Stubbs) Maddock (1812–1878)

In 1832, two years before his marriage, young Joseph Maddock took a trip to visit Friends and family who had settled in Indiana and "the Western country." His account of that trip in 1832 became the first entry of a diary he kept the rest of his life. Many of his early diary entries summarize an entire year in a paragraph or two; later entries relate specific events in more detail. In 1850, he organized existing entries, added a brief family history, and related how his parents had emigrated to Preble County, Ohio.

In a brief autobiographical section, Maddock offers a disclaimer regarding his education, which, he writes, "was rather a limited one, as good schools were scarce and good teachers were few and seldom. A teacher never taught more than one school in the same neighbor's house and some of them poorly qualified to teach the letter . . . it was, as then thought, quite a competent education." An 1881 history of Preble County describes the kind of school he would have attended.

> THE FIRST SCHOOL was doubtless kept by the Friends in the southern part of [Gratis] township, but the exact date cannot now be ascertained, nor the name of the teacher of the same. The earliest school of which recollection is had, however, is one which was kept in the northeastern quarter of section thirty-three,[8] by Jesse Hobson,[9] in the year 1806. . . . The early schools were all taught by subscription.[10] Schools were held in deserted log cabins for many years. These would be occupied during one winter term, and at the next opening, the school would be located elsewhere.[11]

As an adult, Joseph served many years on the School Committee for Elk Monthly Meeting, whose members were tasked with recruiting Quaker teachers to come teach Quaker children in Preble County for a term and occasionally two terms. Eventually, when a "district school" was built in West Elkton—a nice brick building with several classrooms and regular teachers—Joseph and Mary sold their farm and moved into town in part so that their daughter could more easily attend classes.

Later in his diary, Joseph Maddock describes being deeply affected as a child when his father read aloud the works of George Fox and written testimonies of earlier Friends. Such works "raised a secret desire" in him to be like "those Worth[ies]." The inspiration he felt from reading Quaker journals may have been one motivation to keep his own diary. In times of

8. This section is just south of West Elkton on property across the road from John Maddock's farm.

9. In 1804, some Hobsons from Cane Creek Monthly Meeting in North Carolina received a certificate to travel to Miami Monthly Meeting in Waynesville, Ohio, a common stopping place for Quakers migrating West. In 1806 they may have stopped a while in Preble County, but that was before Elk Monthly Meeting was formally established.

10. Subscription schools were common in rural schools in the nineteenth century. Parents paid per each child enrolled, but only for the days the child attended. Children were needed to work on the family farm, so schools were usually open only during the winter.

11. "Gratis Township, The First School." *History of Preble County.*

distress, he writes (a little self-consciously) about his spiritual challenges and struggles, but rarely shares details about the cause or nature of them.

Maddock's writing is not eloquent, and at times he clumsily adopts the lofty, sentimental style of nineteenth-century writing or struggles for vocabulary. But the simple sincerity in his writing reveals him to be a generally kind, genial, outgoing man, on occasion thoughtful and reflective, averse to conflict, and habitually conservative. He did not like change, which led him to remain an "Orthodox" Friend during the 1828 separation of Midwestern Friends, and to side with the "larger Body Friends" of Indiana Yearly Meeting (Orthodox) over the question of *how* to oppose slavery.[12]

All his life, Joseph Maddock was an active and dedicated member of Orthodox Friends in Elk Monthly Meeting, Westfield Quarterly Meeting, and Indiana Yearly Meeting.[13] He liked to travel, took every opportunity to visit Friends near and far, and seems to have been acquainted with just about every Quaker in the region.[14] In 1847, when he was thirty-six and in his fifth year as Presiding Clerk of Elk Monthly Meeting, the meeting called him to serve as an Elder, a call he accepted with deep humility and answered for the next twenty-five years.

During his lifetime, Maddock witnessed 1) the bitter separation over theological differences among Midwestern Friends that began *circa* 1828 (the Orthodox/Hicksite split); 2) the beginning and growth (from the 1830s to the early 1860s) of the Underground Railroad route through Preble County to Levi Coffin's home in Indiana; 3) the rise of the radical (in his eyes) Orthodox Indiana Yearly Meeting of Anti-Slavery Friends and Elk Monthly Meeting of Anti-Slavery Friends; 4)

12. His brother, John Maddock, was an Orthodox Friend and an Underground Railroad "station master" and "conductor" in West Elkton who did not join the Anti-Slavery Friends, though no doubt he cooperated with them. Other members of Joseph and John's immediate family actively participated in helping fugitives on their journeys to freedom. The fact that Joseph seems to have not done so may have to do with Nathan, his mentally challenged son, who would not react well to strangers showing up in the middle of the night, nor understand the need for secrecy.

13. Quaker meetings in southwestern Ohio belonged to Indiana Yearly Meeting.

14. Joseph Maddock mentions by name hundreds of his contemporary Quakers—local, regional, national, and occasionally international Friends. His diary is thus a gold-mine of information for genealogists who can use it to trace the movements of Quaker families through the nineteenth century from North Carolina, Georgia, New Jersey, Pennsylvania and Virginia to Ohio, Indiana, Iowa and Kansas, all the way to Colorado Territory, where relatives of West Elkton Quakers homesteaded.

the tumultuous years of the Civil War which challenged the peace testimony of all Quakers; and 5) the changes that post-Civil War Evangelicalism brought to Elk Monthly Meeting (Orthodox) which remained *unprogrammed*[15] until years after his death.

In his later years, he grew increasingly frustrated with the influence of Evangelicalism on traditional Quaker unprogrammed worship. His diary entries grumpily detail occurrences of hymn-singing, reading the Bible (in lieu of quoting passages from memory), and loud preaching. He bemoans changes that made Quakers more like other denominations with hired ministers and structured worship. In 1884, after attending Indiana Yearly Meeting (Orthodox), he wrote of the gathering that it was "about as large as usual" and many of the sessions were "seasons of divine labor and a good degree of harmony . . . Yet some of the Meetings in the morning and evening were more like Methodist than Friends."

15. From the beginning, traditional Quaker worship was held in silence without a hired minister or an "order of service," relying instead on a higher source/the Divine to inspire whoever might speak from the silent "waiting" worship. Midwestern Orthodox Friends like Elk Monthly Meeting continued this practice until the late nineteenth-century.

# Early Quaker Written Dates

In the diary and letters, Joseph and Martha Ann use the original (now archaic) Quaker way of writing dates. Rather than using names derived from pagan gods or rituals (e.g., Wednesday/Woden's Day, January/Janus, etc.), early Friends used numbers 1–7 to refer to days of the week and 1–12 to refer to names of months.

In handwritten documents (such as Quaker minutes, diaries or letters) format and punctuation vary, but the rule-of-thumb-order is Day, Month, Year. The following key may be helpful to readers. Sometimes the words "m/Month" and "d/Day" are written out. Sometimes abbreviations for "month" and "day" are capitalized ("Mo" "Da") and sometimes they are not ("mo" "da"). Sometimes they are punctuated with a period ("Mo. "Da."). And sometimes they are not ("Mo" "da)." Essentially, if you can tell what date is referred to, it's correct enough.

Quaker Days of The Week

| | | |
|---|---|---|
| First Day or | 1st Day | = Sunday |
| Second Day or | 2nd Day | = Monday |
| Third Day or | 3rd Day | = Tuesday |
| Fourth Day or | 4th Day | = Wednesday |
| Fifth Day or | 5th Day | = Thursday |
| Sixth Day or | 6th Day | = Friday |
| Seventh Day or | 7th Day | = Saturday |

Quaker Names of Months

| | | |
|---|---|---|
| First Month or | 1st Month | = January |
| Second Month or | 2nd Month | = February |
| Third Month or | 3rd Month | = March |
| Fourth Month or | 4th Month | = April |
| Fifth Month or | 5th Month | = May |
| Sixth Month or | 6th Month | = June |
| Seventh Month or | 7th Month | = July |
| Eighth Month or | 8th Month | = August |
| Ninth Month or | 9th Month | = September |
| Tenth Month or | 10th Month | = October |
| Eleventh Month or | 11th Month | = November |
| Twelfth Month or | 12th Month | = December |

### Sample Quaker Written Dates

| | |
|---:|---|
| Fifth Day 18th | = Thursday the 18th |
| Fifth Day the 8th of 8th Month | = Friday, August 8 |
| Fourth Day, 20th of 10th Mo | = Thurs, Oct. 20 |
| latter part of 5th Month, on a | = latter part of May, on a |
| First Day p.m. | = Sunday afternoon |
| 8th Month, 5th and 6th | = August 5–6 |
| 1st of 1st Month 1811 | = January 1, 1811 |
| 2nd da of 1st month 1850 | = January 2, 1850 |
| 15th da 2nd mo | = February 15 |
| 28th da. 3rd mo. 1835 | = March 28, 1835 |
| 12th Fourth Mo. | = April 12 |
| 21st da Fifth mo | = May 21 |
| 10th of 6th Mo. 1889 | = June 10, 1889 |
| 7th Seventh Month | = July 7 |
| 26 Eighth Mo. 1850 | = August 26, 1850 |
| 13th Da Ninth Mo | = September 13 |
| 31 Tenth Mo. | = October 31 |
| 23rd Eleventh Month | = November 23 |
| 25th Twelfth 1865 | = December 25, 1865 |

# Diary of Joseph Maddock (1811–1889)

*Joseph Maddock's punctuation and grammar have been retained as he wrote them. The original handwritten diary (along with a photocopy of a typewritten copy and now a digitized copy) is housed in the archives of the Preble County Historical Society, Eaton, Ohio.*

## Some Accounts of the Maddock Family

By accounts related to me by my father, Nathan Maddock, and grandmother, Rachel Maddock. Appears that the Maddock Family were originally from England. Appears that Nathan Maddock, great-grandfather to my father came to America some time in the first part of the Seventeenth Century with his parents, whilst very young, and settled on Brandywine Creek in the Colony of Pennsylvania. He became a tailor by trade. It was at this place that his son Joseph was born and whilst a young man removed to North Carolina and settled at Cane Creek in Orange County. It was here his son Samuel (my grandfather) was born.

Joseph and his family in time removed to Georgia then a colony under England. They were amongst the first emigrants in those parts. They settled at or near Wrightsborough in Colombia County. This was a short time before the Revolutionary War, so called. Joseph held some very important and prominent offices in the Colony at that time under the King of England. One of them was Justice of the Peace, Deputy Governor, as well as some other places of trust, which he discharged to credit and satisfaction to all concerned. He was also engaged in mercantile businesses and had become very wealthy.

The war was breaking out, and he having previously exercised the laws on a lawless class of men for their misdemeanors, there was a chance now to take revenge on him for so doing. They commenced with their revenge and plunder, burning his house and barn and took off his horses and cattle and destroyed much other property so that he was reduced very low in his circumstances. After a while debts commenced coming on that had been contracted in the time of prosperity. He was broken up and had to fail but not until he had paid off all his dues, as I understand, to satisfaction and died a very poor man as to the things of this world.[1]

His son Samuel secured a piece of land, about 220 acres, in time for a home, and it being pretty well improved. He was also burnt out of home by the same lawless set of men. Besides his horses and cattle taken, he came very near several times of losing his life, but was prevented by an overwhelming providence. He became very much in need in his circumstances, in so much at one time that the Friends of Wrightsborough Monthly Meeting bought a home for him, which he in after time was able to return to his kind donors. It was here that his son, Nathan Maddock (my father), was born in the time of the said war in the year 1778.

[For a fuller account of Joseph Maddock in Wrightsborough, Georgia, see the Appendix, "The Quaker Migration to the South" by Ralph Hayes.]

In the year 1805 Samuel Maddock and family including his son and daughter and one son and daughter married came to the conclusion to remove to the then far off North Western Territory. They with many other members of the Society of Friends (being the last) started in the 4th Month and left the land on account of the baneful influence of slavery and arrived at Cincinnati about the 15th of 6th Month. Going up farther north in the country about 25 miles, stayed at Cotton Run in Butler County, Ohio a while, and in the Autumn of that year settled on land that had been previously entered near where West Elkton now stands in Preble County, Ohio, where he continued to reside to the end of his useful life, which was in the year 1814.

He was a man of deep religious experience and greatly beloved by his Religious Society and those who had the privilege of forming an acquaintance with him. He had a gift in the ministry and was beloved for the Word's sake. It may be truly said of him he feared God, worked righteousness and no doubt but was one that was gathered as a shock of corn fully ripe into the Heavenly Farmes [*sic*].

1. See Smith, "Whatever Happened to Wrightsboro?"

This much I feel like contributing to the memory as well for information respecting my ancestors, and the information of my relatives hereafter.

5th Month, 1850, Joseph Maddock

## Brief Autobiography, 1850

I, Joseph Maddock, was born near West Elkton in Preble County, Ohio, the 10th of 2nd Month, 1811. My parents were Nathan and Sarah Maddock, who were members of the Society of Friends. My father emigrated from the State of Georgia in the year 1805. My mother was daughter of John and Mary Fouts, who emigrated from North Carolina about the year 1804 and settled on Twin Creek in Montgomery County, Ohio. John Fouts was son of Michael Fouts, the Dutch Friend mentioned by Job Scott in his journal where he had a meeting at his house when he was on a visit to the Southern States in the year 1789.

My mother was not a member of Society at the time of her marriage but requested to become one, as appears from the records of Elk Monthly Meeting. She was received with myself and brother John, when I was about two years old. I understand she was an exemplary virtuous woman. As she died when I was quite young, I have a very little recollection of her, being only about four years old at the time of her death. She went over to see her mother in time of her last sickness, which was about 7 miles from our residence, and was taken down sick herself after her mother's death, of which she never recovered. She died the 16th of 5th Month 1815 and was buried in the family burial ground near grandfather's residence.

This was very sorrowful to my father there being four of us small children left to be cared for. Myself, John, Henry, and sister Rachel, she being only a few months old. Our Aunt Mary Fouts came over and stayed with us and kept house. Our grandmother Rachel Maddock stayed occasionally with us, until father married again, which was in 1817 to Martha, widow of Elijah Mendenhall.

Our stepmother was an exemplary pious Christian woman. She endeavored to care for us in our many wants in providing for us, as with a mother's attention and regard, in cultivating our minds as we grew in years. She taught us obedience to the spirit of Divine Grace in our hearts and trained us in wisdom's ways. Her counsel and influence towards us, particularly myself in my young years and at times when my wayward course, I vividly remembered and will as long as memory lasts.

As to my education it was rather a limited one, as good schools were scarce and good teachers were few and seldom. A teacher never taught more than one school in the same neighbor's house and some of them poorly qualified to teach the letter, let alone anything of Christian principles. But as it was, as then thought, quite a competent education. Our reading books, the first we had, were New Testament Bibles, those in the more advanced days reading the Bible.

As I grew up to man estate and began to discover the operation of the spirit of Divine Grace in the heart, I saw at once the great advantage of a pious education and also of religious training in the families. My father and stepmother were careful to have us attend Religious Meetings as well on week days as First Days, Father often telling us on First Day morning that if we did not attend Meeting we should not visit our playmates in the afternoon.

Our living in about one mile of the Meeting House made it more easy for us than for others who were not so favorably circumstanced and we often had Ministers who attended our Meeting, and it often raised in us an anxiety to attend such Meetings, when it was at time of Quarterly Meeting[2] or Monthly Meeting. We always had a Monthly Meeting ever since my earliest recollection. The Quarterly Meeting was established about the year 1823. At the time of these Meetings we often had at Father's, company which we considered as a privilege to have, and often were times of encouragement to us smaller children as well as to parents. Many of these sermons are vividly remembered by me and some of my older Friends. If we kept our places and ranks in righteousness, we would have to occupy in a future day the place of those honored ones.

This raised in my heart a secret desire that I might be as one of those faithful worthy [*sic*] that we often read of in Luvely History [*sic*]. George Fox's Journal, the writings of Friends, were more read in those days in Father's family than any other reading. I well remember the

2. Quarterly Meetings, like Yearly Meetings, were several-day events when Quakers from around the area or region gathered to worship, conduct business, and socialize. When West Elkton Friends attended Westfield Quarterly Meeting at Salem Monthly Meeting in Union County, Indiana, about twenty miles away, it took most of a day to get there by horseback or horse and buggy, and another day to return home. Friends stayed over several days in the homes of members of the hosting meeting. Indiana Yearly Meeting in Richmond, Indiana, lasted most of a week. Besides serious business meetings and shared Meetings for Worship, Yearly Meeting provided an opportunity for young Friends to meet prospective marriage partners, i.e., other young Friends less likely to be related to them than those in their home Meetings.

time when but very few newspapers were taken amongst the people, particularly with Friends. How much better it would be now with us if the writings of our early Friends were read more instead of spending the time in reading the news of today.

In the year 1828 there was a separation in our religious society known as the Hicksite Separation, headed by the late Elias Hicks of Long Island, New York. Hicks and his adherents adopted a new Unitarian Doctrine and principles in which some of them went out into near open infidelity. In Elk Monthly Meeting, which was at that time a large one, the particular meeting at Elk and a small one called West Union—held about four miles west of Elk—comprised the meeting.

About one fourth of the members seceded and set up a meeting to themselves, meeting at 1:00 p.m. on First Days and at usual hour on Fourth Day. Our Meeting being first established and held on First and Fifth Days at 11:00 a.m. There was not many that separated who had been or were active and prominent members of Society in our Meetings for Discipline. Their Meeting, being not very well attended by other people or our young Friends, concluded to change the time on First Day to usual hour of our Meeting and asked for one end of the house to accommodate them, which was not granted by Friends.

Some Friends became excited and warmed up with an untempered zeal and locked the House. This was very trying to other Friends, for instance, a son locking the door against his father and mother. The separatists staying out a while and held their Meetings under the shade of the trees. They then commenced breaking in and holding their Meetings in the House. This was pretty high times, one party locking the door and the other breaking in, which continued for some time, perhaps near two years. This was very trying times to some on both sides and had a discouraging effect on Society to see those that were at one time united in church fellowship so at odds with each other, very discouraging to us young people and caused some to entirely leave Society. Yet most of us remained attached to Friends and kept their principles.

After a while, report came of the decision of a suit at law in the State of New Jersey that a school fund was awarded to Friends by the Supreme Court in Chancery. The Hicksites concluded to leave the Meeting House and built one for their accommodations near by about half a mile distance, where they continued to hold their meetings for a few years. One of them removing, others died; the Meeting became very small and discontinued.

# 1832–1840

## 1832

In the year 1832 I left home to transact some business for my father in Indiana, and also I wished to see some of the Western country, and therefore left home on the 8th of 10th Month in the p.m. Rode to Stone's on Paint Creek. Third Day 9th rode on to Richmond, stayed at Yearly Meeting awhile, it being in session. In the p.m. I started on and lodged near Centerville. On Fourth Day 10th rode on through rain that fell through the day. We saw about 150 Indians who were going to the west of the Mississippi having sold their homes in Ohio. They were the first of the red men, so called, I have ever seen.

Lodged near Greenfield. On Fifth Day 11th rode on to Uncle J. Flaps' near Indianapolis, a pleasant day to what it was yesterday. Uncle J. Flaps lives about 4 miles North West of town. When he knew who I was, he received us being kindly. Aunt Nanny reminisced of the features of my mother and told me she was about the same sized person as herself. After staying overnight with them, we concluded to go on next morning expecting to call on [them] and stay longer when we returned. On the Sixth Day 12th we left and rode on to Thorntown and arrived at A. Davis' about sunset.

On Seventh Day 13th, Isaac Cook, who was with me, concluded to go on to his brother's at Rockwell and accordingly left. I expected to meet him in a few days. I was left alone and went around with the boys a-hunting and looking at their land through the day and on First Day, spent the time about as yesterday, visiting some with their neighbors as we did not hunt any.

Stayed at night with H. Moffitt, he and three or four other families being the only Friends living here. There is quite a large Meeting 12 miles below on Sugar River. On Second Day morning 15th settling some business for my father with A. Davis, I concluded to leave in the p.m. It was trying to see the parents of this family so at variance with each other and the effects it had and would have on their children. I accordingly left and rode to Dr. Theodore Brown about 11 miles down Sugar River.

On Third Day 16th rode on for Rockville, a distance of about 40 miles. Arrived late in the evening at Eli Cook's. Met a very kind reception, he being one I had spent much of my time in early days in school on through farming and various other ways. On Fourth day 17th I rested in town and spent some time in visiting other connections and acquaintances. In the p.m. I rode out to Al Holiday's. I had a very agreeable visit and returned in the evening and lodged at J. Guest's that night.

On Fifth Day 18th we started up the Wabash River for Lafayette, a distance of about 70 miles. We rode that day to Covington, County seat of Fountain County, Indiana. We stayed at Rawls Inn. On the Sixth Day 19th rode on up the Wabash through some prairie until we arrived at the Weaive Plain, a beautiful prairie indeed. I think the most beautiful farm on it I ever saw. It is about 8 miles square and nearly all in cultivation except a few lots in the middle. This was the most pleasant and agreeable day we have had since we left home. Arrived late in the evening at Job Hawkins' and lodged.

On Seventh Day 20th went to Lafayette, a flourishing town and County seat of Tippecanoe County. We lodged at Levi Hawkins'. It was distressing to see him in a state of intoxication all the time we were there. It is a sorrowful example for his children. They lived on a fine farm, well situated, and might do well if their father would only let that poison alone. It is destroying his body and I fear the ruin of the soul.

On the First Day 21st rode about visiting some of our acquaintances and lodged at William Hollingsworth's. On Second Day 22nd spent as yesterday. Isaac left for Nashville [Indiana] this p.m. We expected to meet at Indianapolis in a few days. I lodged at Baker Juentz. On the Third Day 23rd, I started for Indianapolis alone and rode to Dr. L. Brown's near Crawfordsville on Sugar River. On the Fourth Day 24th, after settling some of my father's business with him, I rode on again about 14 miles in the p.m. and lodged near Jamestown. On the Fifth Day 25th rode 32 miles to Uncle J. Fox. On the Sixth Day 26th stayed with them all day, very agreeable.

On Seventh Day morning 27th, I thought I would have to go home alone as Isaac had not arrived yet. After the morning had passed, Isaac came and we concluded to go on for home. At Indianapolis we took the Rushville Road which was better than the National Road we went out on. We got to Buckness Inn on Blue River about 35 miles and lodged. On First Day 28th rode on through Rushville and Connersville to Liberty and lodged at Estep's Hotel. On Second Day 29th, we rode on to J. Jones' and got there about noon. After staying a while in the p.m., we rode on for home. Arrived late in the evening, being absent from home 21 days and rode 500 miles, and was glad to meet again in the family circle. After escaping many dangers or at least apparently so, both seen and unseen.

## 1833

On the morning of 13th of 11th month 1833, a very strange phenomenon appeared in the heavens, of stars shooting or meteors bursting in every direction in the firmament. It was a beautiful sight indeed. It began sometime in the night about 2:00 or 3:00 a.m. and continued until daylight. The scene presented a beautiful excitement to spectators. I think it was the most rare sight I ever beheld and will be remembered as long as memory lasts.

## 1834

In the 23rd year of my age, I engaged in the very solemn covenant of marriage with Mary Stubbs, daughter of Joseph [Maddock] Stubbs. She was a member of our Meeting and about one year younger than myself. Her exemplary deportment and Christian virtues far exceeded mine. Our marriage was solemnized in Elk Meeting of Friends the 20th of 3rd month, 1834, before a large Meeting of Friends, relatives and others. I trust we had the prayer of many for our preservation through life's journey, whether short or long. I believe we felt it to be so in the solemn compact. A short time after we removed on the First Day of 4th Month to our new house on a farm that my father had bought of A. Davis for myself and a brother. There were but few of our Society that lived near us. We felt somewhat alone in our new situation for awhile. But, a family of relations living near, we soon found in our social visits as well as helping one another in our temporal affairs, very agreeable and kind neighbors.

A short time after we came here a very trying and awful circumstance took place. A steam sawmill nearby took fire one night and burnt down. A young man that I had formed some acquaintance with was sleeping in the office room of the mill and was burnt to death. It was thought that he died trying to escape through the door into the mill. The room being on the second story, he found the mill on fire and threw his bedding out the window and attempted to make his escape through the flames and perished. I was one that helped to take his mangled body from the burning timber. It was a shocking sight to behold. Only the evening before he was enjoying life's gaieties and pleasures in a high degree, but now was called to bid adieu to this world and appear before Him, the great judge of Heaven and earth. A solemn thought; it seems as though sometimes going through the busyness of life we are in the midst of death.

As time progressed on and our temporal concerns prospered, we were permitted to enjoy a large share of peace and generally made it a practice to attend one religious Meeting both on First and as well as Fifth Days. Also we had visits from Ministry and occasionally from committees appointed by our Monthly Meeting to visit families for their help and encouragement in the support of our various Christian testimonies. Many of these were persons of strength and encouragement in our isolated home. As we lived about three miles from Meeting with very bad roads, it was difficult to travel in the winter season. I have had to remember the remark made by our aged and honored Friend Thomas Talbert, who said we lived about far enough from Meeting to make it profitable to attend. He said he never enjoyed himself more satisfactorily than when it caused him to make some sacrifice to attend Religious Meetings.

Although in one sense we were favored and strengthened in our Heavenward Journey, we had in many other things to contend with an opposite character. It was a time when Friends were hampered and tried with military demands for several years, and all that kept to their religious scriptures were preserved and a kind of providence made up our temporal losses by way of increase, so that we seldom felt the loss of property taken very long. But it was very perplexing to be asked for such demands every year and trying to the officers who done it. They often took three or four times the amount of property to satisfy the demand, and it was seldom that any person would engage more than one time in such business if they could evade it. There was one old man that called such fines from me two or three times, which in after times, he said he had to regret as he became very poor and had to have the charity of his neighbors to help him; he said it was something he did not expect from me, but I felt as much bound in delivering his wants as if he had done no wrong to me. Remembering it was more blessed to give than take, for in doing so, it was heaping coals of fire on his head, as he thankfully acknowledged.

## 1839–40

As time went on, our Meeting was much reduced in the year 1839 to 1840 by several families of Friends removing to Indiana and Iowa. After a while, several requested to join us in membership, and several of those became useful and were concerned Friends and faithful standard-bearers in the Church. Our Meeting came to be as large as ever and a lively and interesting Monthly Meeting, and I trust held to the honor of truth and the propriety of the great cause of truth and righteousness in the earth.

Our righteous and honored Friend Thomas Talbert, who had been a faithful father, a pillar in the Church for many years, was summoned from us by death in 8th Month 1841. This loss was very sensibly felt.

# 1842–1847

## 1842

In the year 1842, there was much unsettlement in our religious Society on account of slavery in many places, and there was a class of our members who seemed to want to push the emancipation cause to a great extreme. There was much excitement among a number of the antislavery party who were manifesting a very warm and active zeal so that there seemed to be danger of us tampering on our testimony on war. It was so extreme that the Yearly Meeting in 1841 issued an Epistle of Advice to the subordinate Meetings and members, cautioning the Friends against joining the overactive zeal of the antislavery societies and against opening our Meeting Houses to lecturers, which was warmly approved by some when the advice came down to the subordinate Meetings. It seemed to cause a good deal of concern for us, as by many Friends, that we might be enserviced [*sic*] in all our testimony, as well as on the subject of the freedom of the Colored Man. We were neither to run too fast nor to relax into a state of apathy and unconcern on this momentous question.

At the Yearly Meeting in 1842, things were as had been the past year. Very much of a party spirit was getting up in some places and some were denouncing advice issued last year and condemning Friends and using their influence in promoting dissension and discord amongst Friends in places. Also supporting a proposal on the emancipation cause which denounced all those who did not join in with them as pro-slavery, both in church and state, so that the Yearly Meeting came to the judgment to please some of their members who had been in these dissentions as they were manifestly not with us.

Accordingly, four members of the Meeting for Sufferings were released, who stood appointed by the Yearly Meeting. This caused considerable excitement at the time. Perhaps if the Meeting had extended charity and more patience in this, it might have been better. But the zeal of some of those released was up to such a pitch they would not hear. The late Charles Osborn appeared to be the main leader in this sorrowful dilemma.

A committee was appointed to visit the subordinate Meetings with an Epistle of Advice. The committee in 11th Month met at New Garden Quarterly Meeting. It was the main seat of the insubordination. Those appointed to the proceedings of the Yearly Meeting also met as well as many Friends from other places, which was an uncommonly large attendance. The Meeting proceeded to its business and there was quite a warm time. Yet Friends were preserved in a good degree of patience. The Advices were read and accepted by Friends generally, and some that were opposed to these were released from Stations they had previously occupied in Society. Agreeable to the Advices, the Meeting slowed [*sic*] and other Quarterly Meetings proceeded the same way.

The disaffected part, seeing but little chance for theirs, called a meeting or conference, which met in 2nd Month 1843 and decided to separate and organize a separate Yearly Meeting of Antislavery Friends. They proceeded after their Meeting to omit the Subordinate Meetings and organized four Quarterly Meetings out of thirteen Quarterly Meetings subordinate to Indiana Yearly Meeting. One in New Garden called Newport, one in Westfield called Salem, one in White Water [*sic*]... one in Spiceland called Dutch Creek, and one in Northern called Northern [*sic*]... They manifested much zeal in the cause, visited their Meetings quite frequently, and held conferences amongst themselves.

They sent corresponding Epistles as prepared at their Yearly Meetings to all the Yearly Meetings of Friends on the Continent and to London and Dublin. They expected to be acknowledged at least by some of them, the proceedings of Indiana, or especially by London. But when the subject became to be considered in all three Yearly Meetings, they [i.e., London Yearly Meeting] returned their Epistles with the information that they could not acknowledge them as Friends, which had a tendency rather to soften down their zeal. The London Yearly Meeting, in the year 1844, appointed a committee to visit the antislavery Friends in Indiana with an Epistle of Advice offered by their Meeting, which they attended the later part of the year 1845 and first part of 1846, attending our Yearly

Meeting previously. The antislavery Friends expected the English Friends would advise the reinstating of them back again into Society and allow their occupation of the Stations they held when they separated. Yet when [English Friends] visited them and read the Advice for them to relinquish their Meetings and return back again to the body, they were much disappointed in their expectations and [were] denounced as strongly as Indiana Friends [had done]. Yet after a while, a considerable number of [Anti-Slavery Friends] left their Meetings and returned as advised, and many of them were glad of the chance to return, as several of them expressed they were not satisfied with the course they had taken.

Many of them became again valuable members of Society. Those of them left behind still continued to keep their Meetings both for Worship and Discipline until about the year 1858. Then at their Yearly Meeting they came to the conclusion to dissolve their Meetings and return back to Society. A few still in places declined and kept up very small Meetings, yet in two or three years they dropped all of their Meetings and generally returned. Many of them once again became valuable members which was the cause of rejoicing with the honest-hearted of every class amongst us as well as them.

## 1843

In 7th Month, 1843, our beloved stepmother, Martha Maddock, was taken away by death. One evening while walking along in the yard near the house, she fell and broke her thigh or fractured the bone. With her poor health other ways, it caused her death after some two or three weeks' sickness. She manifested much peace and serenity of mind. She said she was fully prepared to leave this world and found nothing in her way. Making many lively and solemn expectations on her death bed, and envincing [*sic*] to those who visited her the declaration, "Oh, that I could die the death of the righteous and my latter days be as theirs."

## 1844

In 2nd Month 1844, our sister [i.e., Mary's sister] Hannah, wife of Joash Stubbs, died at our house. They came over on a visit to us and stayed a while with us. She being in the last stages of consumption, after staying a few weeks, she was taken worse and died. Suddenly one evening, being taken worse, the connections were called in and she seemed weakening away and sinking. On waking up out of a sleep, she remarked that she had been at Meeting and should not be here with us long, and desired us to prepare to meet her in Heaven as she was going, and quietly faded away. No doubt she was one that was permitted to enjoy one of those mansions prepared in the Heavenly Father's Kingdom.

## 1845–46

Our Friend Enos Pray having returned again and settled in our Meeting and was acknowledged as a Minister in 8th Month 1845. He was a young man about of my age and married and settled down about the same time we were. He removed a few years afterward to Westfield, Indiana and after staying there a few years returned back here with us. He had ever since his marriage spoke some in our Meetings by way of ministry. It seemed the time had come to record him as a minister. In 10th Month, they obtained a Minister to visit West Branch Quarterly Meeting and the meeting belonging thereto, and the beloved people of Mercer County, Ohio. He made the visit to satisfaction to himself and friends and returned accordingly. In the spring of 1846 he removed to Mill Creek Monthly Meeting in the limits of West Branch Quarterly Meeting.

## 1847

In 5th Month 1847, my name was proposed by our select preparative to our Monthly Meeting as a suitable person to be appointed to the Station of an Elder. This was a very unexpected thing to me until a few days before the Monthly Meeting. I was informed by two of the Elders. It struck me like a death stroke to think why I should be appointed to such an important Station in the Church, as it seemed to me to be one of the most important Stations. I pleaded to be excused and thought I could not give up to it, but was later told the proposition had passed the Quarterly Meeting of Ministers and Elders without a dissenting voice, and that it would be laid before the Monthly Meeting. This was done and was generally united with, some two or three others of our non-active members keeping silent in the Meeting. A few days afterward they came to me and wished me encouragement. I felt in good degree to submit to it, and felt as an honored Friend. I once read of John Churchman, who was proposed on a similar appointment, to submit rather than refuse to stand.

Having been Clerk of our Monthly Meeting for about five years, I requested to be released and the committee accepted thereto. It's [i.e., clerking is] a very important place to fill in Society. I have often thought one that requires close attention to the intimations of the spirit of truth. A clerk that is rightly qualified to fill the Station may do much to settle uncalled-for sentiments that are in Meeting by those who are not so guarded as would be best in their explanations. I also afterwards served in our Quarterly Meeting for Discipline about seven years; I think I may say to the satisfaction of Friends as well as myself. It's a place where we are fully prepared to fill that brings a degree of that peace which we often experience in our journey through life, and I have often thought by several years' experience, that it was the only place I was qualified to fill (if I was for any) in our Society.

*NOTE: A characteristic of the Quaker decision-making process is the time and deliberation involved. Though Joseph was named an Elder in May, and some time after that requested to be released from his position as Clerk of Elk MM, it took six months to complete the process. In the excerpt below, Joseph finishes his term as Clerk, though he served as Clerk several other times later in his life. D.H.*

### *Excerpt from Elk Monthly Minutes, 20th 11th Mo 1847*

Those appointed to prepare a testimony of disownment against James Denny have produced the following which was read and approved and signed. Joseph Maddock, Jr. and Elisha Stubbs are appointed to write to Salem Monthly Meeting of Friends, Iowa, and request it on our behalf to offer him a copy thereof, inform him of his privilege to appeal and report their case to next meeting ~ Testimony ~ James Denny who has had a right of membership in the Society of Friends has neglected the attendance of our religious meetings, deviated from plainness in dress and address, attended places of diversion, and having been concerned in an affray which ended in blows, for which he has been treated with without the desired effect. We therefore disown him from being a member with us.

Signed by direction and on behalf of Elk Monthly Meeting of Friend, held the 20th day of 11th Month 1847. Joseph Maddock, Clerk.

Those appointed to propose the names of Friends for Clerk and Assistant Clerk propose William Taylor for Clerk, who being united with, is appointed accordingly in room of Joseph Maddock, Jr., who requests to be released, and proposed Levi Lane for Assistant. He not being present, his appointment is referred to next meeting.

# 1850–1859

## 1850

In the 9th Month 1850 at our Quarterly Meeting we had the very agreeable company of our friends, Benjamin Seaborn and Robert Lindsey from England. They were greatly loved by Friends everywhere wherever their lot was cast. They have been four years on this continent visiting all the Yearly Meetings as well as their subordinate Meetings. Their labors will be remembered by many in the wide spread of our religious Society in this country.

## 1851 or 1852

About the year 1851 or 1852, our Friend Naomi Coffin[1] of Whitewater Monthly Meeting visited our families. It was to our satisfaction and encouragement and left a good interpretation on many minds. These visits, when performed in the spirit of divine wisdom, and when visitors as well as visited seek to be profited by it, they are special reasons of encouragement and improvement in our pilgrimage journey through this world.

Some two or three years after this, our Friend Eli Newlin visited many of our families to the satisfaction and encouragement of all. I think he appeared particularly qualified for this very important engagement and left a good feeling amongst us which will be long remembered.

1. Among Quakers, ministers whose gifts of ministry were "recorded" by a congregation were not given titles such as "Reverend," or "Pastor." But whenever Joseph Maddock refers to a recorded minister, he uses the phrase "our Friend" + the person's name, as he does here with "our Friend Naomi Coffin" and "our Friend Eli Newlin."

## 1856

In 3rd Month 1856, our Friend Thomas Jay of West Branch Monthly Meeting attended our Quarterly Meeting and afterwards visited all the families belonging thereto. A satisfactory visit to many that left a good impression on many minds.

In the 1st Month of this year, 1856, we sold our farm that we long lived on and bought one of Robert Stubbs about one mile from West Elkton where our Meeting House is. On the 2nd of 4th Month, we left our old home, having lived in it twenty-two years to a day, and removed to our new house where we are much more conveniently situated in attending our religious Meetings, also in respect to schools. I think we may say it was our only motive in changing our residence. With daughter growing up we think it will be a help to her being now in her eleventh year, and we being very conveniently situated in respect to a good district school, as well as the Monthly Meeting School, which was generally kept up in the winter and summer. We feel much better satisfied in changing our residence. It seemed almost providential that we made the exchange as we did. Perhaps if we had not a [*sic*] done it as we did, we would not a [*sic*] made the change at all. I think we may have some intentions of our various duties, even in arranging to that which may advance our Christian prophesy in this life and ultimately crown all the final wind of time here. Oh, may this be our chieftest concern whilst pilgrims here on earth.

In the latter part of the 6th Month, our Friend Nathan Stacy of Wabash Monthly Meeting, Indiana visited our families. I accompanied him to most of our families on the eastern side of the settlement. He seemed to get along to pretty good satisfaction and afterwards visited the families at Salem.

Sometime, I think it was in the 8th Month of this year 1856, I had one of the most trying and severe dispensations to grasp through that I ever remember to attend my pathway through life. I seemed to be tempted by Satan, that old deceiver, (at a time of some trial outwardly) to give up all hope of ever attaining to a state of acceptance with my dear Redeemer and should be forever lost. I was permitted in some degree to see the bewildered state he gets some in, who are entangled in his snarls and baits, even to commit suicide. I thought I could see and feel this bewildered state and condition, and even thought there was no harm in committing this horrible sin in my forlorn condition. But, oh, thanks be to Him who rescues those who abide in the patience and stands in the path of self-denial and those severe trials. He was pleased in His own time to raise my almost lost hope and forlorn condition and make known His will for my deliverance whilst [I was] out in the field under the shade of a tree. Oh, this was precious to my soul, and I, poor and unworthy, I was permitted in some degree to feel the ministering angel of His presence to be near for my help and encouragement, so that nature seemed to have another aspect. Late in the evening, I returned to the house under feelings of gratitude to Him for His mercy extended to me once more, and have a fortune of the joys of the redeemed in Heaven. Oh, this was a precious season to my soul.

## 1857

On Fifth Day, 11th Month 4th 1857, myself and Mary left home to visit connections and Friends in Indiana and Illinois. We took the train at Camden in the morning and arrived at Indianapolis about 12:00 p.m. After waiting about two hours, we took the train for Noblesville and arrived in about two hours and met our nephew, A.V. Talbert, who took us to his house in Westfield Village, about six miles. Met a kind reception with our relatives. Visited amongst them some on Sixth Day. On Seventh Day, attended Union Quarterly Meeting, very large and solemn Meeting though quite a rainy day. We were also at their large Meeting for Membership. The number of plain, and I trust concerned, Friends here was truly encouraging. They appear to retain more of ancient plainness and are more domestic in their manner than Friends are in eastern Indiana and Ohio.

On Third Day, we left our relatives and started with our nephew, A.V. Talbert, in a carriage for Indianapolis. On arriving at White River, it was so swelled with the late rains, we had to go around by the bridge. We were kindly entertained at Jonathan Harvey's, a relative.

Next morning, we visited the Blind Asylum and spent some time there and heard the pupils read; it was interesting. A large building is erected at the expense of the State and the institution is doing much good for this class of our fellow beings.

In the afternoon, we left for Terre Haute and arrived there about sunset. We found no one to take us to Brother Samuel Stubbs [Mary's older half-brother], as we expected to a [*sic*] been there yesterday, as no one expected us now. We then took the Alton train for Sandford Station about two miles. We got off and went to M. McDonald's, a distance of about one mile, and stayed all night with them. Fourth Day morning, we walked about two miles to Brother Samuel's, who was glad and rejoiced to see us, as well as we to see them. We spent the day very agreeably with them. This is in Edgar County, Illinois, about ten miles from Terre Haute.

On Fifth Day afternoon, Brother Samuel and wife took us in his wagon to Uncle James and Aunt Eleanor Cook's, about six miles, in Clark County. They had been living here some two or three years and had greatly settled on land they bought in the woods. There were little improvements on it, and it seemed far from being a comfortable home as they once had in Ohio. Yet they appeared pretty well satisfied and glad to see us as well as we them. We spent the night very agreeably with them. On Sixth Day, we parted with our aged relatives and felt for their lonely situation, and it may be the last farewell with some of us here on earth.

We went to Samuel's and took dinner with them, and in the afternoon, he took us to Terre Haute. After parting with him, we put up at the Terra Haute House for the night. It was a very agreeable place to lodge. First Day morning, we took the train for Indianapolis and got off at Amos Station about 9:00 a.m., walked about one mile to Uncle N. Harvey's, who were just starting to Monthly Meeting, so that we got in the carriage and went along with them. A pretty large Meeting, and a large number of well-concerned Friends, it appears, belong to it. A case of difficulty came up and it unsettled the Meeting very much. After Meeting we returned home with them and spent the evening and night very agreeably with them. Next morning, after taking breakfast with them, Uncle took us in his carriage to Uncle Robert Harvey's, where we were also very acceptably received and stayed with them all day and night. It was a very agreeable time spent with them as well as to us. The next morning, Third Day, Uncle took us to Pecksburgh Station, about one mile, and we parted with him. We got on the train about 10:00 a.m., and we started for home, going directly on through Indianapolis. We arrived at Richmond late in the evening and took the Hamilton train, arriving at Camden a little after dark. We met our expected conveyance and arrived at our home about 8:00 p.m. We found children and others well, and that all things had been doing well in our absence, which caused our gratitude to the great Giver of all for His thoughtful care over us.

## 1858

In 8th Month 1858, our aged and honored Friend, Jesse Kenworthy, died in the 91st year of his age. He had been from the first settlement of this place and settling up of our Meeting. He was an honest Friend and worthy citizen and Elder in the church for many years, worthy of double honor. He had been prevented by age and bodily infirmity for several years of the latter part of his life from attending our Meeting, yet retained to the last his attachment to Friends and their principles.

## 1859

In 1st Month 1859, our Friend Mary Roberts[2] laid before our Monthly Meeting a concern to visit the family of Friends and some not members of our Quarterly Meeting, which was held by united feeling, and she encouraged to attend to the concerns as Way might open, which service she attended to the later part of 1st Month, fore-part of 2nd Month. Following, our much-esteemed Friend, John Miles of Milford Monthly Meeting, joined Mary in the latter part of the visit in our Monthly Meeting, having a sense of the visit and concern, although he had no outward knowledge of it before he arrived here. It was to much satisfaction to them both, yet at times trying in some families, as things were brought to light and judged accordingly. This is one of the most important labors that engages the faithful laborer in the ministry of our Society. Yet when faith is relied on, the Great Maker is able to carry through to the praise of His ever-blessed Name.

I accompanied Mary with her companion to a visit in Salem Monthly Meeting. We set off on Sixth Day morning, the 25th of 2nd Month, and drove through the extremely back roads and arrived at Hugh Maxwell's late in the evening. We had a favored opportunity that night in the family. The next morning we paid one visit and attended the Monthly Meeting. It was small, yet satisfactory. In the afternoon we made several visits to satisfaction. We stayed with David Huddleston. First Day morning, we paid two or three visits and attended Meeting, and afterwards made several visits more, and all in all, 16 or 17 families to satisfaction, I trust, to both visitors and visited. On Second Day, we returned home with peace and satisfaction which was worth all consideration of an earthly nature.

2. Mary (Puckett) Roberts, a recorded minister, seems to have had a close personal friendship with Joseph and Mary Maddock. She was the younger sister of Martha (Puckett) Wooten, the noted Quaker minister recorded many times and by many monthly meetings in Indiana Yearly Meeting, as well as the older sister of Jane (Puckett) Jones. All three sisters were ministers recorded by Elk Monthly Meeting.

In 5th Month, our Friend Mary Roberts again obtained another minute to visit Meetings belonging to Fairfield Quarterly Meeting [in Clinton County, Ohio]. The committee appointed myself and beloved wife to accompany her; although we had short notice, we concluded to do so. On the Seventh Day morning, the 25th of 5th Month, we left home and rode to John H. Pyle's near Clarksville and lodged. On First Day morning, rode to Martinsville, a distance of about ten miles and attended Newberry Meeting. It was middling-to-large and satisfactory. We dined at William Betts'. In the afternoon we visited Mary's brother, David Puckett. Mary stayed with him all night. We lodged with Eli Newlin.

On Second Day morning, we visited our Friend, Henry Moon. He is quite indisposed. It was a satisfactory time and will be remembered in days to come. His counsel and fatherly advice was encouraging. We went on and attended Northfork [illegible] Meeting at 10:00 a.m. and dined at Stephen Hussey's. At 4:00 p.m., we attended Clear Creek Meeting. Both were satisfactory, the first small. We lodged at John Akers'. On Third Day, 31st, we rode about ten miles to Fall Creek and found no notice had been given of a Meeting. We dined at John Cowgill's with some Friends of a committee appointed by Fairfield Monthly Meeting who were visiting families, after which we went on to Hardin's Creek and attended Meeting at 4:00 p.m. It was pretty well attended by its members and others. Close labor extended to some, as well as encouragement to others. We lodged at James Hadley's, a quiet, resting place.

Fourth Day, 1st of 6th Month, attended Fairfield Weekday Meeting, a small, dull Meeting yet encouragement was held out for the few concerned members and trust the labors would not be lost. Fifth Day 2nd attended Walnut Creek Weekday Meeting, a satisfactory and encouraging time to the members of that Meeting. Their number is small. We dined at Gershorn Purdue's in Martinburgh. In the afternoon, we went on to Job Smith on Lee's Creek and lodged. On Sixth Day at 10:00 a.m. attended an appointed Meeting for our friends, Eli Newlin and Mary, in a schoolhouse nearby, which was well attended by Friends and others and proved a satisfactory time to all, both visitors and visited. We dined at John McPherson's and had a precious sitting in the family with other Friends, a time I want to remember. We went on in the afternoon to Daniel Puckett's, called on the way to see our young Friend, Daniel Hunt, in the last stages of consumption. We had a satisfactory opportunity, encouraging to the young man as he had little or no prospect of recovery. He appeared entirely resigned and willing to go if it was the Master's will.

On Seventh Day 4th, we attended Westfork Meeting at 10:00 a.m., a good Meeting and pretty well attended. There seems to be a considerable number of Friends here who make a very commendable appearance, more so than any Meeting we have attended in Fairfield quarter.

In the afternoon, Eli Newlin being with us, and who also attended the Meeting this morning, with Job Simcock and his wife and their daughter, we started down into Clermont County. We rode about twelve miles to where Friends once had an Indulged Meeting, but had lately been discontinued by removal. Some of us lodged at Isaac Miller's. On First Day morning the 5th, a very hard frost appeared and brought much hurt with it, as well as to all other vegetables.

At 11:00 a.m. we attended Meeting with the few Friends here at Samuel Miller's in the village of Cynthiana. It was to satisfaction. Few others attended besides Friends. In the afternoon we attended a Meeting at 4:00 p.m. in the Methodist Meeting House appointed by our Friend Eli Newlin in which he had much to say to the people. It was a solemn Meeting and I believe the people felt it to be so. The attendance was large and the people appeared well satisfied. After Meeting we parted with our Friend Eli Newlin and the other Friends. It being late in the evening we rode home with our Friend, John Malone, near New Boston about seven miles and did not reach his hospitable home until after dark. The next morning, Second Day the 6th, we parted with our kind Friend and family and started for home.

It was perceivable as we pushed on that the frost yesterday morning had done much damage to the growing corn crop in some of the bottoms. It appeared entirely killed. It seemed it might be a lesson to those who raised so much of their grain for distillation and that a kind of Providence was not satisfied with. The improper use made of this staple article of our country while His judgments are in the land. May the people live righteous. We pushed on through Goshen, Deerfield, on to Lebanon where we fed our horses and took dinner at the hotel. We arrived home about dark, having traveled about fifty miles in the day and found all well and doing well. In looking back over this little visit to Friends of Fairfield, it has raised in our hearts gratitude and thanks to Him that cares for His dependents only, which is joy unspeakable for the favors we are permitted to take. May all praise be given unto Him to whom it is due.

In the latter part of 7th Month this year, our beloved Friends, Hannah Pierson and her husband, Thomas, of Lockport, New York, paid an acceptable and satisfactory visit to the families and Friends of our

Monthly Meetings. She expected to visit all the families in our Yearly Meeting. A great and arduous undertaking to her, yet the reward of faithfulness is to be the purpose before anything of temporal nature. May He who sends His servants into the field to labor be with her unto the end of the visit and she be favored to return to her family and Friends with the reward of sweet peace.

In 8th Month at our Monthly Meeting, our beloved Friend Mary Roberts laid before the Friends a concern to visit the Meeting of Friends in North Carolina and attend the Yearly Meeting there in 11th Month next, which was united with, and she encouraged to attend to the concern as Way may open. The Quarterly Meeting in 9th Month following very firmly endorsed her ministry, and much feeling of Christian sympathy was expelled with her in her concerns, and she expects to start immediately after our Yearly Meeting.

In 10th Month attended Yearly Meeting at Whitewater which was large and favored. Although there was cause of regret in respect to some things that are amongst our religious Society, which I fear are not working for the best. The proposed change of the name of our Boarding School to the name of "Earlham College" was largely decided in the Yearly Meeting and finally the changes made. Although not satisfactory to a large number of Friends, yet submitted to, I fear there is too much of a disposition in some amongst us to join into the customs and maxims of the day, which our forefathers in the truth were called upon to refrain from. It is true there is nothing in the name of a thing, yet we may almost imperceptibly be led away if not very watchful into things that are not for the best, and which Friends as a Society never went into in the early days of the church. The name "College" has never been given to any of our Boarding Schools under the superintendence of a Yearly Meeting before, at least as far as I'm aware of.

Soon after the Yearly Meeting our much-esteemed Friend, David Kenworthy, was taken down sick with liver disease and attended only one Meeting with us afterwards, which also was the last our Friend William Stubbs attended.

David was confined to his room and bed some five or six weeks, manifesting much Christian recognition, his friends not thinking him dangerously bad until a few days before his death. Yet he seemed to be going down all the time. We visited him several times during his sickness; he seemed to have much to say to those who visited him by way of counsel, advice, and admiration as well as encouragement.

Many of his expressions will long be remembered by me as well as many others. He had acceptably filled the Station of Elder in the church for 18 years. A father indeed, in the church an Elder: worthy of double honor though young in years. He quietly passed away on the 29th of 11th Month 1859, aged 49 years. This loss to his family and friends is great. His seat in our Meeting is vacant—on whom will his mantle fall? At one time when his physicians had left his room, he enquired what they thought of his case, and observed some hesitation on the part of his friends in answering him, he said, "You need not fear to tell. I feel quite resigned to the will of the Lord." His funeral was largely attended by Friends and others. After the internment, a very large Meeting was held on the occasion, solemn and much tendered were many hearts. Our Friend had been one that had been looked up to.

# 1860–1869

## 1860

Our beloved Friend, William Stubbs, who had been in declining health for several years, was ordered otherwise, by Him who knows what is best, to leave us. William Stubbs, still continuing quite poorly and in a declining way, gradually sank under disease (dropsy) and peacefully closed his useful and exemplary life on the First Day of 1st Month 1860, aged about 65 years. He had acceptably filled the Station of an Elder for 24 years. We visited him frequently during his confinement in which time he suffered much at intervals, yet appeared cheerful and resigned. Some of his fatherly advice and counsel to me is vividly remembered and will be as long as memory lasts. The loss of these two honored Friends above is much felt amongst us.

Joseph Doane and wife of Center, Ohio, were at our Monthly Meeting in 11th Month [1859]. They were very acceptably with us. Afterwards they visited several families under afflictions, particularly the families of our two late Friends who had been called from works to rewards. Our beloved Friends, Joseph Wright and Eli Newlin of Fairfield Quarter, were acceptably in attendance at our Quarterly Meeting at Salem in 12th Month and also attended our Monthly Meeting. A few days after, Joseph visited several families of our younger Friends. In 8th Month 1860, our beloved Friend Mary Roberts laid before the Monthly Meeting a concern to visit Friends in Canada. Much unity and sympathy was felt and expressed for her, and she was encouraged to attend as way opens. The Quarterly Meeting in 9th Month very cordially endorsed her and left her at liberty to proceed.

In 10th Month, attended our Yearly Meeting, which was large and mostly satisfactory. Our Friend, Joel Bean[1] of Red Cedar, Iowa, laid before the Meeting of Ministers and Elders a concern to visit in the love of the Gospel the Sandwich Islands, which was very feelingly united with, and he was encouraged to attend to his concern as far as way opens. It was a time of encouragement and renewing of strength to many exercised minds, and supplication was offered up for the preservation of our dear Friend that He who called him to the service might go with him and be his support in every trial he might have to pass through. He is quite a young man and has been acknowledged as a Minister only two or three years.

The proposition for establishing a Yearly Meeting in the State of Iowa was weightily considered and resulted in granting the request of Friends in that state, if concurred with by other Yearly Meetings, to be open at Oscaloosa in Mahaska County in the 9th Month, 1863.

In the 11th Month, there was much excitement at the time of the Presidential election. The times portend serious thoughtfulness on a careful observer of things with us as a nation. It has been for two months that a great stir and much parade by the two parties respecting their candidates for office. Yet the Republican ticket was successful and Abraham Lincoln elected President of the United States.

Soon after the result of the election was known in the Southern States, South Carolina declared herself an independent state, as it was thought by the South that Lincoln would be more favorable to the interests of the Northern States, as several of the former presidents had given their influence to the South, especially on the subject of slavery. The excitement ran quite high at the convening of Congress, and still the Northern members were mostly calm and deliberate yet firm in their movements. It was a pretty stormy beginning.

## 1861

In the 1st Month of 1861, the excitement still continues and things are getting worse, and several other of the Southern States are about to join

1. Joel and Hannah Bean, prominent members and traveling ministers of Iowa Yearly Meeting, resisted changes to Quakerism brought about by the late nineteenth-century revivalist movement. In their later years, they founded the College Park Meeting in California, which was unprogrammed and non-doctrinaire, and tried to stay closer to the early Friends in its faith and practice. "Beanite" Quakerism became a model later adopted by many meetings around the United States.

South Carolina, and the Senators and Representatives from those states are leaving Congress. Trials and difficulties are anticipated and the Separationists are forming what they call the "Southern Confederacy" and demanding the evacuation of Southern forts. Bold and highhanded threats are made if [the forts are] not given up to them, all on account of Slavery not being tolerated and upheld according to Southern dictation.

On the 4th of 3rd Month, Abraham Lincoln was installed into office and took his seat as President of the United States. There were a large number of troops for several weeks before stationed about Washington City for the protection of the capital and order amongst the people. It was one of the most exciting times about the city and country that had been experienced since the days of the Revolution, the seceding leaders still demanding the surrender of the Southern forts and the President refusing to comply with their demands. They commenced storming Fort Sumpter near Charleston and continuing for several days, [until] the Union troops surrendered up the fort to the Secessionists. There were only about 150 men in the fort at the time. This caused great excitement amongst the people.

The President immediately imposed a proclamation to raise 75,000 volunteers and to convene the members of Congress. On 4th of 7th Month, in less than one month, 100,000 men were reported as ready, and many of the troops were on their way to Washington and other points of defense.

On the 1st of 6th Month, attended our Meeting for Sufferings, having been lately appointed to fill the vacancy of our beloved Friend, William Stubbs, deceased. The subject of the rebellion and war seemed to engage the solid and deliberate attention of the Meeting, and a short address of caution and counsel on the subject was offered to our subordinate Meetings and members.

Congress met on 4th of 7th Month and there appeared a very determined disposition in the members to put down the rebellion by force as the Secessionists or Rebels would not hear or consider to any thing that could be done, only to acknowledge them as a nation and government. The Rebels were still collecting their troops and preparing for defending their cause, having large numbers about Richmond in Virginia as well as at other points between there and Washington City. There were considerable skirmishes amongst the government troops and Rebels in places. About the 19th of the month, a bloody battle was fought near the Manassas Junction on the railroad from Washington to Richmond. A considerable number on both sides were killed and wounded. This was sorrowful tidings to the Christian believer to see the disposition that men may get into or come to, this day of gospel light and knowledge. How long will it be before the sword will be beaten into plowshares and spears into pruning hooks, and the people learn war no more, and righteousness cover the earth as waters do the sea?

In 10th Month, attended the Yearly Meeting. It was large and favored. Our Friend John Hodgkin from England attended, as well as other Friends from different Yearly Meetings on this continent. A few days before the Yearly Meeting, our Friend John Hodgkin held a Meeting with the soldiers in the Meeting House, there being about 1000 in camp near Richmond [Indiana]. It was a satisfactory meeting to them. During the sitting of the Yearly Meeting, there was much excitement and stir amongst the people about the war. Yet Friends generally, I believe, kept out of it at the time, and we had many interesting and favored sittings of the Meeting for Discipline as well as those for Worship. One Meeting for the youth appointed by our English Friend was an interesting season and will be remembered by many in days to come.

The request to set up a Quarterly Meeting in Kansas was granted. It is composed of three Monthly Meetings—Kansas, Spring Grove, and Cottonwood—lately established in that territory, many Friends from Tennessee having removed there since the commencement of the rebellion.

In 12th Month, there were many reports going that Friends in North Carolina have been very much tried since the rebellion amongst them, and some reports that several individuals were executed on account of their opposition to war and the rebellion, as maintaining their conscientious scruples thereof. Yet after a while, the report proved false, and we learned that Friends there had not been molested up to the time of their Yearly Meeting but were favored and held it in the quiet, and the attendance as large as could a been expected. The mail having been stopped as well as other communication with the rebellious states, so that there is but little information going, only what is received from rebel sources.

## 1862

In 3rd Month 1862 our Friend Thomas Jay of West Branch attended our Quarterly Meeting, which was a favored season. We are but a small Meeting for Discipline, there being but few members composing it to what there once was, yet I trust there is left a body of concerned ones who feel the responsibility that rests on them of holding a Meeting to the honor of truth and the prosperity of the great cause. Thomas Jay and companion afterwards visited all our families composing it as well as several others who had been members—about 60 families of members and 20 that were not members. A very satisfactory visit it was to all and left a good impression and will be remembered in time to come. I accompanied him to most of the families on our part of the settlement to my satisfaction and encouragement. He like-wise visited Salem Monthly Meeting families. About seven years ago he paid a similar visit to the families of our Quarterly Meeting, which was then, as well as now, to our satisfaction and encouragement.

In the 5th Month, much excitement about the war's two bloody battles lately fought by the government troops with the Rebels, one at Fort Donaldson, the other at Pittsburgh Landing on the Tennessee River in the State of Tennessee. Many lives sacrificed to the demon of war. Many being killed as well as a large number wounded. It is awful to think of the destruction of human life in these two battles, especially in the last where it is said that there were more lost slain than in any battle ever fought on this continent. Still there is two large armies of the Union or government troops, as well as of the Rebels waiting for one another. One is at Corinth Mills and the other near Richmond, Virginia.

Awful to think of the depravity of human nature and where and what war will lead to many on both sides, in groping to be the followers of the Prince of Peace yet take up carnal weapons to defend their conceived rights. What will be the consequences of all this in the awful day of reckoning? It is to our Divine Maker we are accountable whether we stand or fall. But they go into the war as a horse rushes into the battle. Solemn considerations indeed to think of. The Savior declared that his Kingdom was not of this world, and therefore his servants could not fight, and further, that they were ashamed of Him and his sayings before a wicked and adulterous generation. He would be ashamed of them before his Father and the Holy Angels. How awful are these considerations when viewed in the light of the Gospel which breathes peace on earth and good will to men.

Very few peaceful men, it appears, have kept to their principles in these perilous times—from information received from different parts of our country—except the Society of Friends. Many of their young members in places have enlisted in the war, which is cause of sorrow and regret. Yet with us here in our Meeting, there is but few who went into the military service. Three have gone into the regular Army, one into the Commissary Department of forwarding stores, and two or three were gone a few days at the call of our Governor, out of about 40 members subject to the draft or conscript.

Whatever may be the end of this war, it is hoped it will be to the downfall or extinction of slavery, "the sum of all villainess," as attested by that eminent Divine and reformer, J. Wesley. Although it may be a sore remedy, yet we as a nation or government, particularly northern states, are implicated or have given our support to this atrocious system, and now, an over-ruling Providence has taken the cause in hand as I verily believe, and will work for the deliverance and ultimate emancipation of the oppressed, as well as other high-handed wickedness in our land connected to slavery. Oh, may it be applicable to us as a nation as it was formerly, that when the judgments of the Most High are in the earth, may the people have wisdom and virtue.

In the 10th Month, attended our Yearly Meeting. It was middling to large. The subject of drafting men for the war was brought before the sitting of the Meeting. The war kept several of our young men from attending, as no person was allowed to leave his residence and go out of the state. Yet a considerable number of them from our state as well as Indiana attended as the excitement was somewhat abated. It was a solemn time to many of our dear young men as well as others. And many were prepared to suffer for their peace principles and their Divine Master rather than go into the war. Martial law being declared in Cincinnati a short time before, on account of the City was going to be taken—it was thought—by Southern invaders, caused much excitement in the country.

Yet Friends were favored to hold our annual solemn Quarterly Meeting in much quiet and without molestation, and it was a season of Divine favor to not a few.

Joel Bean returned his certificate to prepare a visit to the Sandwich Islands, granted by the Yearly Meeting of Ministers and Elders in 1860, with satisfactory information that he had performed the visit to the peace of his mind. After the close of the Yearly Meeting, our Friend, Joshua Douglas from Maine, returned home with us and appointed a Meeting next day. It was to satisfaction. He is a little humble man and refrains more than many other Ministers do. He believes in the ancient simplicity in dress and demeanor.

Our Friend, Arneat Black of Greenwood Monthly Meeting, Indiana, daughter of the late, honored Nathan Hunt, visited the families and parts of families of our Monthly Meeting the latter part of the 10th Month. It was to the satisfaction and encouragement of all I trust. Many sittings were times of favor and renewing of strength as the rain on the thirsty grounds. May it bring forth fruit in due season to the praise of the great Husbandman. Myself and wife accompanied her and companion, Ana M. Pennington, to the families on our part of the settlement to our satisfaction and encouragement.

Our aged and honored Friend father, Joseph Stubbs,[2] having been quite poorly and weakly during the summer, became more feeble in the fall, and his strength failing, he gradually went down and quietly and peacefully passed away without much suffering on the 25th of 10th Month. His funeral took place on First Day, the 26th, in the afternoon. It was largely attended by relatives, Friends and neighbors. After the interment, a large and solemn Meeting was held on the occasion in the Meeting House, where he had been a humble worshipper of his Savior for more than half a century. He was not a member of the Society at his death, having been for many years a constant attender of our religious Meetings and an honorable man in the community in which he lived. He was disowned from the Society many years ago, some high-spirited zeal getting up amongst some of the members and him, which resulted in his disownment.[3] It was thought by some Friends at the time, as well as years afterwards, that he was partially treated with. How often is it applicable in such times, and we to remember that it is better to err in mercy than in judgment.

The 11th Month was a time of some trial and conflict of spirit in which it seems faith was tried to a hair's breadth, and my poor soul almost overcome with the subjections of the old Enemy of all good. So that for many hours one day, it seemed I would have to give up and fall by the way. Yet after I endured for a season and kept in the patience, light sprang up and—praised be the name of Him who never was foiled in battle or beaten in the field. Towards evening, a ray of light of His was seen and

2. Joseph Maddock Stubbs was Joseph's father-in-law, i.e., the father of his wife, Mary (Stubbs) Maddock.

3. Joseph Maddock Stubbs was disowned by Elk Monthly Meeting (Orthodox) in 1830 during the Orthodox/Hicksite separation. Apparently he did not acknowledge error in what he had done, so was not accepted back into membership with Elk Monthly Meeting (Orthodox). His son-in-law's diary, however, reports that later, he was a "constant attender" of the Orthodox meeting in West Elkton until his death. (It should be noted that one did not have to be a member in order to attend a Quaker Meeting for Worship.)

felt by the inner man to that degree that I was once again permitted to enjoy something of a foretaste of Heavenly good, and my tribulated soul in some degree made to leap for joy on the banks of heartfelt deliverance, going on my way, rejoicing in His once-more extended mercy to me, an unworthy creature. Praised be His ever worthy Name.

12th Month, the President, Abraham Lincoln, in 9th Month last, introduced a proclamation declaring all slaves free belonging to Rebels after the first of the year 1863 unless they [the states] returned to their allegiance. It was to all loyal slaveholders who wished to free their slaves, which caused much excitement with the Rebels, but was favorably received by members of Congress. The Rebels being much engaged since the issuing of the proclamation appear to be trying their utmost to sustain their cause and are concentrating larger numbers of troops at and near Richmond, Virginia. The government troops are marching on towards that place so that there is at this time, and for several days past, a bloody conflict going on near Fredericksville, in which several thousand have been slain and likely many more will be before either side surrenders. The awful calamity of war seems to hang over our country at this time. All that can be said or done by man seems to have but little effect in allaying [*sic*] with the engaged troops. May He who holds the destiny of nations in His hand interpose for the relief of and the freedom of the Colored Man, and the awful scourge banished from our once-peaceful yet now-divided land and the peaceable reign of the Messiah.

## 1863

Much excitement during the forepart of this summer, respecting the raids of the notorious J. Morgan into the states of Ohio and Indiana, taking many horses and burning barns, mills, and other buildings in his route. Governor Todd of Ohio ordered out all the militia and all other able-bodied in the counties of southern Ohio for the protection of the state, and many in our midst responded to the call to endeavor to capture him and his company, of which it was said there was several thousand. After a few days, they mostly returned as more came than was wanted and the excitement went off in a short time, and Morgan with some of his principal men were taken prisoners in the northeastern part of the state. How little dependence is to be placed in military operations as Morgan came very near making his escape. After being taken he was put into the State Prison. After staying there a while, he succeeded in making his escape. In the excitement, some three or four of our members went into the hurry and hustle, which shows how unstable the mind is when not placed on Him who said, "My Kingdom is not of this world," and therefore his servants could not fight.

Our Friend, Mary Roberts, with a woman Friend, paid a visit to Governor Todd this year, respecting the drafting of our young men into the military service. He heard her attentively and said he could not do anything to relieve them and regretted it, and said all relief could only be obtained from the Department at Washington. He further remarked that he had been furnished with a copy of our Book of Disciplines and had read it with much interest and appeared to understand our religious scruples.

Some frost the latter part of the 7th Month, which nipped the vegetation and on the 29th of 8th Month, a pretty hard frost, which done considerable of damage in some places.

9th Month, a remarkably good season and a large yield of corn—as well as good crops of other kinds of grain—and vegetables. The like having rarely occurred in the past, which no doubt caused the hearts of many to give thanks and praise to our Almighty Father in Heaven for His many favors towards us. It seems that our lives at the present time are cast in pleasant places to what many are who are near the contending armies of this desolating war raging in our now-divided land.

On account of the indisposition of my aged father, I was prevented from attending several of the first sittings of our Yearly Meeting this year. Some of the latter sittings I attended were favored seasons, and through the condescending of our Holy Head many hearts were made to rejoice in secret, although a backsliding people I fear we are in this day.

A few days after this, our nephew Allen Stubbs' remains were brought home and interned in our burial ground. [Actually, Allen was Mary's half-brother.] He had enlisted into the military service in 8th Month 1862 and was marched off in a few days and into battle at Richmond, Kentucky and was taken prisoner. He received a slight wound by a spent cannon ball which did not disable him much. Being paroled, he returned to his father's house to the no little joy of his brothers and sisters. He had for several years previous lived with an uncle in Iowa and some months before his enlistment lived at Westfield, Indiana, so that his return was mixed with joy and grief, and it appeared evident he regretted the course he had taken. A sister said to him, whatever made him enlist. He said he hardly knew for what and remarked he would give all he had in this world to be out of the difficulty.

Being shortly afterwards exchanged [*sic*], he returned to the army and then marched into Tennessee, afterwards down further into Alabama and Mississippi to near Vicksburg where he was detailed. He went on to a field hospital on the river where he continued several months as an assistant to the physician in the hospital, preparing to take care of the sick and wounded. He wanted to be there rather than be instrumental in taking the life of his fellow man. In the 8th Month following, he took the chronic diarrhea and was removed up to a hospital at Memphis, Tennessee, where he only lived a few days after his arrival there. His younger brother, John F., about the 1st of 11th Month went down to Memphis and had his remains brought to his father's residence where a large company of relatives and Friends attended his funeral, after which a large and solemn Meeting was held on the occasion where much counsel was held out to those present. Although he was a young man who gave much promise of usefulness in his day, but like many other young men was taken in the excitement, and through unwatchfulness partook of forbidden things. Yet after all, his relatives and Friends have more cause for joy than grief, and hope through the pardoning mercy of a dear Redeemer, he was entered into everlasting rest.

12th Month, First Day, the Meeting for Sufferings called a special meeting of their members to consider the subject of drafting our members for the war. As there appeared a disposition in some members in Congress to favor the conscientious scruples of Friends, a proposition was received from Baltimore Friends to consider the propriety of all the Meetings for Sufferings on this continent to send delegates to confer on this important subject. Accordingly, four Friends were appointed to meet in Baltimore in a few days at such a Meeting or conference and we adjourned to meet on the 22nd. I was prevented from attending at this time on account of indisposition at time adjourned to. There were about 40 members in attendance. Those appointed to attend the conference at Baltimore reported they attended and that committees were present from New England, New York, Baltimore, Ohio, Indiana and Western Yearly Meetings; Iowa having not had time to call the Meeting for Suffering together, North Carolina being cut off by the Rebellion. The report of the proceedings of the conference were read and the ancient grounds of our Christian testimony were alluded to in the report, and much counsel and advice was held to the faithful in the report of this important testimony on all wars and fighting. Many Friends were encouraged in this important movement of Friends in this perilous time.

## 1864

In 2nd Month, Congress so amended the Conscript Law so as to allow the conscientious scruples of Friends and others the privilege to go into the hospital or amongst the Freedmen or pay $300 for the use and benefit of the Freedmen, which was very trying to some Friends. There was in some places Friends who were willing to go in, and some paid the $300. Yet it was evident that there was in it a compromise of principle. This was very trying to all rightly concerned Friends. Although there was no occurrence in our Meeting except in one instance: a member removing here from Indiana was drafted and Friends mostly helped make up the money. I was one that paid some towards it. Yet afterwards had to regret it and if I was to do it again, I should not or could not pay anything in that way. But sometimes in the excitement, we look too much to others and do not go down into a close examination and judge for ourselves the wisdom of truth, which principle leads out of all error of slavish fear into that Light which makes manifest and in which no deception can live.

Our Friend, Mary Roberts, obtained a Minute from the Monthly Meeting in this month to have some Meetings amongst those not proffering with us in the villages and larger towns in the country around. (Myself and wife having felt a concern to accompany her and her husband in these visits.) The first was held at Seven Mile on a First Day p.m. and was a memorable time to all the people and they seemed well satisfied and invited her to come again. On the following day at 3:00 p.m., we attended a large Meeting in the Protestant Meeting House in Middletown. The last two Meetings were seasons of Divine Favor and were made to exclaim in language of the Apostle, "I perceive of a truth that God is no respecter of persons, but in all motions them that love and fear Him and wish righteousness are accepted with Him."

Also attended on a First Day afternoon a large Meeting in Somerville and one on the same day of the week at Hamilton with the Colored People. I attended their scriptural school in the morning and after it the Meeting in their Meeting House. Rather a novel sight to us to see so many of this people in a company together. They made a very commendable appearance and appeared satisfied with our visit to them. Their scriptural school is an interesting one and is well conducted. They have a school for common education amongst themselves and manifest quite an interest in their privilege of our state laws in allowing them to organize schools amongst themselves. They have a sufficient number to do so. I suppose there was about 300 present at the Meeting.

In 3rd Month, much excitement about drafting, as a draft was expected to take place as the calls of the President had not been filled up by volunteers. The people are raising among us a bounty to induce volunteers to offer to go which is trying to Friends who feel bound to the support of our ancient Christian testimonies, and many are strongly solicited to help make up the bounty fund. A few of our young men as well as older ones contributed to the fund and the money was at last made up, and the people relieved of a draft at this time.

The latter part of 4th Month, the people were again called upon to furnish more men. There being large companies of militia organized into what was called "State Guards" in our state, who had gone into their organizations expecting to be relieved from being drafted, the Governor of Ohio offered the guards to the service of the President. They were accepted and they were at once ordered out to meet in a few days at different places to continue for 100 days' service. This seemed to be the most trying time of any that had took place. Having never thought of being taken in such a difficulty, but so it was, they had to go or furnish substitutes; some left their families very destitute of anything to live on for they were not able to hire substitutes. Those that were left generously contributed to the support of their families.

Soon after this there was another large draft ordered by the President, if not filled up by volunteers by the 1st of 8th Month. It is like when one woe was over, behold a greater one came, which caused a very great excitement and was a very trying time with the people. The former remedy again had to endeavor to raise a large bounty to induce volunteers to offer and ward off the draft. The draft was put off from time to time so that the vacancy was filled up without a draft in our Township, a few being drafted in other places in the County. Yet after that we were relieved from going by volunteers and by paying large bounties from $400 to $500 and $600, and part of it to be raised by taxation on the people. So that it appears that the system of war is fought with many evils, inconveniences, and oppressions, as well as tyranny in the extreme, and well may the old adage be applicable, "The tender mercies of the wicked are cruel."

There was a large number of Friends drafted in different parts of our Yearly Meeting. Most, or perhaps nearly all, availed themselves of the provisions of the Conscript Law to pay $300 for the benefit of the Freedman, but so far there has not been any of our members drafted except one or two instances in Butler County, and they were [not] called upon to appear as the quotas were filled without calling on any. We were grateful to the people as well as Friends to be relieved. Yet others viewed the conscript clause for Friends in some degree of jealousy, and it did not set so well as we could a wished. I believe that Friends as a religious body would a fared better and the peace principles advanced more if we had of laid still and simply petitioned our national government with the real scruples we as a religious society held on the subject of all wars and fighting. Although we might a had to suffer, for it is a tried and a proved people the Lord will have. The church of Christ has ever prospered under deep and sore persecution.

The past summer has been a time of an unusual occurrence. To see how we have in this vicinity been relieved from going into the deadly conflict. May we ever take it as an interpretation of all-Divine Providence and remember His protection and regard towards us in these perilous times. May we be so watchful and in the fear of Him to conduct ourselves. We are endeavoring to follow the dear Redeemer and are subjects of his peaceable Kingdom here on earth.

10th Month, attended Yearly Meeting. It was not so large as usual on account of the war, and drafting of Friends caused them to stay away, yet it was satisfactory. Friends were favored to transact their business in much harmony and brotherly consideration. The Committee appointed last year to consider the scriptures of our discipline reported amendments and some changes on which the Meeting sat for two days and received deliberate consideration. The Meeting approved and a good degree of unity and good feeling was expressed by Friends at the adopting of it. There was two subjects which claimed more deliberation in the Meeting than all the others did. The war was considerably discussed, but was left nearly as it had stood for many years. The others on our members joining secret societies or connecting themselves with such was considerably denounced. Also some amendments were made but not as much restrictions as perhaps might a been. But there was a disposition in many Friends in places to join in things that are not for the best, especially the young and inexperienced in these perilous times. There is an improvement in many of our youth in our various Christian testimonies, especially in younger families that are coming up. May they be strengthened and encouraged to hold on their way. Several Ministers from a distance attended and much counsel and advice was given. The Meeting closed under a very solemn feeling.

After Yearly Meeting we concluded to send our daughter, Martha Ann, to the Boarding School, or Earlham College as it is called, the winter term commencing the 12th of 10th Month, and she entered as a pupil in the preparatory department.

My aged and honored father was quite poorly and feeble during the latter part of summer and for part of 10th Month, and about the middle of the month he was taken much worse and continued to get weaker and gradually declined away and peacefully closed a long life on the 30th of 10th Month in his 87th year. He prayed through some very trying seasons during his last sickness, and at times had some gloomy foreboding of his acceptance with his dear Redeemer. But he made his close and seemed much more resigned. He peacefully closed his time here on earth and we are consoled in the belief that in the pardoning mercy of the Savior, he found acceptance with his dear Redeemer and entered into everlasting rest. His funeral was on Third Day morning, the 1st of 11th Month and was pretty largely attended. After the internment a large Meeting was held. The people generally coming in to the Meeting House where he had been a diligent Attender for near half a century. It was a solemn Meeting. He was the last survivor of the Friends who had families that emigrated from Columbia County, Georgia in the year 1805 on account of the baneful effects of slavery. He, in the autumn of that year, settled on a farm about one mile south of West Elkton where he lived nearly fifty years. The last eight years, he lived with John, his son in the village.

In 11th Month this year, Ann Marmon, a young Minister of Whitewater Monthly Meeting, visited the families of the Meeting; also about fifteen families of some of those who were not members, but who were in the practice occasionally of attending our Meeting. In all about 67 sittings. A satisfactory visit and leaves a good impression on many minds.

In 12th Month, attended our Quarterly Meeting at Salem. Five Ministers were in attendance from other places, both far and near, without any previous knowledge of each other attending, to wit: Daniel Williams [and] Nathan Douglas of the State of Maine; David H. Bennett of the State of New York; John Elliott of Ohio; and Eli Newlin. It was a rather remarkable time, especially on First Day. The testimonies on First Day were directed pretty closely to the unbelievers and those that are endeavoring to invalidate and do away with the plan of salvation and atonement of our dear Redeemer. This class, of whom several were present, were powerfully sermoned. This doctrine might do well to live by. But when the trying hour came for us to leave this world, it would not do to die in vain. It would be for us to call on the rocks to hide us from the frowning of an offended God. It was an alarming time.

## 1865

1st Month, the 5th, I left home early this morning to visit Earlham College, Martha Ann wishing for some of us to come up again (her mother being up some time ago). I got on the morning train at Camden and arrived at Richmond in about an hour and walked out to the College about a mile. I arrived just before Meeting set. It was an interesting occasion to see so many young people collecting at their usual weekday Meeting and the comely order and sittings that pervaded this large and beautifully open young people. A pleasing sight indeed. The Meeting was held in silence except a short supplication by one of the teachers, after which the meeting was loud, the scholars leaving in relation as when they took their seats.

We afterwards went down to the parlor where Martha Ann and Sally Jones came in to see me and appeared glad that I had arrived in time to attend Meeting. We pretty soon went down to dinner where the same order was observed as at Meeting in taking their seats. I spent the afternoon walking about the premises and heard one or two classes recite. I spent some time in the evening in social intercourse with the superintendent, very agreeably, respecting the school. In the evening before returning to rest, we all collected in the reading room. After a suitable praise, the superintendent read the 12th Chapter of Numbers, which after a solemn praise, we all retired to rest.

In the morning at breakfast, after all had eaten, the 4th Chapter of Acts was read. All returned to their different apartments in their usual order as before. After returning to the parlor and spending a few minutes with Martha Ann and Sally, we took leave of each other and I started for home.

After spending a day and night in the interesting institution of learning I was glad of having the privilege of spending time talking with the superintendent as well as teachers on the committee appointed to the charge of the Yearly Meeting for the improvement of the pupils, manifest both in literary learning as well as religious instruction. It was time well spent by me and will be remembered in days to come. There is about 175 pupils in attendance: 100 boys and 75 girls. The largest attendance since the school was opened.[4]

In 2nd Month, our brother, John Stubbs,[5] died very suddenly. He had been complaining some for about two weeks. In going in to see him on Fourth Day morning, pretty early, I saw he was quite poorly. A few hours after, I again called and saw he was getting worse. The Doctor being present said he appeared to be in a critical situation and wished counsel sent for, which could not come until next morning. It seemed little or nothing could now be done to retrieve him. He gradually weakened away and peacefully closed his life on Fifth Day morning about 2:00 a.m., the 16th of 2nd Month, 1865, aged about 64 years. He seemed unconscious for several hours before he died and never spoke after the morning he was taken worse. It was a very trying time to his family to have to part with him in so short and unexpected time. Yet his family and Friends have the comfortable hope and belief that he is at rest with his dear Redeemer in the mansion's eternal rest. His funeral took place on Sixth Day after a large attendance of relatives and Friends. After the internment a large and solemn Meeting was held.

Our friends, Sam and Jane Jones, having removed some time ago from Honey Creek Monthly Meeting settled with us, Jane being a minister. In 2nd Month, our Friend Jane Jones obtained a Minute from our Monthly Meeting to visit the families belonging to our Quarterly Meeting which she attended. She had some public Meetings in several of the villages around.

In 4th Month, our Friend, William Beard of Salem Monthly Meeting, and David Huddlestone, his companion, visited the families generally in our Monthly Meeting, besides several families that once had been members. A satisfactory visit I trust it was to all. He was much favored in some families and his labors leave a good impression on many minds and it will be remembered in days yet to come.

A time of much excitement in our Country. The reported victory gained by the troops of our government over the Rebel Confederacy seemed to rain acclamation of joy in many hearts at the termination of this cruel war and rebellion. As the Rebel armies surrendering and the prospect of the return of peace once more to our beloved country was very consoling to every Christian patriot and statesman.

4. These paragraphs from the diary are copied in context between 1st Month 1st and 1st Month 10th in the letters to and from Mattie.

5. i.e., Mary's half-brother, John Maddock Stubbs.

But alas, our high expectations of peace were frustrated by the sorrowful tidings of the assassination of our honored President Abraham Lincoln on the night of the 14th of this month. He was shot in one of the theaters in Washington by a wicked man by the name of Boothe [sic]. The sorrowful news spread like lightening through the land. Everything was wrapt in gloom and mourning for the loss of so great and good a statesman. Time passed on and the shock seemed to pass away, and the Vice President Andrew Johnson was installed into the office of President, and I hope it was a good lesson to the nation, not to put more confidence in man, but place all in Him who holds the destiny of nations as well as individuals in his hand.

A very extremely wet season for planting. As much so that there was but little done until very late. Yet after a time, the weather became better and planting and sowing was done through very late in 6th Month. After which the rains came on again and injured our wheat considerably so that there was not more than half a crop.

1st of 6th Month, attended the Meeting for Sufferings at Richmond, the members were generally in attendance. The suffering conditions of Friends in the South, particularly in Tennessee, claimed the sole deliberation of the Meeting and resulted in appointing two Friends to visit Tennessee and relieve them as much as possible and as our subordinate Meeting directed. Two Friends were appointed to visit our Friends in Tennessee and render all the relief they can for their comfort who have been favored to maintain our Christian testimonies in regard to the Great Preserver of Man for His watchful care over them in these severe trials.

After my return, the subject of offering funds for our Friends in Tennessee was opened in one of our weekday Meetings and over $60 raised.[6] Our Friend, Owen Edgerton of Whitewater Monthly Meeting, paid a satisfactory visit to many of our Friends in the first part of 6th Month this year.

A time of deep wading, as it were, in the mindly [*sic*] waters of discouragement, which was no doubt permitted in mercy to attend my pathway at times for several weeks, so that I was almost ready to give up all hopes. Yet in some of these smart tries and proving reasons, the patience and responding confidence in the arms of power, which has never failed to relieve His humble dependent children. I was made to rejoice on the banks of true heartfelt deliverance of which I was in some degree

6. Sixty dollars in 1865 was the equivalent of $1,193.09 in 2025.

permitted to experience, unworthy as I feel to be and to rejoice in His ever-worthy name, who is forever worthy of all honor, praise, domination, and majesty, not only now but henceforth for evermore.

At Monthly Meeting in 8th Month, a committee, having been appointed in Quarterly and Monthly Meetings previously, attended our Meeting as our new discipline to review the appointment of Elders. The committee proposed that a large number be added to the number of Elders now standing, which was somewhat trying to many families, but after an expression of unity of the former Elders, when the subject was laid before the Meeting, it was proposed that the appointment stop here and that it was a sufficient number. This was freely united with by Friends generally. This caused some of the committee to reflect on the Meeting and become excited. Yet Friends were favored to maintain their ground deliberately considering the subject, and all appeared satisfied and quietly passed away from it, except a few of the committee who were the cause of this unpredicted subject. When we undertake to do the honest work in our own wills and strength, we are sure to fail, which was the cause of the instance before us.

In 10th Month, attended several of the sittings of the Yearly Meeting, which were interesting and solemn seasons. Our English Friends, Joseph B. Bealthwait [*sic*][7] and Joseph Craftsfield, were present with several Ministers from other Yearly Meetings on this continent. $30,000 was directed to be raised by our subordinate Meetings for the benefits of the Freedmen. Our Friend, John Henry Douglas of Center, Ohio, was liberated by the select Yearly Meeting to attend the extension service in the ministry to Friends and others in Great Britain and other parts of the European Continent.

11th Month 7th, attended a called Meeting for Sufferings on the subject of the Colored People. An interesting and appropriate memorial [i.e., memorandum] was prepared to be laid before the legislature of Indiana on the rights of the Colored People and asking them to repeal the obnoxious laws which bear heavily and oppressive on them who incline to settle in the state. Also a memorial was prepared to be presented to Congress at a suitable time respecting the rights of the Freedman of the South and the Colored People generally.

7. Joseph Bevan Braithwaite (1818–1905) was a conservative, evangelical English Quaker minister who traveled in America to counter the teachings of Elias Hicks. In 1887, Braithwaite was largely responsible for drafting the Richmond Declaration, a statement of faith widely used by Evangelical Friends.

12th Month, attended Quarterly Meeting at Salem, a satisfactory Meeting. A committee was appointed to attend the Monthly Meeting with the Advice and visit the families as far as way opens. The committee attended our Monthly Meeting on Fifth Day 21st. Their company and services were satisfactory and encouraging, after which they visited all (or nearly so) four families to satisfaction and their encouragement, I trust.

25th of 12th Month, our long absent brother and sister, Robert and Delilah Stubbs,[8] who after several sojourns in Iowa for the last four years and living in the Colorado Territory, arrived at our home. We had a joyful greeting, being about 10 years; although joyous in some ways, yet other ways painful. As several of the connections came in during the afternoon and evening, that loved ones once here had left this state of probation and gone to the land from where no traveler ever returned.

Our brother and sister look well and not much broke in the time since leaving here. Their daughter, Hannah, was with them. She is an amiable young woman about 22 years old. William A, a small lad, and their little girl, Flora about 4 years old, is with them. They seem to enjoy the visit to their native land very much with their Friends and relatives. They left Denver City about the 1st of 10th Month and were about 6 weeks crossing the plains to Iowa. They stayed in Iowa a short time, then went to brother Joseph H. Stubbs [another of Mary's brothers] in Lake County, Indiana. They stayed two weeks there, coming to Wayne County, and stayed awhile before arriving here.

Some two or three weeks after arriving here, they had the very shocking and heart-rending intelligence of the death of their daughter, Lucy Ann, wife of Phillip Miller, which occurred about the 20th of 12th Month, after a very short illness. It seemed almost for a while to overcome them, as they never had an account of her sickness before her death. Yet after a while, they became resigned to the sad stroke and bereavement, believing that the dear departed was, through the mercy of the dear Redeemer, into a mansion.

## 1866

Our relatives stayed during 1st Month and 2nd Month of 1866, visiting their connections as well as many Friends and neighbors and enjoyed

8. Robert Harvey Stubbs was the brother of Mary (nee Stubbs) Maddock and Joseph's brother-in-law.

much satisfaction in their sermons of social intercourse. They attended many of our religious Meetings and received much interest with us as well as we with them. Yet the time arrived when they had to leave us for their far-off, distant home. We all attended Meeting on First Day, the 10th of 3rd Month, which was annually a solemn and favored Meeting, and allusions made and petitions offered up by Mary Roberts and others to the Throne of Grace for the preservation of our dear relatives who were about to leave us for their home. After Meeting, many came forward and bid them a long, and perhaps a final, farewell. It was a solemn time. They, with many connections, came to our house and took dinner with us. Many came in during the afternoon and evening to bid them farewell. The others came next morning, and we too took our final leave with desire for each other's preservation; it was a solemn parting. I furnished them with some books—Stephen Grellet's *Life Journey and Observations.*

In 2nd Month, our Friend, Mary Roberts, laid before our Monthly Meeting a concern to visit in gospel love the Meetings of Iowa Yearly Meeting as far as way opens, particularly remote Meetings and some Meetings in Western Yearly Meeting. Much unity and sympathy was felt and expressed, and they encouraged her to attend to the prospect as truth opens the way, which was fully endorsed by the Quarterly Meeting. In 3rd Month, Delilah Stubbs[9] was liberated to go with her as companion; also our young Friend, Eli Kenworthy, as assistant companion.

In 5th Month, our brother and neighbor, Joseph Mendenhall, died of an illness of some two weeks. He had a birthright in the Society. (He was my stepmother's second son.) But moving out of Society he suffered himself to be disavowed for more than 30 years in much of an unconscientious and indifferent state of mind, and he raised a large family of children. But being taken down very sick, he seemed apprehensive that he should not recover and lamented very much his folly and misspent time, and the duties he should have attended to, but now it was too late. I almost daily during the latter of his sickness visited him. He frequently told me if spared to live, he should endeavor to live entirely a different life to what he had lived. A life devoted to his Lord and Master. He frequently wished to hear the Bible read through the day and seemed comforted in these sessions of reading retirement. He gave much comfort to his

9. This Delilah Stubbs was the wife of William Stubbs, brother of Newton and Jesse Stubbs. In 1846, Delilah and William made a trip to Wrightsborough, Georgia, to see about bringing free people of color to Ohio.

children and near his end expressed that his peace was made with God. A large and solemn Meeting was held at his funeral.

In 6th Month attended our Quarterly Meeting held at Salem. A pretty good Meeting. Milton Winstow of Back Creek attended. He had an appointed Meeting with us at Elk Creek on Second Day. It was pretty well attended, a comfortable Meeting. At Monthly Meeting on Fifth Day following, our Friend William Beard of Salem attended, a satisfactory time. At 6:00 p.m., he had a Meeting with the Colored People. Several of them attended. An interesting opportunity for which they appeared thankful. On Sixth Day 22nd in the afternoon, he had two small Meetings with the refugees lately from Kentucky on Elk Creek, a mixed race of human beings. They appeared satisfied with what was said. I hope it will do some good. They never had any education. They are now sending their children to school.

On Seventh Day 23rd at 3:00 p.m., we had a Meeting on Brown's River with the Colored People. A considerable number attended with some white people, a satisfactory Meeting. There is several Colored People living in this place at the present time. They are mostly engaged in chopping wood. They are getting along pretty well. They are an interesting class of their race, temperate and industrious. We parted with them under feelings of deep sympathy and Christian regard. They appreciated much attachment to us as well as we to them. Lewis and Martha Ann Taylor, as well as myself and wife, attended with William and his companion, John Davis.

On First Day 24th, we went as companions with William Beard and other Friends to Hamilton to attend the Colored Scriptural School at 9:00 a.m. and also the Meeting for Worship with them at 11:00 a.m. Both the school and Meeting were satisfactory. We dined at the Widow Lymms', an interesting woman.

On next First Day, 7th Month 1st, attended with the aforesaid Friends, also with J. and M. Kenworthy, at Oxford with the Colored People at their scriptural school at 9:00 a.m. A large and interesting school, about 100 in attendance. A more interesting scriptural school I never attended amongst white people. We attended Meeting at 11:00 a.m., a pretty large attendance. A good outing to us and appeared satisfactory to them. Much was said, and may it fasten on the minds as a nail in a sure plank. We arrived at J. Jacksons', an interesting family of Colored People. We returned home in the evening and felt well-satisfied with our visit to Oxford. There appears to be a very interesting class of Colored People living there who appear to manifest much interest in the education of their children, which was encouraging to us.

In 9th Month at our Quarterly Meeting, our Friend, Wright Book and his companion from Vermillion, Illinois, and Charles Fleoffers of Richmond attended. Our Friend, William Beard of Salem Monthly Meeting, laid before us a concern to visit in gospel love the approaching Yearly Meeting of Friends in North Carolina and its subordinate Meetings, which was weightily considered and sympathy and good was felt and expressed for him, and he was encouraged to attend to his prospect. It seemed it might be an evening sacrifice required of him, he being in or near his 80th year.

In 10th Month, my brothers, Henry and Samuel from Iowa, were in here on a visit and also to get the balance of our aged father's estate. I endeavored to settle with them as well as I could, but not to as much satisfaction as an Executor as I could a wished, after giving way to and sacrificing more than justice demanded.

In this month, Samuel and Jane Jones removed to Duck Creek, Indiana after staying over two years with us. At our Quarterly Meeting in this month at Salem, Elwood Ashburn from Iowa and Mary N. Hadley of Springfield, Ohio attended a pretty satisfactory Meeting. They attended an appointed meeting at Elk on Second Day. Also Elwood attended our Monthly Meeting on Fifth Day following.

## 1867

At Monthly Meeting in 3rd Month, our Friend, Mary Roberts, was liberated and obtained a Minute to attend Fairfield, Center, and Miami Quarters and to appoint some Meetings in towns and villages around in our country. Also to visit the Infirmaries of Preble and adjoining counties. Martha Ann Taylor is to be her companion. On the 24th we attended with them an appointed Meeting at Jacksonburg at 3:00 p.m. Although small it was satisfactory. Also on First Day at 3:00 p.m., 4th Month 21st, we attended with our Friends an appointment at Green Bush near where we formerly lived, pretty large and satisfactory.

5th Month, attended Miami Quarterly Meeting with my wife, she being one of the committee appointed by last Quarterly Meeting to visit the three Eastern Quarters on account of a request for the privilege of holding a Yearly Meeting to be held at Wilmington, Ohio. Several of the committee were present and it was a pretty large Meeting. Having not attended it for several years, it was indeed satisfactory to mingle with many Friends again. We lodged last night with our friend, Achilles Pugh, in Waynesville and after Meeting today, dined with our friend. We rode to Springboro, eight miles in the evening and stayed with our kind Friends, David Miller and family. We attended Friends Meeting on First Day of 6th Month at which our friend, Irone Jay of Indiana, attended. Also Zeri Hough of New Garden and Isaac [?] had Meeting. It was a pretty good Meeting though the attendance small. Dined at John Hadley's and went for home in the p.m. And arrived late in the evening, about 16 miles.

In the 6th Month, attended our Quarterly Meeting at Salem, satisfactory and encouraging Meeting, particularly on First Day. Our friends Elkanah Beard from Cherry Grove, and John Jessups of Dover attended. Our friend Elkanah had an appointment Meeting with us at Elk on Second Day at 1:00 p.m., pretty large and satisfactory. John Jessups attended our Monthly Meeting on the Fifth Day following. We visited several families on Sixth and Seventh Days. On First Day, attended two of Mary Roberts' appointments a few miles distance. In the evening attended a Meeting at the funeral of our young friend, Sally Jones, a solemn and good Meeting, pretty well attended. On Second Day morning, our friend John had a Meeting for our members, pretty well attended, yet not as satisfactory as other Meetings had been, that Christian charity was wanting in some of his expectations.

9th Month, our Quarterly Meeting held at Elk was a pretty good Meeting on Seventh Day. On First Day, it was very largely attended by other people, which is generally the case at this time of year with us. Thomas Jay of West Branch very acceptably in attendance.

10th Month attended our Yearly Meeting. Pretty large and most of its sittings were solemn and encouraging sermons. There seems to be a class raising up with us in many places who appears very active and proffers much concern for the cause. Yet it is to be feared that they have not got deep enough to be established on the immutable foundations, the Rock of Ages. Several Minutes in attendance from other Yearly Meetings on this continent. Our young friend, John Henry Douglas, returned to the Yearly Meeting of Ministers and Elders the Minute granted him two years ago in order to perform religious services and a visit to England, Ireland, and three other parts of the European Continent. Soon after Yearly Meeting we organized again our First Day School for Scriptural Instructions, with a prospect of keeping it up during the winter, which has been pretty largely attended.

11th Month 3rd, our aged friend and brother, Charles Swain of Eaton, Ohio, a Minister of the Methodist Church, attended our Meeting on First Day. Very acceptably. Had much to communicate. Pretty good attendance of Friends and others.

12th Month 15th John L. Fall, a Minister of the Wesleyan congregation of New Paris, Ohio, had an appointed Meeting with us on First Day p.m. at our Meetinghouse. Pretty well attended and satisfactory. A few days after attending Quarterly Meeting at Salem, our nephew, Job Smith of Cedar Creek, Iowa, returned with Friends here a First Day evening and visited several families during the week, until Fifth Day. At our Monthly Meeting which he attended, the proposition for recording our friend Martha Ann [Taylor], a Minister in the Gospel, was laid before the Meeting. While considered and labored with, she was acknowledged accordingly. It was a good Monthly Meeting. Our Friend Job Smith visited several more families during this week and again attended our First Day Meeting. Also our friend, Martha Watkins of Goshen, Ohio, attended and Nathan Ogleby, a Minister of the Methodists in Middletown likewise attended. A large and favored Meeting, in which all the Ministers exercised their gifts to the satisfaction and encouragement of all present.

## 1868

Cold weather during the 1st of 2nd Month this year. The ground hard frozen all the time, considerable snow fall. Allen Jay, a Minister of Greenfield Monthly Meeting in Indiana, attended our Monthly Meeting in 2nd Month. A good and favored Meeting. Also Stephen H. Leas of New Garden attended with a prospect of visiting some of our younger families. He was encouraged to attend to this concern. Our friend Allen Jay is a young Minister and appears much concerned for the cause and I trust is doing much good in the exercise of his valuable gift. May his labor have the right effect with us. In the latter part of the 2nd Month and first part of 3rd Month, Warvel L. Francis, a United Brethren Minister, and D. Lancaster, Methodist, attended some of our weekday Meetings. He had some short communications to deliver amongst us which were satisfactory. They with others were attending a "protracted Meeting," as they called them, at the Union meetinghouse in West Elkton, which continued for several weeks in which there seemed to be much excitement and many joined in prosperous conversation. Some few of our young members joined in it. It was hoped that there would be a change wrought and amendments of life begun in some at least of the reckless youth of our vicinity. But I am sorrowful to relate that most of them pretty soon went back into their former habits of sin and frivolity. A few seemed to continue in their preferred conversations and seemed to be changed in heart.

In 3rd Month, our Quarterly Meeting was pretty well attended by Friends here as well as by a few from Salem. Levi Jeppart from Richmond and Rufus King of Walnut Ridge attended and Vienna Johnson of Cherry Grove attended. A satisfactory Meeting. Much was communicated and I hope lasting impressions made on some minds.

Our young friend Rufus King seems to have a very peculiar gift and speaks with much feeling, yet not an acknowledged Minister.

He is a native of North Carolina and in the late rebellion was pressed into the Rebel Army and afterwards made his way into the Union Army. Although he says he was sensible when first taken that war was wrong and inconsistent with the Gospel, yet having no knowledge of the Quakers and their principles. He says he could never raise a gun or weapon to kill a human being. During a skirmish or battle while in the Rebel service, he was ordered to fire on the enemy but refused. The officer broke out in very profane language that if he did not attend to orders, he should be shot. Rufus told him he could not take the life of a fellow being on no occasion whatever. Whilst they were conversing, a ball hit the officer on the head and killed him instantly, which made deep impressions on his mind, confirming the attitude of his course.

Soon after, he got into the Union Army, and being released he came to Indiana where he joined a religious society, but not feeling satisfied, he became acquainted with Friends and their principles, which were in accordance as he believed, especially in respect to war doctrine, and he soon joined the membership with them. He seems now to be an able advocate for the cause of his Redeemer, although only engaged in the work of the Ministry for but a few months past.

Our young people as well as many of our older Friends seem very much interested in him and his labors. I saw him at last Quarterly Meeting at Richmond and felt much for his getting along and advancement in the cause. He seems to have improved in his gift very much since then; as some young people, a few of our members included, attending Meetings in the village became awakened, or perhaps somewhat excited in relation to the salvation of their souls, it was no doubt a solemn time with some. At least it will have some effect on their minds for good. Some few of them have appeared in our Meetings in communication with a spreading of the goodness of the Lord in their souls, which was encouraging, and I trust will have some effect with them in turning them from their evil ways to their Redeemer who is waiting to be gracious to all who sincerely call upon His name.

At our Monthly Meeting a few days after Quarterly Meeting, Jesse L. Hartley, a Minister of Gilead Monthly Meeting, Ohio, was with us. Levi Francis, a United Brethren Minister, asked permission to sit with us, which was granted. It was a favored Meeting. Several of our young Friends attended and I trust were encouraged and strengthened in their Zion-bound journey. It was an interesting Meeting to all. The Meeting appointed in the evening by our friend Jesse L. Hartley was largely attended by our young people. A remarkable and favored opportunity. There was a singular circumstance that took place in the Meeting.

Rather an unusual affair. Lewis Francis attended and spoke considerable and at one time proposed to sing a Hymn, as he thought in the way that R. Barclay treated singing in his valuable Apology. After making some remarks on his exercise before commencing the Hymn, at beginning he was touched by one of our Elders sitting by his side and whispered to that he was out of order, and he was taking up too much of the time of the Meeting, which was our friend Jesse L. Hartley's appointment. He then said to the Meeting that it was suggested to him he was taking up too much time of the Meeting and sat down.

It was very trying to several present. Our friend spoke considerably afterwards to several present. The Meeting closed pretty satisfactory. Lewis' sermon very much tried the members, but after a pretty free interview with him after the Meeting and next morning, he seemed to be sensible that he was out of his place, and if he had understood things better, he would not have attempted such an exercise. I think it was more for the want of information of our principles, and perhaps self-activity or anxiety with him, that caused him to do all he did. He had been looking forward to joining Friends and had withdrawn from the Brethren. I believe he was an honest seeker after the good and the will of his Divine Maker. May he be preserved in the patience and simplicity of the truth which leads out of all self-activity and anxiety. He attended our Meeting occasionally. Living several miles off, he finally left off and continued to preach as an independent Minister.

On the 2nd of 4th Month, Murray Shipley of Cincinnati brought several children from the Home in that city to our weekday Meeting in order to put them out amongst Friends and others to raise. They all found homes except one or two. We took one to raise, a girl; Ann Eliza Brown is her name, about ten years old. She appears to be an intelligent and interesting little girl. She was only at the Home a few days, and it appears she was born at Charleston in Virginia and was one that has been raised well, far above the common children in the streets of our large cities.

Our Quarterly Meeting in 6th Month at Salem was pretty well attended. At our Monthly Meeting in the following week, William Brown of Salem attended with a Minute from his Monthly Meeting to visit our families, which he attended to, and some Meetings with Colored People in Brown's Run, Hamilton and Oxford. He still appears lively in his gift and much concerned for the prosperity of our religious Society and retains his mind in a remarkable degree, he being 80 years old or upwards.

The committee appointed, in the late Quarterly Meeting, to join committees in Monthly Meetings to review the Elders in the 7th Month, reported all the former Elders with an addition of two more, which passed the Meeting pretty satisfactory—my beloved wife once more on the women's side and Marmaduke Mendenhall on the men's.

In 8th Month attended Monthly Meeting at Salem with others of the committee appointed in the Quarterly Meeting to review the appointment of Elders. After conferring with their committee from their Monthly Meeting, we were united in proposing that some Friends be continued in their Stations (except two who had lately removed) with one that had been left off heretofore who should be added to their number, which passed the Monthly Meeting satisfactory. This new rule adopted in our discipline seems to not work so well in many places in the limits of our Yearly Meeting. I think it will be sent up for recommendation by some of the Quarterly Meetings to the Yearly Meeting. It is a rule that has never been adopted by any Yearly Meeting, either in Europe or America, only Indiana. Some Friends of other Yearly Meetings accept the belief that the sooner it is removed from our discipline, the better it will be for us.

Quarterly Meeting in 9th Month was pretty well attended. Jesse Johnson and companion from Cherry Grove, Indiana attended. A favored Meeting on First Day, not so large an attendance as is the case at this time of year on account of much rain having fallen. Our friend Jesse visited some families of the aged and infirm.

Attended Yearly Meeting this year. Pretty large and many of its sittings were seasons of Divine favor. Much business came before it. On the subject to assist Friends in North Carolina and the subject of education and schools. About $1000.00 was subscribed in the Meeting and the same sum directed to be raised by the subordinate Meetings the ensuing year to aid the Baltimore Association in the good work going on in the South. The subject of reconsidering the Clause of Discipline on the Appointment of Elders as contained therein came up on the reports of three of the Quarterly Meetings, which was committed to a committee taken from all of the Quarters and to report to next Yearly Meeting. The committee met at the close of the Meeting, and it seemed the rule had not touched well in many of the Quarterly and Monthly Meetings from the expression of Friends. They adjourned to meet in 6th Month next. Although there appears to be some contention amongst us and confined to some extent to Ministers, which was a cause of sorrow. The subject of establishing a Yearly Meeting at Wilmington, Ohio came up on the report from three Eastern Quarters. After receiving some consideration, it was referred to next Yearly Meeting. The Meeting closed on Third Day under a feeling of solemnity.

In 10th Month, our friend Martha Ann Taylor was feeling liberated to visit Friends in Tennessee, which service she performed in about three weeks and returned her Minute to the next Monthly Meeting, expressing that she attended to the concern of the peace and satisfaction of her mind. Friends in those parts suffered much during the war. Some of their Meetings were dropped under severe trials to which they were exposed. The Quarterly Meeting at Lost Creek was suspended for some time, but now their Meetings are reviving and some that went to the North are returning. Both the cause and prosperity of the Society is increasing not only in Christian interest, but in numbers, which was cause of encouragement.

Our Quarterly Meeting in 12th Month at Salem was a pretty good and favored Meeting. Miles Mendenhall of Springfield and Priscilla Hedgecock of Ripe Creek, Indiana attended three services. They were satisfactory and encouraging. Priscilla had an appointment at Elk on Second Day and visited some of the aged and infirm to satisfaction and their encouragement.

## 1869

In the 1st and 2nd Months of this year, there was again efforts made by Friends to secure further subscriptions for building a new school house as the subject had been laying for some time. There seemed much more interest manifested by other people as well as by Friends, so that at the

Monthly Meeting in 2nd Month, report was made that about $2000.00 was subscribed. After being deliberately considered, the subject was left with a committee to solicit further subscriptions, and that if $3000.00 was secured so as to put up such buildings as to make it a grade school. At next Monthly Meeting, the committee reported about $2850.00, and the Meeting felt an interest in the concern of education and, many Friends not being willing to drop the subject, went into further subscriptions; and $156.00 more was added by men and women Friends, and a building committee appointed to proceed with the work.

Our Quarterly Meeting in 3rd Month was held here at Elk and pretty well attended by Friends here and from Salem. William Laughton of Raysville, Indiana very acceptably in attendance. He had a Meeting at the Union Meeting in West Elkton at 3:00 p.m. on a First Day, which was largely attended by Friends and others, as well as the Meeting in the morning at Friends Meeting House.

In 6th Month attended our Quarterly Meeting at Salem, although small it was satisfactory. Thomas Hannate of Miami and Thomas Miller of Springsboro attended. Visited families at Salem and in a few days afterwards came back to Elk and proceeded in visiting our families and attended our Monthly Meeting during the week. Also had an appointed Meeting in the Union Meeting House in our village, which was small though satisfactory. I accompanied them to most of the families and it was truly an encouraging and satisfactory visit. They had much to communicate in some families and left a good impression on many minds. Our Friend Thomas Arnett being in his 78th year, it seemed like being a farewell visit to us here. He has long been engaged in his Master's service.

In 8th Month attended Salem Monthly Meeting as one of a committee in care of some difficulties in that Meeting. We found, in examining things, that Satan had in some way sown the seeds of discord amongst them. In committee, I trust, we were favored to reconcile in a good degree the difficulties and misunderstandings amongst them and left them with peaceful minds. On the 7th of 8th Month, there was a very singular eclipse of the Sun. The most total darkness of any eclipse for a number of years. A person could barely see to read. It reminds us how the great planetary system of worlds moving on in such harmony from time to time by the great Author, that man is brought to explain in the language of the Psalmist, "What is man that Thou are mindful of him, or the son of man that Thou does visit him?"

At Quarterly Meeting in 9th Month, Thomas Jay of West Branch attended a satisfactory Meeting. The Meeting on First Day large and interesting to all, no doubt as they are frequently large this time of year. 10th Month attended Yearly Meeting. The first sitting rather smaller than usual. Several of the representatives failed to attend on account of sickness and for want of means to pay traveling expenses. No Friends or representatives from Spring River Quarterly Meeting in Kansas.

Another Quarterly Meeting by the name "Hesper" was established, and committees appointed to attend the opening thereof in 3rd Month. The name of Kansas Quarterly Meeting was changed to the name of "Springdale." A proposition from the Quarterly Meeting in Kansas was introduced by them regarding the Yearly Meeting for the establishment of a Yearly Meeting at or near the City of Lawrence. It was considered and referred to a committee appointed to visit them and report of the possibility of granting their request next year. The subject of the Wilmington Yearly Meeting in Ohio, after being deliberated considerably, was under very good feelings of brotherly considerations. At Monthly Meeting in 10th Month, the building committee, appointed in 3rd Month last, reported that they had endeavored to attend their appointment and that our neighbor and worthy citizen, Richard W. Randall, had donated a lot of 2 ½ acres of land for a building site valued at about $250.00, adjoining the south side of our Meeting property, and that the committee had erected a good substantial building. It is 52 feet long by 32 feet in width, two stories high, with a vestibule or stairway in front two stories high, at a cost of about $5,200.00. The lower part is to be in two rooms of about 30 feet by 24 feet each, for school rooms. The upper [part] to be in one for a lecture room as well as other purposes. $224.00 was realized from the sale of the old school house and lot. Also seats for about 30 scholars, and 2 stoves that had been procured from the legacy left by my aged father's will to Elk Monthly Meeting, amounting to about $175.00. A few other small donations amounting to about $3500.00, [about $92,000 in 2026] the whole cost of the building. A committee was appointed to superintend the school, which is expected to commence the 1st of 11th Month.

A few days after Monthly Meeting, according to instructions by others outside of our Religious Society, the committee met and called in A.W. Randall and Dewitt C. Stubbs to form a Board or Committee; their names (to wit): Asa Talbert, Hiram Stubbs, William J. Kenworthy, and Joseph Maddock on part of Friends. It was the understanding that the school is to be under the care of the Society of Friends of Elk Monthly Meeting.

# 1870–1880

## 1870

In our 1st and 2nd Month Meetings, whilst the School was in session, the committee frequently attended and were pretty well satisfied with the progress of the scholars in their library studies. Their conduct at Meetings were generally satisfactory though some few scholars declined to attend the Meeting on weekdays. Two or three scholars left after the first week because they thought it having too stringent rules. But the School progressed on to the close with but little interruption, which was under the care of William Kenworthy as Principal and Sally Neddish, his assistant.

On the 11th of 3rd Month our aged and worthy Friend, Elvira Townsend, who had lived with her children in West Elkton a number of years with Elisha and Elizabeth Stubbs, died age 102 years and 4 days. She was a remarkable woman; she retained her mind in a good degree to nearly the last. She was sick only a few hours. Her funeral took place on the 13th. A large attendance of Friends and others on the occasion. A solemn Meeting was held (it was First Day) on the occasion. Our School closed about the 1st of 3rd Month, having been in session 18 weeks with a vacation of one week. There was a large attendance. It seemed pretty satisfactory. The average in attendance was about 48. A summer session is to begin in a few weeks. Our Quarterly Meeting in 6th Month at Salem was small as to members, several families of members of Salem having removed since last fall. Miles Mendenhall of Springfield, Indiana, attended the Yearly Meeting. Although small on Seventh Day, it was solemn and satisfactory. On First Day, the Meeting was large and a solemn and interesting session. It seemed in the declining condition of our Quarterly Meeting and it would have to be discontinued. Yet I trust we will be indulged with the privilege of a Quarterly Meeting as long as the Yearly Meeting thinks it right and the truth will justify. This seems to be, I believe, the feeling of the committee at this time.

Many times during the summer, my mind has been very thoughtful concerning the awfulness of death and a future state. I have at times had to examine myself and past conduct very closely as a man accountable to the Great Judge of Heaven and Earth, whether I was filling up my place in the militant [*sic*] Church or the world, and was fully prepared to meet Him with acceptance. I am now in my sixtieth year and feel the infirmities of age coming on. It seems at times that I am making but slow progression in the Christian course. At times, there is a feeling Christian solitude that I am endeavoring to progress on in the Way everlasting. If I continue faithful to the end of the race, there is a crown of glory laid up for me, and not only me, but all who love the Dear Redeemer and His Cause in sincerity. O may this be my chief concern whilst I sojourn here on earth and continue so from day to day. When the time comes, steward, give up the stewardship, for thou shall be no longer steward; and hear the welcome answer and enter thou into the joys of thy Lord. There to join that company which joins the Divine.

In 9th Month our Quarterly Meeting was pretty well attended. On Seventh Day, Joseph Pemberton of West Branch was very acceptably with us; also Enos Pemberton was with us. He is a young man of much promise, and if he keeps his place, may make a notable advocate for the cause of his Redeemer. A suggestion was introduced by the Yearly Meeting committee of the propriety of holding a General Meeting for Worship at Salem the last Seventh Day next Month, which after being appointed, to superintend such a meeting, if concurred with by the Yearly Meeting committee.

Our Yearly Meeting this year was largely attended and was an interesting occasion I understood. This committee appointed last year to visit Friends in Kansas reported in favor of granting their request for the privilege of holding a Yearly Meeting in that state and was concurred by other Yearly Meetings.

I was prevented from attending the Yearly Meeting this year. Our son Nathan having had several epileptic spasms or fits in the last few years, it seems best for me to stay at home and let Mary attend. Nathan had the first fit or spasm the 23rd of 12th Month, 1865, and the next was the 7th of 11th Month, 1869, and the third the 10th of 6th Month,

1870. The last was a very hard one, so that he was not able to be about or do much for several days.

On Sixth Day p.m., 10th Month 21st, myself and daughter Martha Ann went out to Salem in order to attend the general Meeting for Worship. On Seventh Day morning, the Yearly Meeting committee met and conferred on the prospect of our meeting. Much good feeling and love prevailed. The Meeting assembled at 10:00 a.m. A favored and good Meeting, although the attendance small. At 3:00 p.m., we held another favored Meeting with a large attendance. In the evening, we attended a lecture on peace delivered by our Friend Robert W. Douglas. It was a large attendance at the Chapel. On the First Day morning at 9:00 a.m. our Friend Daniel Hill had a Children's Meeting. A pretty good attendance and favored, many young hearts were contrite before the Lord. All were much interested on the occasion. At 10:00 a.m., the Meeting assembled for worship. A very large attendance of the people of the surrounding country who seemed interested, a day of reward and favor again extended. In the p.m. we left for home. Yet another Meeting was held at 3:00 p.m., also one in the evening, both large and satisfactory. So closed the General Meeting. It seemed a time of favor both to Friends and others, and I trust will be remembered by many in days to come. Several Ministers from other places very acceptably attended and many of them exercised their gifts to the edification and a demonstration of the Spirit and power of the Gospel. Many interesting truths were delivered to the gathering of Christian believers as well as our own household of faith.

At Quarterly Meeting in 12th Month attendance was satisfactory. Our Friends Hazel D. Green and Gershom Purdue of Fairfield, Ohio attended. A committee was appointed to have the subject of holding General Meeting under care and respect one year hence. Our Friends had appointed a Meeting at our Meeting House on Second Day. It was pretty well attended and satisfactory.

## 1871

Our Quarterly Meeting at Elk in 3rd Month was attended by Isaac Roberts of Richmond, Mordecai M. Gilbert of Hopewell, and Ruth Johnson of Cherry Grove. It was very acceptable with us. Pretty good attendance on Seventh and First Days. On Fifth Day following, 23rd of 3rd Month, our Monthly Meeting was held. Our Friend Isaac Roberts attended; also Amos M. Kenworthy of Richmond, Indiana attended. Isaac had visited several of our families since 2nd Month and expects to visit all before he leaves for home, which I trust will be to our strength and encouragement in best things. It was throughout a favored Monthly Meeting. Our Friend A.M. Kenworthy gave much good counsel and encouragement to us. It was a favored time with our young people as well as others.

On Sixth Day 24th, our Friend Amos M. Kenworthy had an appointed Meeting. Attendance was large and a solemn and favored sermon. Our Friend seems to be largely and rather singularly gifted in the ministry. The people seemed much attached to him. In the evening, another large and good Meeting. Isaac Roberts also attended the aforegoing Meeting and in this evening Meeting, bid us a solemn farewell at the close. Having finished his visit to our families, I trust, to our strength and encouragement in best things. May his labors be remembered and practiced with us. Our Friend Amos M. Kenworthy still being with us had an appointed Meeting on Seventh Day at 1:00 p.m. at Allen Reeves' near our dwelling. Although small it was satisfactory. At 4:00 p.m., we had another Meeting at the Meeting House, pretty well attended. At the close of the Meeting, our Friend proposed a Meeting with the heads of families on Second Day at 10:00 a.m., which was pretty united with.

On First Day 26th, they attended our usual Meeting. Very large and much crowded. Our Friend and neighbor Nathan Gifford having died, was buried this morning at the public cemetery. The people after the internment came to our Meeting. Much close testimony was delivered and all had to say Gospel truths were communicated. In the p.m. at 3:00 we had a Meeting at Roberts' School House, about 3 miles' distance, a favored time. On Second Day 27th, the Meeting for heads of families assembled. A pretty general attendance, another day of renewed favor. A Pentecostal shower to all, I trust, in which we were made to rejoice together in the evening. Another very large and crowded Meeting, and it may be said another Pentecostal shower was experienced again amongst us, to our further strength and encouragement. This was a day in which many were made to renew their covenants to a covenant-keeping God. A time to be remembered as long as memory lasts, may all praise be unto Him to Whom it belongs.

On Third Day 28th at 10:00 a.m. and in the evening, very large Meetings were held much the same as yesterday. Many were made to rejoice and speak well of their Divine Master's worthy Name; both old and young had to speak of it. Those Meetings today were the most solemn of deep feeling I think that I ever experienced beyond the control or wisdom of man. All praise to Him to Who it is due.

On Fourth Day 29th, we had another large Meeting at 10:00 a.m. It was much the same as yesterday in which we were made to rejoice in God our Savior and Redeemer and said in our hearts it was good that we were here. In the p.m. we had a solemn and good social Meeting at the house of Jane Kenworthy. Many young people were present and many were made to renew covenant with their God, an interesting and good time it was.

On Fifth Day 30th, I attended a large weekday Meeting, very satisfactory and encouraging to all present. In the evening, another Meeting at Allen Reeves', rather small but satisfactory. Some closing remarks were delivered, may they be practiced by them to whom others belong.

On Sixth Day 31st, we went to Salem and had an evening Meeting. Another Meeting on Seventh Day at 10:00 a.m.—both were small—and returned to Elk in the evening. On First Day, the 1st of 4th Month, I attended our usual Meeting, large and satisfactory. In the p.m., I attended a Tract Reading Meeting at Samuel Roberts', which was largely attended and satisfactory. Many hearts were made to rejoice in the cause of their Dear Redeemer. On Second Day 3rd, our Friend A.M. Kenworthy left us and went to Springboro.

The Board of Managers and Advisory Committee of our School has procured the services of our young Friend, Edwin C. Ellis of Martinsville, Ohio, as superintendent and teacher. He arrived some time ago and is now settled with us with his wife and little son. The School opened on the 10th of this month with about 28 scholars and increased to 35 with a prospect of a few more coming in. He appears to be an interesting teacher and a talented young man other ways. He has been acceptably engaged in communications or ministry in our Meetings since he came amongst us, and I trust will be a strength and encouragement in the instruction of our youth as well as in social and religious influence with the people of this vicinity. May the cause of the subject of education prosper under his supervision during his sojourn amongst us, and desire that parents may patronize and support him in his arduous undertaking. A Certificate for himself and family was produced to our Monthly Meeting on Fifth Day the 20th from Newberry Monthly Meeting and received that they are members, and very acceptably too.

At Monthly Meeting in 5th Month, a committee was appointed to hold Meetings in various places in our limits whenever opportunity offers and the wisdom of truth should dictate.

At our Quarterly Meeting at Salem in 6th Month our Friend Amos L. Kenworthy attended; although small was satisfactory. The public Meeting on First Day was large. Our Friend had very close doctrine and rather singular service in the Meeting.

At our Monthly Meeting in 6th and 7th Months of this year, we had large applications for membership in our Religious Society, in all, some 25 or 30 persons including children, which was cause for encouragement to us. I hope that many of these are truly convinced of our principles and will make valuable members with us and will increase our joys and numbers.

At Quarterly Meeting in 9th Month, it was pretty well attended. Joseph and Enos Pemberton of West Branch were very acceptably with us. On First Day attendance was quite large. After the House was filled, a large company assembled under the trees. Both were satisfactory Meetings and instructive occasions.

Our Friend Mary Roberts at Monthly Meeting in 9th Month laid before Friends a concern to visit the few scattered Friends and others in the Colorado Territory, which was feelingly united with, and she encouraged to attend thereto as far as truth offers the way. It was a good and solemn Meeting.

In 10th Month I attended Yearly Meeting. It was pretty large and a good feeling prevailed during the several sittings thereof. There was cause for mourning in some sittings of the manifest departure of some from the primitive simplicity in dress, and in a few instances of the plain language, and it is sorrowful to say it is not confined to common members, but has found its way amongst Ministers and Elders.

Our General Meeting for Worship, a proposal at our last Quarterly Meeting, commenced on Fourth Day, 20th of 10th Month at 2:00 p.m. Enos Pray, William Roberts, Jane Jones, Elijah Hodson of New Garden, with some other Friends from Salem, were acceptably with us at first sitting. On sitting down and after an introversion of Spirit, prayers were made that we might have a good time together during this General Meeting. It was a favored time, our own members being generally in attendance. In the evening pretty large attendance, much was communicated and an interesting occasion. On Seventh Day morning 21st, met again at 10:00 a.m. Joseph Moore and Susannah B. Pedwick arrived; very large attendance and Meeting much favored. Many Gospel truths were acclaimed to the contributing of many hearts. A Pentecostal shower of celestial rain experienced on many minds. Met again in the evening, a large and favored Meeting similar to the one in the morning.

First Day morning 22nd, had a large Children's Meeting. The Union Scriptural School in the village adjourned and met with us. A lovely sight to see such a large number of youth meet together, which was an interesting occasion. Enos Pray, Joseph Moore and others addressed them, which made deep, and I trust, lasting impression on young hearts and will be long remembered. The Meeting for Worship began at 11:00 a.m. The large number assembled soon filled the House and Lecture Room of the Academy, Enos Pray, William Roberts, Jane Jones going to the Academy. Both were interesting and solemn Meetings, many people attending from different parts of the country around and seeming much awakened and interested on this solemn occasion. Probably about 800 people were present. At 3:00 p.m. we met again in the House, which was much crowded; a good Meeting and made, no doubt, good and lasting impressions on many minds. We met again at 7:00 p.m. in the evening. The House was crowded, a memorable occasion and the general Meeting closed under deep feelings of solemnity. Many hearts were made to rejoice in God, their Savior and Redeemer.

At Monthly Meeting in 11th Month, our Friends Mary Roberts and Martha Ann Taylor made report of their visit to Colorado Territory, Martha Ann being liberated by the committee as companion. Also Jesse Kenworthy and Mary, his wife, as assistants. They were favored to attend to the concern, to the peace and satisfaction of their minds, some 10 or 12 Meetings in different places in the Territory, which was satisfactory in the Meeting. Also informed that five applications were forwarded by them to be received into membership with Friends, which was very deliberately considered and much unity expressed in granting their request. Several of them being disowned by our Monthly Meeting several years ago and were desirous to be again attached to us. Their names: Robert and Delilah Stubbs, Isaac and Henry Hutchins of Fountain, and Reuben Francis of Cañon City. A committee was appointed to inform them thereof and have care and oversight of them by correspondence.

In 12th Month attended our Quarterly Meeting at Salem; small yet a favored Meeting. Owen West of Fairfield, Ohio and Levi Jessup were in attendance. The small pox being in the settlement of Salem caused it to be small. Several deaths having occurred previously to the Meeting, we returned home on Seventh Day evening with other Friends. The public Meeting on First Day was small. Our Friend, Owen West, after attending, returned with Friends to Elk the same evening and visited several of the families of aged and infirm amongst us until Monthly Meeting on Fifth Day the 21st, which was pretty well attended and satisfactory and a very cold day. By information from the Committee appointed in 8th Month last to solicit subscriptions for building a new Meeting House reported about $1,600. About $500.00 more was subscribed in the Meeting. The estimate of a new House would be about $3,000.00. They were continued to solicit further and report when complied with.

## 1872

At Quarterly Meeting in 3rd Month, pretty well attended by Friends of Salem as well as by us here. A favored Meeting on Seventh Day. David J. McMillan and Robert Hodson from Bridgeport and Plainfield, Indiana acceptably with us. A large satisfactory Meeting on First Day. At Monthly Meeting in this month, the committee to solicit funds for building a new Meeting House reported about $2800.00 subscribed and that a new House would probably cost about $3000.00 or more by using the material in the old House. The Meeting after a careful and considerate deliberation were united in appointing a building committee to take action towards erecting a new House and report when complied with.

At Monthly Meeting our friend Mary Roberts laid before the Meeting a concern to visit Friends in Tennessee which was feelingly united with and she encouraged to attend thereto as best wisdom may dictate. It was a good meeting. Jesse and Mary Kenworthy accompanied her.

On Seventh Day, 5th Month 4th, myself and wife went out to Salem [in Union County, Indiana] to attend a Meeting at Quakertown or Millsborough as it is called, appointed by our Quarterly Meetings Committee. We stopped at H. M. Davis' near Liberty and took dinner and then went to the Meeting about 8 miles – attended at 2:00 p.m. in Stanton's Hall. A goodly number attended. Also at 7:00 p.m., attended another Meeting somewhat larger, both satisfactory. On First Day morning at 10:00 a.m. we attended another pretty large and satisfactory Meeting. William Mobert having arrived this morning. All have been interesting and solemn occasions, and I trust they will have a good effect on the people. One more Meeting this afternoon and another in the evening are to be held. There seems to be much satisfactory with the people. After the morning

Meeting, we left our kind friend Eli Stanton's and rode five miles to our friend R. G. Kenworthy to dinner. In the p.m. we rode home, arriving about dark, well satisfied with our visit to that place. It is the place where our late friend Samuel Lest formerly lived who had mills and a woolen factory and where other Friends lived.

On Fourth Day morning 5th Month 8th, my friend Marmaduke Mendenhall and myself, on behalf of our committee, rode up to old Westfield settlement to attend the Hicks Friends Meeting. Only 8 were present of their members, it being their weekday Meeting. They treated us kindly and it seemed there was good feelings amongst them at the close of their Meeting. We introduced the subject of holding a general meeting in the settlement. They seemed thoughtful and considerate, but did not incline to join us in the concern. We went home with our aged friend William Brown and took dinner with him and family, who treated us with much kindness, but told us that their Meeting House could not be had, as some of their members would object to it. We made arrangements for two Meetings on First Day the week following at the School House. Joseph Borredile and Jesse Brown offering to give notice and make accommodations as seemed satisfactory.

On First Day morning 5th Month 19th, went up to Westfield to attend the Meeting. Considerable rain having fallen the evening before, it looked somewhat discouraging this morning, yet we found several present. At 10:00 a.m. we sat down with them and divine good seemed to attend us in coming together and was a favored meeting. At 2:00 p.m. we again met, quite a large attendance. Our aged friend William Brown and wife being with us. After sitting down, our friend William Roberts came in and had such to say to the people who seemed to be interested and proved a satisfactory and encouraging Meeting. After it closed, several came to us and desired the committee to hold more such Meetings in the future.

5th Month 25th myself and brother John went over on Twin in order to place some grave stones to our mother's grave[1] and turf it over, which seemed to produce solemn feelings over our minds.

In 6th Month attended Quarterly Meeting at Salem, a pretty satisfactory Meeting. Sarah Ann Linton of Center, Ohio, and William Gilbert

1. Joseph's mother, Sarah *nee* Fouts, was buried "in the family burial ground near grandfather's residence." This would have been John Michael Fouts' home "over on Twin," i.e., Twin Creek north of West Elkton in Twin Township or in neighboring Montgomery County near Germantown, Ohio.

and Rebecca Talbert attended. On First Day, a very large attendance and good meeting. All seemed solemnly impressed. Yet our individual objective which seemed to startle some, but did not affect the quiet thereof. There has been for several years in this settlement a few individuals who make or endeavor to throw aside the Bible and its teachings, and one or two even deny its authority and the existence of the great supreme Redeemer and openly disavow them. A few years ago, they built or erected a hall or building near the Meeting House for holding their Meetings. Some time past, their hall took fire and burnt down. Since that time, they have built a larger and more costly Hall some distance off, but some difficulties arising amongst them, they do not meet so frequently as formerly and their hall is not so much occupied.

On First Day morning 7th Month 7th, we went with our friend Martha Ann Taylor to Salem and attended Friends Meeting at the usual home, a quiet, good Meeting though small. There was a very large attendance at the Hall of the people around in the country, a noted speaker from Chicago being present who discarded the Bible and its teachings and it was said many were disgusted at his objections. It is thought they are weakening in their influence and losing in number. After Meeting we rode three miles to our friend R.G. Howarth to dinner. Afterwards we went to Millborough to attend the appointment of the committee; attended Meeting in Stanton's Hall. Quite a large attendance and good, quiet Meeting. Many seemed interested in the committee holding Meetings here as they are appointed the First Day in the month. The people seem to attend more generally when Friends appoint Meetings than when other Meetings are held.

The committee appointed in 3rd Month last to superintend the building of a new Meeting House, having made arrangements for building, procured brick from Hamilton, which were mostly hauled the latter part of 5th Month and delivered on the ground. Also stone was delivered so that we entered into written contract with Joseph Loop of Camden on the 11th of 6th Month to put up our House. The committee to furnish stone, brick and sand on the ground, and he to find all other material and finish it in good workman-like manner for $2, 373.00 to commence the 1st of 8th Month.

At Monthly Meeting in 7th Month, the committee informed the Meeting of the arrangements made for the building and that the brick and stone of the old House would be wanted to work in our new House. The new House would set north and south lengthwise and take in some of the east end of the old House. Friends were very united and agreed to adjourn all of our Meetings for worship and discipline to the hall of our Academy building after First Day the 29th of the month.

At Monthly Meeting in the 8th Month, our friend Martha Ann Taylor laid before the Meeting a concern to visit Friends of Iowa Yearly Meeting, which was very feelingly united with and she encouraged to attend to her prospect. Also our friend Edwin C. Ellis laid before Friends a concern to visit the inmates of the Ohio Penitentiary at Columbus, which was very freely united with and he also encouraged to attend to his prospect as truth opens his way. Whilst his concern was claiming the attention of the Meeting, I felt such a flow of good will and interest that I offered to accompany him, which was approved by Friends. This was a very satisfactory and encouraging meeting. Many minds were made to rejoice in God our Savior. Also Enos Pemberton of West Branch attended. He had an evening Meeting with the youth, quite satisfactory, and visited families with us to satisfaction.

On Seventh Day morning 9th Month 7th I left home by previous engagement in company with our beloved young Friend, Edwin C. Ellis, to visit the State Prison at Columbus, Ohio. We rode to Middletown and took the train for Dayton where we arrived in about an hour. After conversing a few minutes with Joseph Galloday, a brother of Mary Ann, an interesting young man, we took the train for Xenia. After delaying some four hours, we started for Columbus where we arrived about half past five in the evening. We walked up through the city to the State House, after spending a few minutes walking through the House and yard, we went to the U.S. Hotel, entered our names and residence on their register. The clerk being an acquaintance of Edwin's, gave us a kind welcome. After supper we soon retired for the night.

On First Day morning the 8th, after a good night's rest and eating breakfast, we started for the prison about one mile distance. On arriving at the gate, we were questioned some by the porter, who after learning our business, kindly directed us to the office of the Warden, Raymond Burns.

On going in we were offered seats by the clerk, there being some company in. Soon after, the Warden came in and we introduced ourselves to him. There having been some correspondence between Edwin and him, he at once gave us a kind welcome and seemed interested in us spending the day with them in the prison. In a few minutes, we went into the prison chapel, a large room well seated, in order to attend their scriptural school. Soon after they began to come in, each guard bringing in his division so that I suppose it was half an hour or more before they all were seated.

It was a solemn sight to behold, their coming in such good order, their hair cut short and beards shaved off and dressed in their common clothing of gray color. It reminded us at once of the Scripture text, "The way of the transgressor is hard."

After a few minutes all were still. The Chaplain, O.H. Newton, invoked a blessing and a short hymn was sung. Many prisoners then came forward and took their books and went to their seated class. As there is a great lack of teachers, many have to go without instruction, of course, only what they hear from others, so that it is a great treat to them. We were solicited to take a class, of which I did one, and read with them from Luke and had as interesting a time with them as I ever experienced on the subject of forgiveness of injuries done unto us. The humble and contrite disposition some of them seemed in was grateful to my feelings, they manifesting no disposition of resentment or bad feelings towards those placed over them. They kindly spoke of them with the silent tear running down the cheek. I think I never felt more freedom in concurring with any one than I did with those dear souls, even if they were inmates of a prison.

The exercises of the School being over, the prisoners retired to their cells. At 11:00 a.m. the prisoners again began to come in to their Meeting for Worship; all are required to attend. It was indeed a solemn sight to see them again coming in, each guard bringing his division in the same good order. When all were seated, the Chaplain invoked blessings and singing a hymn and prayer was offered.

The prisoners were informed that Edwin C. Ellis of the Friends Church would address them and they should pay good attention as he had come in love to see them. After a short prayer, he arose and commenced in the language of the Apostle, "Christ Jesus came into the world to save sinners" and was favored to acquit himself as a workman that needed not to be ashamed. The prisoners seemed to pay great attention to the young man's communication to them and appeared much interested; it was a good Meeting.

Several of the people of the city attended. I suppose altogether more than one thousand people were present. After one or two short exercises, the Warden read his monthly report respecting conduct of prisoners, and it was an interesting account, after which the Meeting closed and the prisoners went to their cells. After all had retired, the Warden kindly invited us to take dinner with him and his family, which we very willingly accepted and enjoyed ourselves very much with them; an interesting time it was with us.

At 2:00 p.m. we were invited by the Warden to go with him to the female prison and found 27 inmates. They do not associate on any occasion with the male prisoners. This being the time of Scriptural instruction with them, we found them seated in becoming order, and we read verses aloud with them and the Warden. After which he spoke to them at some length on the duty we owe to God and to one another and the consequences of sin and disobedience and the reward of virtue and holiness. Some of them seemed to pay but little attention and looked like pretty hard cases. After he was through, he gave Edwin an opportunity to relieve his mind to them. He was favored to take their attention and the conscience of those who seemed indifferent became changed and all appeared interested with his communication. Brokenness appeared among them. After giving a tract to each one, we bid them affectionately farewell. Many of them at parting responded and said "The Lord bless you for the visit paid us this day, poor beings as we are." This was truly an interesting occasion.

At 3:00 p.m. we went into the Chapel to attend the meeting of the Christian association, a society formed amongst the prisoners for religious improvement. Some 300 were joined and united together in this society who seemed in earnest in the cause of the salvation of their souls. Truly there was converted souls amongst them. Many of them spoke feelingly of the favors expressed in the morning Meeting. As several prisoners were to leave before another Meeting, their time being about to expire. It was a peculiar time with them and probably they would never meet again in this world which seemed to call forth much counsel and earnest for themselves and encouragement, to those left behind to be faithful to their Lord to the end of the race. It was a very solemn and interesting time to them as well as to us. I think I never heard any Minister or any person more earnestly engaged for the flock than many of them did for themselves and those left behind that they might be faithful in the performance of every duty to their Lord and Savior and receive the comforting language at the close of time here on earth.

After their exercises were through, we felt like holding out a few words of counsel and encouragement to them to be faithful to their Dear Redeemer and at the end, the reward would be sure, and affectionately bid them farewell. A few more addresses were made by other visitors and the Meeting closed. This was one of the most interesting occasions I ever witnessed and truly it may be said that the Lord was with us.

After this we had permission of the kind Warden to distribute tracts amongst the prisoners in their cells. On passing around amongst them and offering a tract, which they seemed joyfully to receive, and also to see us again. Edwin taking one way and I another, we passed on amongst them. Many on receiving a tract said, "The Lord bless you for your visit to us this day."

On going around I found one William Thomas who asked where I was from. Being told from Preble County, he seemed glad in meeting one from his native county and said he was here for the awful crime of murder, of which I remembered of the circumstance his being sentenced for life. Having a spite against a man, in a fit of intoxication and being in a crowd, shot at him and killed a young woman. He seemed sensible of his great error and said he believed that through regretance [*sic*] and faith in his Lord and Savior, he had found forgiveness and acceptance with his God. He spoke of his conversion and acceptance with that degree of assurance that there seemed no doubt of his having experienced sincere acceptance in the anointing blood of Christ. He was visited by our friends, Mary Roberts and Martha Ann Taylor, whilst in Eaton jail awaiting his trial and spoke of the visit in terms of respect, although he said he was a hardened criminal at the time. We parted from him under much feeling of sympathy in his lonely cell that he might be preserved from evil to the end of life and at last find acceptance with his Dear Redeemer.

In passing amongst the prisoners, many of them seemed much interested in again meeting with us and spoke in a feeling of their being associated as they were in their Christian association and the help they were to each other. We left them under a feeling of much solicitude and interest and were rejoiced in believing that the kind Chaplain and Warden had more at heart than a Christian interest and welfare of these outcasts than anything of a temporary nature. We hope they will, in due time, reap a rich reward.

On going into the Warden's office before parting, we made acknowledgment to him for his kindness to us in mingling with the prisoners as we did and to hold out the language of encouragement to him in his arduous and responsible position and affectionately bid him farewell.

It being late in the evening we feeling clear and well satisfied in mingling with the prisoners and officers, we went to our hotel. After supper we soon retired for the night. I being somewhat restless got but little sleep, wishing to leave on the early morning train. We were called up at 12:00 a.m., settled our bill with the clerk and left our kind host and walked to the depot and got on the train at 2:00 a.m. after which I got some sleep.

We arrived at Xenia about daylight; after waiting about an hour, we started for Dayton. On arriving there, we went on immediately for Middletown and arrived about 8:00 p.m. After waiting some time, took the Hack for West Elkton and arrived about 11:00 p.m. at home, thankful for the favor we enjoyed whilst mingling with the inmates, Chaplain, and Warden of our State Prison and will be remembered by me as long as memory lasts. There were 925 inmates in the prison the day we were there—898 males and 27 females. Some 68 were in for life. A large number were quite young; three-fourths under 25 years.

Our Quarterly Meeting in 9th Month was pretty well attended. Having to meet in the Hall of the Academy and being somewhat crowded, men and women clerks having to occupy the same table, it was thought we hardly could transact the business to satisfaction. But after Meeting, it seemed we got along satisfactory under the circumstances in which we were placed. Joseph Wright and William West, Joseph and Enos Pemberton, also Rebecca Talbert, were in attendance.

On First Day, two quite large Meetings were held—one in the Hall and one at the Union Meeting House in the village, it being offered for Friends. Both satisfactory meetings. Joseph and Enos Pemberton went to Hamilton in the morning and held a large Meeting in the Court House yard and visited prisoners in the jail. In the afternoon had a large Meeting in Hall, also one in the evening; satisfactory Meetings. Joseph and Enos returned and attended in the evening.

On First Day morning, 10th Month 20th, went up to Westfield settlement to attend a Meeting appointed by Quarterly Meeting committee; met at 10:00 a.m. in the Schoolhouse. Meeting rather small yet satisfactory. We met again at 3:00 p.m., a much larger Meeting and satisfactory. Many seemed glad to attend these Meetings. Many desired us to hold more such Meetings in the future.

Our beloved and much esteemed friend, Eloria, wife of Asa Talbert, died on the 31st of 10th Month. She was an Elder in the Church and generally beloved by all who knew her. Her funeral was largely attended on First Day and was a solemn and good Meeting held on the occasion.

Our new Meeting House being about finished and seated. The first Meeting held in it was our monthly meeting on Seventh Day the 23rd of

11th Month. On First Day 24th, it was opened for public worship. A large attendance of the people in our vicinity and the county around. House pretty well filled. It will accommodate between 400 and 500 people (that latter number will crowd it), and seems well adapted to our needs. It is pretty well arranged so that we will find it a great accommodation to us of which I trust Friends feel thankful to an all-wise Providence for His mercies and care over us, so that we have got along with our contractor and others in building it to entire satisfaction. It has cost us up to the present time about $3500.00. We still need a partition for discipline, which will probably be arranged in the future. The subscriptions, if paid up well, with other means realized from material in the old House, would be about sufficient to pay the expense in building.

On account of the severe disposition of our daughter Martha Ann, we were deprived of the privilege of attending our Quarterly Meeting at Salem in 12th Month this year, which we understand was small yet satisfactory. There being some time previous to it a disease amongst the horses called the Epizooty[2] which caused some of our members to stay at home. People began to realize, to some extent at least, the value of this animal, the horse. In the time of said disease in many places in the east, it was said, as well as here in the west, that all kinds of work done by this useful animal was stopped both in town and country for some time.

## 1873

On First Day morning 1st Month 12th we went with Martha Ann Taylor to Eaton in order to attend a Meeting appointed by our friend at the County Infirmary for the inmates. Arrived about 11:00 a.m. We met with a kind reception of Superintendent Homan and wife and two of the directors. We went into the room filled up for Meeting and School purposes and had a satisfactory and encouraging Meeting with them. There being at this time about 55 persons as inmates, several of them not being able to be out from Infirmary, and we went around and visited them in their rooms. They seemed to be comfortably provided for and expressed satisfaction of their home and the provisions made for them by the county. Afterwards we took dinner with the Superintendent and family and expressed satisfaction of the visit and invited us to attend in the future.

2. *Epizooty, epizootie, epizootic*: "pertaining to a disease affecting many animals at once." *Merriam Webster.*

We had pretty cold weather in the 1st and 2nd Months this year, as well as the first part of 3rd Month. Our Quarterly Meeting in 3rd Month was pretty well attended, and a good Meeting. John Jessup of Dover, Indiana and Jared Binford of Carthage, Indiana attended.

Our young friend Edwin C. Ellis, on account of poor health at the close of his winter School, resigned his place as superintendent and teacher. He settled up his affairs and removed the latter part of 4th Month to Jonesborough, Indiana. We sincerely feel the loss of this dear young friend since he left us. Since his sojourn amongst us, he has grown in his gift in the Ministry and will make a noble donation if he keeps his place. But as it was he left us. After being at his new home some time, we heard of his being protracted by sickness of disease of the lungs, which saddened many hearts. Yet a few days after, it was more solemn and mournful than ever to hear of his death, which occurred the 2nd of 6th Month having been confined to his room for some 10 or 12 days only. He was much beloved and respected in this vicinity and the information of his death cast a gloom and feeling of sympathy not very common amongst us on the minds of the people. Yet we have assurance that the dear departed one has, through the mercy of the dear Redeemer, made a happy partaker of one of those mansions prepared for the righteous in the Heavenly Father's Kingdom.

Our General Meeting appointed by the Quarterly Meeting commenced on Seventh Day the 7th of 6th Month a.m. Pretty well attended for first Meeting. Thomas Miller of Springsborough, John Jessups of Dover, and William West, Ministers, were present at first Meeting. At noon, Joseph Morgan, J. Daniels, and young Friends were also present. Meetings again at 3:00 and 7:00 p.m., pretty large and satisfactory. On First Day morning 8th at 9:00 a.m., a large Meeting in the Meeting House, also one in the Lecture Room of the Academy. Both satisfactory and interesting Meetings. Amos Kenworthy and Rebecca Talbert arrived at Meeting and attended today. Meeting again at 3:00 and 7:00 p.m. in the House, much crowded and favored seasons. The General Meeting closed.

On Second Day 9th Amos M. Kenworthy commenced a series of Meetings, met at 10:00 a.m. The Ministers at General Meeting attended. At 3:00 p.m. pretty well attended and pretty satisfactory Meeting. Evening Meeting small, it being rainy. On Third Day 10th, Meeting again at 10:00 a.m. and 4:00 p.m. Some of the Ministers left last evening. Attendance large and in a general way satisfactory.

Fourth Day 11th Meeting at 8:00 a.m. for young people and under conversion. Also at 10:00 a.m. and 4:00 p.m., large meeting and mostly satisfactory in a general way. Fifth Day usual Meeting at 10:00 a.m. Quite large. At 4:00 p.m. Meeting for adult members of 30 years and upwards, pretty satisfactory. On Sixth Day 13th Meetings again at 10:00 a.m. and 7:00 p.m. Pretty large attendance and favored. First Day 15th, large attendance. William West being acceptably with us, after this William West and companion, Joseph Morgan, went to Salem and had several Meetings before the Quarterly Meeting on Seventh Day and returned to Elk and our Meeting on First Day. A favored time, though a small Meeting on account of many Friends staying at Salem. On Second Day after Quarterly Meeting, Mahlon Hocket of Walnut Ridge, Indiana and Jesse Pierson of Union had an appointed Meeting; though small, it was satisfactory. On Third Day at 10:00 a.m., our friend Mahlon Hocket had a Meeting at Lows Chapel. The attendance small yet a satisfactory and encouraging Meeting. Myself and Martha Ann attended. After Meeting, took dinner with Sarah Brown, an acquaintance and relative, where we seen her mother, Amar Jones, in her 87th year, very feeble and infirmed, yet she retained her faculties in good degree. She appeared glad to see us, it having been twenty years or more since I saw her.

In 7th Month our friend and citizen Henry Lane died, he being sick and confined to his room for two months or more, requested to be buried according to our order in our Burial Ground. A pretty large attendance at the Meeting on the occasion. Joseph Moore of Richmond was present at his request. A good Meeting, and it seemed a season of great solemnity.

In 9th Month our Quarterly Meeting here was pretty well attended. John Allen of Deerbrush, Indiana, as well as some Friends of Westbranch acceptably with us. Our aged and beloved Friend William Beard we missed very much. He being very sick and not expected to recover; it produced solemn feelings to many of us.

10th Month attended our Yearly Meeting. Not so large as some of the 1st sittings. Yet on the whole a good degree of unity, and brotherly unity considerably provided in the Meeting for Discipline. In the Meeting of Ministers and Elders not so satisfactory as there is evidently a departure in some of the members in our Christian doctrine and practices, as held by our early Friends. And in one or two of the reports, exceptions were made which seemed to claim the attention of Friends so that it was concluded to hold a conference on these and other departures amongst us on the 1st of next month. The day before the Yearly Meeting closed, it was announced that our beloved and honored Friend, William Beard, had quietly passed away, having gradually lingered away since Quarterly Meeting.

Our friend John M. Ellis died of disease of the lungs on the 28th of 10th Month. He had been on the decline for several months and suffered much at times, yet made a happy close. He had requested and was received into membership with Friends only a few days before his death. His funeral took place at our Meeting House. A solemn and interesting occasion, after which his remains were interred at the family lot in the West Elkton Cemetery.

On 8th of 11th Month, Nancy, wife of H.A. Bennett, died, aged about 52 years. A worthy, amiable Christian woman. She was afflicted with a Cancer for several months before her death and went through a surgical operation with composure and patience becoming a Christian, and even admiration of the surgeons. Near the close, she spoke of happy prospects and that a place was prepared for her in Heaven. She requested that her funeral should be conducted according to the order of Friends. A very large attendance at our Meeting House of relatives, Friends, neighbors, and was a solemn and interesting Meeting, after which her remains were interred in the family lot in the cemetery.

In 12th Month attended our Quarterly Meeting at Salem which was small, yet goodness and mercy of the dear Redeemer extended to us. Many could say that it was good for us to be there. We feel the loss of our dear aged father William Beard. It was spoken freely in select Meetings.

## 1874

On Third Day morning, 1st Month 13th, myself and wife left home to attend the conference of Ministers and Elders at Richmond. We took the train at Camden and met with other Friends going up. Arrived a little late. Went on to White Water Meeting House and found a pretty large attendance. A few Friends from the most distant Meetings in attendance.

1st sitting pretty satisfactory. A committee was appointed to arrange business for the future sittings of the Meetings or conference, and it seemed there was a pretty good feeling of brotherly consideration to several. Met again at 2:00 p.m., committee proposed three sittings to be held a day at 9:00 a.m. and 2:00 p.m. and 7:30 p.m. in the evening, and that doctrines and other subjects be considered during the sittings and discussed Fourth Day morning, being White Water weekday Meeting. Friends generally attended and was a good Meeting.

There was [*sic*] two speakers. They took out their Bibles and read their texts and communicated from them their services. It did not seem to have the effect it would a had if they would a went on without reading. It appears that some of our Ministers are trying to advance some new way. In places, there is some exercising done in singing a verse or two, and some sing at considerable length, and it does not meet with much approval, as well as reading the Scriptures.

Yet some Friends think it best to let these kind of Ministers have their way. If their exercises are not worded, the divine influence will come to nought. This class have widely departed from our usages and practices, not only in dress and language, but some are criticizing our doctrine laid down by early Friends. Many subjects were discussed on in a good degree of unity and good feeling, and the conference closed after having eight sittings in three days.

In 2nd Month Lewis Francis of U.B. [United Brethren] and John L. Fall of the Wesleyan Methodists attended one of our First Day Meetings and had considerable to communicate and appeared to be a satisfactory Meeting.

On the 24th of 2nd Month, our friend William Allen of Richmond, Indiana, a Colored Man and member, seemed to be quite a minister with us. Some other young Friends came amongst us and had some Meetings with us under the care of the Quarterly Meetings committee. They appeared profitable seasons, about 13 sittings, and attended our Monthly Meeting in time on the 26th.

The few Friends in Colorado informed us at our Meeting that they were united in requesting the privilege of holding a Monthly departure and Meeting for Worship at Fountain Village in El Paso County, Colorado Territory. The subject was deliberately considered and after due consideration of their distant situation, it was fully united with, in forwarding the subject to the Quarterly Meeting for its consideration and judgment.

Our Quarterly Meeting in 3rd Month pretty good attendance. Our friend Joseph Hobson of Gilead, Ohio and Jaret P. Binford of Carthage, Indiana were acceptably with us. The request of our Friends in Colorado came before the Meeting, and after a full and free expression of sympathy and unity with Friends in that far off isolated place, Friends were united in granting their request. They had held Meetings for Worship for more than two years and were so far separated from any Meeting of Friends that the Quarterly Meeting thought best to grant their desire. A committee was appointed to attend the opening of said Meeting at such a time as circumstances may seem to justify.

A large attendance on First Day, a favored Meeting. On Second Day, our aforesaid Friends attended the funeral of our eternal friend David Taylor. Meeting at 10:00 a.m., pretty large attendance and good Meeting. Our friend Joseph Hobson had a Meeting for our members at 4:00 p.m. and was satisfactory.

At Monthly Meeting on the 26th, a proposition from the Quarterly Meeting of Ministers and Elders was introduced that Rachel H. Maddock be recorded a Minister of the Gospel which was feelingly united with and was recorded accordingly.

At Monthly Meeting in 4th Month, our Friend Rachel H. Maddock introduced a concern which had been on her mind for some time to visit the inmates of our state prison at Columbus, in addition to some other services in that city, which was freely united with, and she encouraged to attend to it as best wisdom may open the way.

The committee appointed some two years ago to attend to the erection or building of our new meetinghouse reported that they had attended to this appointment and had closed up the concern and settled up the account now, and the subscriptions and material in the old house were sufficient to pay off all claims in building the new house. The whole cost appeared to be about $3545, which appeared satisfactory to the meeting.

Some five or six requests for membership amongst Colored People were received and satisfactory.

A very hot, dry summer, yet we are blessed with very good crops of grain. The wheat crop, a very good yield; it should rain thankful hearts to our Heavenly Father for such favors from unworthy beings as we are.

At Monthly Meeting in 7th Month, our Friend Martha Ann Taylor informed this meeting of the prospect of sojourning for a while at Fountain and Colorado Springs in Colorado. It produced a very solemn feeling in the Meeting, and much sympathy and unity was expressed with concern and she encouraged to attend to the service. Her husband, Lewis Taylor is to accompany her. They expect to leave after Yearly Meeting in 8th Month.

We received the very shocking account from our brother, Joseph H. Stubbs in Kansas, of the destruction of their spring crops by grasshoppers, as well as their garden vegetables. It seemed from accounts from other sources, a pretty general calamity in parts of Kansas and Iowa, as well as Nebraska. It seems unusual and much suffering will ensue if relief is not afforded.

Our Friend, Elwood Osborne and wife called on us on their return from the East, he having been liberated by his Friends in Iowa to perform a religious visit to Friends and others in New England and New York Yearly Meetings. They stayed with us several days and attended three of our meetings as they came in course, and it was pretty satisfactory to Friends as well as them.

Our Yearly Meeting in 9th Month pretty well attended, quite large on First Day morning and favored as well as the p.m. meeting; Joseph Pemberton acceptably with us as well as others were in attendance.

On the 14th of 10th Month, our Friends Martha Ann and Lewis Taylor left us for Colorado expecting to sojourn there for some months or a year as way may open. It was a solemn parting; many prayers will be put up to our Father in heaven for their preservation and encouragement in the important missions they are about to embark on in the far-off West.

In 11th Month, attended West Branch Quarterly Meeting. There was a pretty good attendance on Seventh Day. Several ministers from other places were present. It had been nine years since I was there before. It appeared that all or nearly all of the active members had passed away from the scenes of Earth. And those that took the lead now were much engrossed with the things of this world and did not appear to live in that self-denying and humble disposition their fathers did. Some of the Ministers as well as others in this and adjacent Quarterly Meetings in our Yearly Meeting have widely departed from that simplicity in dress and manners that once was so conspicuous in the early days in our religious society. And a few are advocating unsound doctrines and calling in Question Robert Barclay's *Apology* and the doctrines and practices therein contained, which have been the standard of all sound Friends, and acknowledged as such by all the Yearly Meetings of Friends in both Europe and America. Some of the said classes are introducing singing in meetings and placing mourning anxious seats, in series or revival meetings, so that it seems there may be another shifting amongst us unless this class runs entirely out as the Ranters did in the early gathering of the Church. Yet we may, and assuredly do, know that the foundations of God are sure and the Lord knows them that are his.

Attended meeting on a First Day at 3 p.m. appointed by Quarterly Meeting Committee at the Simonson Chapel. Attendance was small, yet it was a satisfactory meeting. In the evening at 7 p.m. attended a pretty large meeting in Jacksonburg. A solemn season much favored; the people seemed sensible of it. Our aged pilgrim James Craig appeared in supplication near the close. Many could say that it was good for them to be there.

In 12th Month, attended our Quarterly Meeting at Salem. It was small, yet a favored time. The meeting on First Day was also smaller than common but satisfactory. A prominent infidel in the vicinity made some startling assertions in respect to his belief, in which he was answered in a plain and candid manner that seemed to abash him somewhat, and it did not disturb the Meeting. William Allen of Oak Ridge, Indiana, very acceptably attended with us.

12th Month 24th, William Allen attended our Monthly Meeting. Also had a series of meetings for several days, generally at 10 a.m. and in the evening. N. McLain and E. Burris, two young men from Indiana, also attend these meetings. Several of the first meetings were pretty satisfactory. The latter ones were not so much so. Yet on the whole, they were profitable meetings. About 10 meetings altogether were held besides our usual meetings. David L. Coppock of West Branch attended some of the meetings.

## 1875

The latter part of 1st Month, Harris Howard, a Unionist of Cincinnati, attended several of our First Day and weekday meetings. He seemed a very pious and devoted Christian man, and has been for some time employed as City Missionary of Cincinnati, distributing tracts and appears quite a talented man. He has a good education and has been preaching for several years amongst the Free Will Baptists in New England as a minister of the Gospel. Not feeling satisfied with their rules and regulations, he withdrew from them and came west. He appears very much attached to Friends. He had several meetings, whilst staying with us, at several of our houses as well as sittings in families, that were satisfactory and encouraging seasons.

Information was received some time ago that our Friends, Martha Ann and Lewis Taylor, had arrived in Colorado. On arriving at Denver City, their baggage car took fire in which their clothing and Lewis's tools were in and burnt up, which was a sad loss. Since then, Martha Ann has had poor health, and she was confined to her room and to her bed for a while, which was quite a detraction to our Friends concern of Gospel labor in that far-off distant western land. Since then, her health has improved so that she is engaged in her mission and work amongst the people and attending the small meeting of Friends at Fountain. We trust her labors will be blessed to the strengthening and gathering of souls into the Heavenly Father's kingdom, is the prayer of many of her Friends and relations here and she be permitted to return to us with the reward of sweet peace.

Our Quarterly Meeting in 3rd Month was held here and a favored season. Benjamin and Louisa Fulghum of Milford, and Hazel D. Green of Fairfield with others, were acceptably with us. At the suggestion of some young Friends and others, with the approval of the Quarterly Meeting committee, a series of meetings was held for several days and satisfactory occasions and much interest manifested. Pretty good attendance in the evening, one or two young speakers engaged at times in the exercise of singing hymns, which was thought by many not to be expressive of the meeting at large.

In 4th Month, winter appears to be breaking and the weather begins to appear as spring-like appearance. It has been quite cold winter-like weather, ever since the year set in—ground hard frozen nearly all time, Mercury down several times 15 to 20° below zero. Wheat much killed out, and much rain and extremely wet rainy spring. In 7th Month, very wet harvest, so the wheat was much damaged and much of it hardly worth hauling in and seemed nearly entirely a failure with us.

On the 8th of 8th Month, our aged and honored Friend Phebe Maddock departed this life having for several years had symptoms or status of paralysis. She had long stood as an upright pillar in the militant church and was no doubt made a happy partaker of one of those mansions in the Heavenly Father's kingdom. Aged about 86 years.

In 9th Month, our Quarterly Meeting was held here at Elk. William West of Caesar's Creek was acceptably with us; a pretty good attendance of Friends and others. Our Friends Martha Ann and Lewis Taylor arrived just in time to be with us after a long sojourn in Colorado. They were kindly welcomed again amongst us. On their return they stayed a few weeks in Iowa with some of their children and attended several sittings of the Yearly Meeting at Oscaloosa.

Our Friend Mary Roberts laid before the Quarterly Meeting a concern to attend North Carolina Yearly Meeting and to attend other services in its limits, which was feelingly united with and she encouraged to attend thereto. Our Friend Martha Ann Taylor made a return or statement of sojourn in Colorado and felt the reward of sweet peace. This was a day of much Christian feeling and interest amongst Friends

10th Month attended our Yearly Meeting. Several sittings were very satisfactory and good meetings. Several Friends from other Yearly Meetings were in attendance. In the Meeting of Ministers and Elders, the care came up from one of the quarters respecting a Minister [probably refers to Murray Shipley] who had, through weakness, gone through immersion or water baptism. It seemed alarming to think that an acknowledged Minister would give way to such weakness. A minute was sent down to subordinate meetings, not allowing Ministers or Elders to submit to such improprieties.

There seems to be some improprieties as well as the inconsistencies with a few Ministers in our Yearly Meeting at time will determine. Rufus King, an honored and beloved young Friend, was liberated to perform religious service amongst Friends and others in Great Britain and Ireland and other parts of the European continent.

At Monthly Meeting in 10th Month, Martha Ann Taylor and Rachel H. Maddock were liberated to visit the meetings belonging to West Branch Quarterly Meeting, and if way opens for them to visit our state prison.

Along about the 1st of 12th Month, Noah C. McLain, a young colored man and acknowledged Minister, came to our meeting with two or three other young men and went to holding revival meetings without advice or counsel respecting such service, and continued their meetings for several weeks, having meetings morning and evening with a pretty large attendance, especially in the evening, and many seemed considerably interested. Yet at times, not so satisfactory as could be desired. Friends expostulated with him about his course. He reflected on Friends in public and threw out accusations which were unfounded, and at times engaged in Congregational singing, which seemed to stop his services and people would not attend, so that he went off and afterwards returned. Yet people did not attend his meetings as they did at first, and he finally closed them. Other Friends came and had meetings appointed and were largely attended and were seasons of favor and encouragement.

## 1876

On the 18th of 2nd Month, Samuel Maddock died. He was a cousin of mine, son of the late Francis and Phebe Maddock. He was a young man of about my age, talented and well-educated in the community branches of an English education and gave great promise of much usefulness, both in the church and community in which he lived. About the 30th year of his life, being of a lively disposition and given to frivolity in some degree, his affections became entangled with a young woman by the name of Hannah Gregg in relation to marriage, who disappointed him and refused the matrimonial connection. It was afeared on account of a wealthy young man interfering. It was a sorrowful and disheartening disappointment, and the cause of our young cousin's insanity. He labored alone in this condition for several years, not getting any relief. He was taken to the asylum at Columbus, Ohio; not receiving any relief after staying about a year, he was brought home and a room being prepared for him, he continued to stay or live in it for more than 20 years. He was at times somewhat noisy or outrageous. I often visited him in his room and found him rational at times. This situation was a sorrowful one. He died aged about 68 years.

On the 20th of 6th Month, Anna Stubbs died; she was the daughter of Elijah and Martha Mendenhall. After the marriage of her mother to my father, she lived in our family for some eight years until her marriage to Nathan Stubbs in 1825. She was a woman of much piety and Christian virtue. I received in early life from her, much instruction in piety and virtue. Under the parental roof, as we then lived, and may say it was at that early day I received the inclinations of conversion and consecration to God, which has continued with me, a poor and unworthy creature, to the present time.

In a few days before our dear deceased Friend's death, she went with me to Salem to Quarterly Meeting and also returned home with me. We had many interviews together on going and returning from the Meeting in respect to life and things connected with our pilgrimage. Neither of us little suspecting it would be our last meeting here on earth. Yet, it proved so as she died of heart disease. The family had little warning of her death. So passed away one honored and beloved by relatives, Friends and neighbors, who no doubt, was one permitted to enjoy one of those mansions of praise for the righteous in realms of never ending bliss. Aged about 68 years, eight months, and seven days.

Many Friends, not being satisfied the way we had been holding our Meeting for Discipline, especially women Friends, since our new Meetinghouse was built. Men's and women's clerks sitting at the small table, often interrupted each other in transacting their business, so that several Friends went into the subscriptions [i.e. took up donations], and shutters were put up so as to separate men and women Friends apart. And we enjoy our meeting much better since they were put up and finished, the cost being about $108.

## 1877

Our Quarterly Meeting in 3rd Month pretty well attended for this time of year. Isaac Jay was very acceptably with us. The Mills of Cherry Grove and Noah C. McLain attended, their company not very acceptable, especially the latter, as they indulged in their singing exercises and unbecoming gestures and other ways that is very trying to many Friends.

Our beloved and honored Friend Benjamin Fulghum of Dublin, Indiana died sometime the latter part of the 6th Month. He was a prominent and valued member and Minister of Yearly Meeting. He will be much missed in the church as he was one who stood as a faithful watchman and pillar in the church for our ancient doctrines and testimonies.

About this time, David Tatum, Minister of Cleveland, Ohio attended one of our First Day meetings, very acceptably with us. In the p.m. he delivered a temperance lecture at our meeting house. A pretty good audience. He and his wife, a Minister, spent last winter in the South in preaching the Gospel and lecturing on temperance and are doing much good in their cause wherever they go, and their services are well received by the people.

On the 7th of 8th Month, our niece, Ella T. died. She was the wife of Thomas G. Jones and daughter of John and Eleanor Stubbs. She was confined to her room several months and suffered much at times. They consulted several physicians to but little benefit. Being young and to some extent participating in the gaieties of youth, yet her relations have the consoling hope that through the mercies of a risen Redeemer she found acceptance with him.

In 10th Month attended Yearly Meeting. Pretty good attendance. Several Ministers in attendance from various parts of this continent, also Stanley Humphrey and wife, also Walter Robinson from England, very acceptably attended. The meeting learnt in sorrow that a small separation had taken place in Western and Iowa Yearly Meetings and a few had withdrawn from Winchester Quarterly Meeting in our own Yearly Meeting. It was a time of deep feeling and concern of many Friends that our members might dig down to the rock and sure foundation on which our fathers were established, and that it would preserve us a people from the world and its many sinful pleasures and pastimes. Many have departed in simplicity and self-denial in the church as respecting dress and to some extent language; what will be the result, time will determine, yet the meeting seemed to provide us with its blessings in the good degree of harmony and consideration. Robert W. Douglas of Center Quarterly Meeting was liberated to visit in Gospel love Australia, New Zealand and many other parts of that far off-country with much success.

## 1878

About the beginning of 1st Month, Noah C. McLain and some other young persons came into our vicinity from Gordon, Ohio and commenced "revival meetings," as they termed them, without any leave or confidence with Friends, which caused some excitement. Many preferred conversion; some made quite boisterous demonstrations of their attainment while they held their meetings in our Meetinghouse. Many Friends, not being satisfied with their doings, they were stopped. Afterwards, they held some in Winchester [Gratis] and several at Somerville. At the latter place, about 40 persons preferred conversion and attainment in religious sense. They generally had congregational singing and their meetings were quite noisy. Noah C. McLain came on with several applications for membership of Friends with an understanding that they must have a Meeting granted them at or near Somerville. The subject was in our Monthly Meeting and was referred to the committee appointed to hold meetings by our Quarterly Meeting. They held Meetings for some time with them every two weeks, and they not inclining to our rules and order, their requests were dismissed

At our Quarterly Meeting in 3rd Month, our friend Stanley Humphrey and wife from England were in attendance very acceptably with us. On First Day, Noah C. McLain attended and encouraged some young men to sing a hymn in a concert way, which was very trying to some Friends as well as others.

For some months past, my beloved wife seemed to be losing her eyesight and became entirely blind by cataracts growing over them, one eye having failed some years ago. About the 1st of 5th Month, we consulted with Dr. Corson of Middletown as well as our own physicians of West Elkton, Doctor Weinland and Dr. Robertson, after which, by advice of Dr. Corson, she concluded to go to Cincinnati and consult some regular opticians of the city. Dr. Corson and Martha Ann went with her. And after a pretty thorough examination by Dr. Joseph Aub, he thought she might be helped by a surgical operation of removing the cataract on the eye that first failed of sight. After she returned to Middletown and stayed a few days, Dr. Aub of Cincinnati came up on the 10th of 5th Month and performed the operation in less than 15 minutes, binding up and all, some eight or 10 physicians of Middletown being present. She suffered little or no pain in the operation. She was confined after the operation in a dark room at our honored and beloved friend, Eva Christiancy's house, whose unremitting care and attention to her is greatly remembered by us as well as Dr. Corson attending. Also Dr. Aub of the city came up twice to see her. After staying nearly 3 weeks, Martha Ann being with her all the time, she concluded with Dr. Corson's consent to return home as she had got along pretty well, or perhaps better than could have reasonably been expected. On the 27th of the month she came home. It seemed to worry her some. But after a few days she got better and seemed to improve some, yet her sight was not very much better, yet she rejoiced to be at home and the comfort it was to mingle amid family society again.

On the Third Day of 6th Month I went up to Richmond as a representative from our Quarterly Meeting to meet with the committee appointed by our last Yearly Meeting on revision of the Discipline and found them assembled in one of the committee rooms at the new Yearly Meetinghouse. We had two sittings a day for three days and were favored to go through all the Rules of Discipline in church harmony and condescension. Some of the rules were changed and others added, as well as a few left off, which will be laid before our next Yearly Meeting. Along the last of the 6th Month, my beloved wife began to fail in her general health, having to be confined in a dark room whilst in Middletown. Also since returning, the extremely warm weather caused extreme prostration of body and her appetite somewhat failing during the 7th Month and forepart of the 8th Month. General prostration of her system seemed to be gaining on her, so that towards the last of 8th Month, and through the 9th Month her situation seemed very critical. Dr. Robertson had thought it needful to attend on her daily, as well as Dr. Corson of Middletown, who attended about every two weeks. So that through the 9th Month, she was entirely confined to her room and bed and manifested great patience and serenity of mind. She said if it was the Lord's will either to live or die, all would be well, and that not the shadow of a doubt was in her mind but what a bright mansion was prepared for her if taken away from the scenes of earth in the Heavenly Father's Kingdom.

Some two or three weeks before she died, her mind became somewhat flighty and continued so until the end. Her strength of body failing, so that for some ten days her suffering was great at times, and she gradually weakened away and passed from the scenes of Earth on Second Day morning about 15 minutes past 10 a.m. in 9th Month 30th. I have the consoling assurance that she was fully prepared to enter one of those mansions prepared for the righteous in the Heavenly Father's Kingdom.

Drs. Corson and Robertson, having done their utmost to raise the dear departed, were at a loss all the time during her sickness to know the real condition of her system and requested a postmortem examination. On Third Day morning 10th Month 1st, Dr. Corson and Dr. Dickey of Middletown, and Dr. William Saylor of Winchester, Dr. Francis of Camden, Dr. Owsley of Jacksonburg, Dr. Weinland and Dr. Robertson of West Elkton, and several students went through an examination and found that there was some frill disease lurking on her system. And that probably she would not a lived more than a year or, not more than a few months at furthest. So that we were satisfied in granting their request for an examination. On the afternoon of said day at half past 2 p.m. the funeral took place, a large attendance of relatives, Friends and neighbors attending. We moved on to the Meetinghouse where a pretty large and solemn Meeting was held in which our dear friend, Martha Ann Taylor, had considerable to say. It was a solemn time to myself and my daughter, Martha Ann. Said the poet, "As I am, so you must be, prepared for death as follows me."

The 11th Month since my dear companion has left us, myself and Martha Ann feel our loss as we take our seats in the family circle, the scriptural school or in Meeting. Her seat is vacant that she occupied. No more to behold her here on earth. After the silent tear trickles down our cheeks unrestrained, in remembrance of the many seasons of social interest and communion that we have spent together during our pilgrimage journey thus far through life.

## 1879

Very cold weather in 1st and 2nd Months of the year. The worst, so it was thought that there had been for 20 years past. The mercury was down several times to 20° below zero. Much snow fell during the winter. Our Quarterly Meeting in 3rd Month was held here, as usual this time of the year. Samuel Pitts of Dover, David Jay Coppock of New Garden, Indiana. Also our young friend, Rhoda J. Thomas of West Branch, Ohio. Very acceptably with us. On First Day the meeting was large by attendance. A very solemn and instructive occasion. In the p.m. not so large but satisfactory.

At our Monthly Meeting in the 4th Month, our young friend, Helen C. Balkwill of England very acceptably with us. Also Anna S. Ritchie of Whitewater attended. They had an appointed meeting in the evening. Attendance, not so large as usual, yet was thought a profitable meeting. On Sixth Day 5th Month 16th, concluded to go out to Stillwater, it being the time of West Branch Quarterly Meeting. We rode up through Winchester [now Gratis], West Alexandria and Piermont, rested at hotel a while and went on in the p.m. Arrived at Riley Davis' near Milton in the evening. Altogether, about 35 miles. Met a kind reception with our friend, Mary Hasket, who appeared glad to see me, as well as John and their two amiable daughters. Mary has been confined to her room and part of the time to her bed for perhaps 20 years with something of a spinal affliction. She appeared cheerful and resigned to her situation. On Seventh Day attended the Quarterly Meeting at the old West Branch Meetinghouse. Attendance not large. A number of Ministers from other Quarters were present, much speaking done with several times exercising in singing in the congregational way by some. After the Meeting for Worship was over they had a recess of about an hour afterwards. The Meeting for Discipline closed about 3 p.m. We went into the grave yard and saw my sister Rachel's grave and the graves of their three children who died soon after their mother. Returned to Riley's after dinner and went over to John Hasket's and spent a pleasant time with him and family.

Next morning parted with Riley's and went to West Branch and attended a very interesting lecture delivered by C. F. Coffin of Richmond to the young people at 9 a.m., after which attended the Meeting for Worship. Very large and interesting in some ways, yet a few indulged as yesterday in singing. After Meeting took dinner with Henry Fouts, a relative and interesting man, with several of his relatives. A very satisfactory time.

About 3 p.m. we parted with their kind relatives and friends and went down to Dayton, about 15 miles, arriving at M. A. Holaday's late in the evening about 3 miles on the Trey Pike. It was quite a surprise to our young sister as she was quite intimate with Martha Ann, having taught school in our district and boarded at our house. So that it was joyful meeting with us in some ways, as well as sadness of the ways she had lost her father and mother the last two or three years, and we had parted with our dear mother at home. Our feelings were in no small degree reciprocal. Martha Ann had visited with her some time ago so that our meeting was to mutual satisfaction.

On Second Day stayed with our kind young sister, who is a Presbyterian, a worthy Christian woman. In the p.m. we went in to Dayton and visited some about the water washes. I went into the Clerk's Office and got a record of my father and mother's marriage, dated March 1, 1810, which was kindly give over by one of the assistant clerks. After a good night's rest, on Third Day morning we started for home. We stopped a while on the road at the Soldiers' Home and went to see several of the animals in the parks. We rode onto Germantown and rested a while, then went on for home. Arrived about 4 p.m. and found all well and things doing well since we left it under the care of our young friend, Alice Gray.

The latter part of 5th Month, on the First Day p.m. Martha Ann and I went up to Goodwin Schoolhouse to attend the Scriptural School. Whilst there, a very hard storm or hurricane came up, and on going out to see to my horse, the carriage was blown over on to me. A tree falling before me and behind us frightened the horse very much. I was very badly hurt. My arm and shoulder somewhat out of place, and several cuts on one arm so that I was very much disabled for several weeks. Seemed a providential escape from death, so that it appears in times of prosperity and health, we are in the midst of death and know not when we shall be called upon to give up our stewardship here below and be in redress to meet the messenger of death.

8th Month, we have had a very prosperous harvest of the wheat crop. The best harvest yields for many years, which turns out, very good since threshing has commenced, which should raise in our hearts Thanksgiving and praise to our Dear Father for his superintending care and protecting hand over the people of this country. When there is in China and other nations at times so much suffering and even starvation.

About the 1st of 9th Month, our beloved Friend, Anna S. Ritchie, and her husband, Samuel Ritchie, very acceptably and satisfactorily visited the families of our meeting, in numbers about 60. Very satisfactory in general, it was to us. I accompanied them to many of the visits. I trust it will be remembered by many in days to come.

On the 7th of 9th Month, our sister and friend Esther Reeves, wife of Alan Reeves, died, aged about 66 years. She had been complaining and confined at home, at times during the summer with a sore leg and being other ways unwell. Some two weeks before her death she had a light stroke of paralysis. She gradually weakened away and said several times she had no fear of death and that all would be well, and a happy home was prepared for her in the Heavenly Father's Kingdom.

Our Quarterly Meeting in the 9th Month was pretty well attended and a satisfactory time. Quite a large attendance on First Day. Our dear friends, Thomas Jay and William West, also Enos Pemberton, very acceptably with us.

In 10th Month attended our Yearly Meeting. Not so large at some of the first sittings, yet afterwards filled up more. Stanley Humphrey from England with his wife very acceptably with the company. He has been on this continent in religious service about four years and leaves a good impression. Wherever he has traveled much good has been done in building up the church. Some of the sittings were seasons of divine favor, particularly the Meeting of Ministers and Elders. Yet many well concerned Friends had to lament of the departure from that simplicity and self-denial that was once so highly held amongst us as a religious society. Some few are separating from the body of friends in Kansas and Iowa since last year, as well as a few in our Yearly Meeting. Perhaps with more consideration and a little more charity on both sides, separations might have been avoided.

11th Month. I feel the infirmities of age coming on more sensibly since I received that hurt in 5th Month last. And I am reminded that my stay here may be short, which causes me often to examine whether the necessary preparation is going on with the day that when called upon to give up my stewardship, that I am in readiness and feel that assurance that all will be well, and an entrance made into the heavenly city. It is my desire above everything else in this world. A poor Pilgrim, I feel myself to be.

Attended our Quarterly Meeting at Salem in 12th Month; although small was satisfactory. Samuel Pitts, very acceptably with us. Also James P. Hayworth of Illinois. He had an appointment at Elk on Third Day at 10 a.m., also one in the evening. Satisfactory, I think, although the attendance was small. Some of our members during the past year have greatly neglected the attendance of our meetings for trifling excuses, because our Meetings for Discipline with some were not satisfactory. Yet lately, there appears some improvement.

# 1880–1889

## 1880

In 1st Month and 2nd Month of this year, very warm and rainy weather. We had little snow or freezing since the year came in.

2nd Month 10th. This day, I have completed my 69th year as it is recorded. I am over average of human life. I feel many weaknesses of body, and imperfections attending the passing of later years. Yet I am thankful to my Heavenly Father for His tender care and regard over me, even from my youth to this time. That his watchful protection may still be with me during my pilgrimage journey through this world and that an abundant entrance be made into one of those mansions of eternal joy in that city whose gates are everlasting praise forevermore is my desire.

2nd Month 24th. This afternoon at 2 p.m. the Ministers and Elders of our Meeting held their usual meeting, in which our beloved friend, Mary Roberts, after commencing our business, had a very hard stroke of paralysis, which prostrated her so that she seemed as helpless as a child. It also impaired her mind and speech some. A doctor was called in, and she was removed to a house nearby and stayed till morning and then was taken to her home, where she remained in somewhat of an unconscious state until the morning of 3rd Month 6th, when she was released from the sufferings of the body for the joys of an eternal inheritance in the Redeemer's Kingdom. It was a sad and awful circumstance and great bereavement to her family and Friends to see her stricken down. It may be truly said, a mother in Israel is fallen; her loss is felt in the church. The funeral took place in the afternoon of next day, the 7th, and was largely attended by relatives, Friends and neighbors. A very large and solemn Meeting was held on the occasion and very appropriate communication delivered respecting the solemn event by her dear sister, Jane Jones and others, on the duty we owe to our dear Lord and Master and the language very appropriately applicable.

Our Quarterly Meeting in 3rd Month attended about as usual at this time of year. Pretty satisfactory occasion, John Jessups of Dover and Isaiah Jay of Indiana in attendance. Meetings on First Day large; Isaiah Jay stayed a few days and had meetings. Pretty good satisfaction with us.

Our honored and beloved friend Elisha Stubbs, having been for the last year very much confined to his room by age and bodily infirmity, quietly passed away from the scenes of Earth on the 4th of 6th Month in his 82nd year. He came with his parents from Georgia in the first settling of this country when quite a lad. After arriving to manhood and marriage he filled several important offices of trust in the township and community and was much respected as an exemplary and useful citizen. In later life, he with his family joined in membership with Friends and continued as a useful and worthy member and Elder in the church. His funeral was largely attended, and we feel the loss of such, as well as dear Mary Roberts. Also that our aged father, John Kenworthy, from bodily infirmity has been prevented from meeting with us the last two years.

1st of 9th Month, attended two sittings of the Cincinnati Methodist Annual Conference at Middletown, Bishop Peck of New York, presiding. It was an interesting occasion to me to hear the advice of the bishop to the ministers about to be sent to their different fields of labor. Some very able and talented and who seemed alive in the cause of our dear Redeemer, and in the extension of their branch of the Christian church here on earth. About 300 members were present.

10th Month, attended several of the first sittings of our Yearly Meeting. Rather small at first, yet after a few days it filled up more. Sarah B. Satterwaite and Mary White from England were very acceptably in attendance, as well as other Ministers from different Yearly Meetings on this continent.

Several sittings and the Meetings of Ministers and Elders were solemn and important sittings, resulting in the proposition to offer to the Yearly Meeting of Discipline, the appointment of an Evangelistic Committee. They are to attend the Quarterly Meetings in order to endeavor to stave up all classes of our members. More particularly the Ministers and Elders, to a more faithful discharge of duty in support of our various Christian testimonies, and the advancement of the dear Redeemer's cause on earth. It received the united concurrence of the Yearly Meeting-at-large at a future sitting of the Meeting of Discipline and a large amount of subscriptions offered to defray traveling expenses of the committee as well as the expenses of Ministers in visiting our subordinate meetings in carrying on the work of the church. The subject of Earlham College having claimed the attention of Indiana and Western Yearly Meetings for two or three years past, an order for joint management of it by trustees appointed by each Meeting was finally settled. The care and superintendence of it is to be surrendered to the Board of Trustees. I hope it may be an advantage both in education and financial points of view.

## 1881

The first part of 1st Month, Myron T. Hartley of Michigan and Rebecca E. Talbert of Spiceland, Indiana, Ministers, commenced a Revival Meeting, which was continued for some two weeks, one meeting at day and one generally at night—about 22 meetings. Also attended four of our usual Meetings. They were largely attended at night and on First Days, and were generally interesting occasions, especially when they treated on doctrinal points as well as counsel and admonition extended. It seemed a time of renewal of strength and encouragement to many, and I hope will be remembered in time to come. Some attempts were made to settle some difficulties and misunderstandings amongst our members, whilst M. T. Hartley was here. They were in a good degree complemented and reconciled. Yet after he left some parties withdrew and held back the promises made and appeared fruitless, so that disunity and trouble exists with a few amongst us.

Our Quarterly Meeting in the 3rd Month was pretty well attended by our members. Thomas Miller of Springborough very acceptably with us. The meeting on First Day was largely attended; a solemn occasion.

The last winter has been one of unusual severity. It set in early and was extremely cold, most of the time up to the 1st of 4th Month. Much snow fell—about 6 feet and 3 inches during winter. More than was ever known in later years. Mercury down several times to 15° to 25° below zero.

At Monthly Meeting in 5th Month, some three or four of our Ministers offered resignations of membership after extending proper care. One declined and three others were accepted. Some since that seem to regret the course they took, and many returned to their church again in the future.

During the summer there seemed to be much apathy and indifference with several of our members in the attendance of our Meetings, more particularly in the middle of the week. Much care was extended to many of them, as well as admonition, with some little fruit of the labor extended. It appears to be a prevailing cause in most all meetings in our religious society at this time. Yet our meetings here at home on weekdays are generally seasons of instruction and encouragement to those who attend them.

Our friends, John C. and Rachel H. Maddock, with their family about the 1st of 4th Month, removed to Newcastle, Indiana to sojourn for the present to labor as ability may be afforded in them. We miss Rachel very much in our Meetings.

This summer has at times been very discouraging on different occurrences that have transpired in our midst. So that it seemed I should hardly be able to survive the trials that seemed to loom up in my pathway. Yet continuing in the patience and looking to Him the Great Preserver of his children in the hour of temptations and trial, I have been kept and made to rejoice in the Lord my Savior and Redeemer in some times of great trial on the banks of true heartfelt deliverance, forever be praised his great and worthy Name.

8th Month, 5th and 6th, a Bible conference for our Quarter was held here by some of the Yearly Meetings Committee on Scriptural Schools, and it appeared some interesting counsel and advice was extended that I trust will be a help to our Bible school.

In 9th Month, our Quarterly Meeting held here, pretty well attended; Thomas Jay and Enos Pemberton of West Branch, and also William G. Hubbard of Columbus, Ohio, all very acceptably with us. The meeting on First Day, large and satisfactory.

The trying situation of my son, Nathan being of unsound mind since childhood, at times during past summer, manifesting symptoms of insanity and offering violence to persons when things did not suit him. Martha Ann and I, after consulting with relatives and Friends, also with two or three physicians, thought best to take him to an asylum. Probably his situation in the future might be worse. Accordingly, I with Joseph Stubbs went up to Eaton. After looking over the Infirmary buildings and the farm of about 200 acres of land and consulting with an attorney and with the directors of the Infirmary, also consulted the statute clauses of Ohio. It appears his case would be one that would come under the provisions of the aforesaid. The clerk of the board at once made out a permit for him to be taken there. On the 20th of 9th month, I went with him up there and stayed all night with him. In the morning we went over the farm and around some. He appeared willing to stay there and I left him without any trouble after he found his clothes were in the carriage box and they wanted work and help on the farm.

On the 28th of 10th month, we had a sale and sold off our stock as well as farming utensils, corn, oats, hay and some articles about the house and prepared to move to West Elkton, having purchased a house and lot some time ago. On the 1st of 11th month, we removed us there, and the house and farm we rented to Levi Stubbs, and longer if I did not sell it.

11th Month, 27th, Mary C. Moon, the Minister of Oak Ridge, Indiana, commenced a revival meeting, which continued about two weeks, mostly two meetings of the day; had altogether about 20 meetings besides attending six of our usual meetings. Mostly pretty satisfactory, yet she with a few others exercised in singing in a congregational way. This was trying to some Friends, and is a departure from primitive order and usage amongst Friends. The Meetings at night were largely attended.

12th Month 18th, John Jessup and Samuel Pitts of Dover, Indiana, had several meetings, about eight in number. Also, William S. Wooten of Danville, Indiana, attended several of them. Several of them were not so satisfactory as could a been desired, but so it seems that some of the Ministers are running into the customs and maxims of the world in dress as well as language, also in their communications in public, for which our forefathers in the truth suffered the spoiling of goods and imprisonment for their testimonies. These are looked upon as nonessential by some who are disposed to speak lightly of ancient doctrines and practices. It is sorrowful to many well concerned Friends to see and understand the way that many of these revival meetings are conducted by some Ministers of our Society.

## 1882

Warm and pleasant weather during the beginning of the year, more so than usual with us, but little snow and rain. It was and has been a very open winter with muddy roads and considerable sickness at times. About the 1st of 3rd Month, I sold my farm, where we had lived for 26 years, for $6,000, as Martha Ann's health had been for several years very poor, so that we thought best, after leaving it, to dispose of it and live in the village.

We think we enjoy ourselves as well and better than we expected and have less care and attention of things than when we lived on the farm.

On the 2nd of 3rd Month, we removed to the Cooper property, which I had lately bought and which was more convenient and better improved and suited us better.

Our Quarterly Meeting in this month was attended about as large as common and pretty satisfactory. On the 31st of this month, I went up to Eaton after Meeting to do some business. I went out to the Infirmary and met a very kind reception from the Superintendent and his wife and took dinner with them. Nathan appeared glad to see me, but did not say much. Yet he enjoys himself quite well and has good health since he has been there, about six months. A new Superintendent has lately been taken in and appears a very suitable person. Both he and his wife and son conduct things very well and satisfactory to the County Directors. There is about 75 inmates, 15 of them children.

Through the forepart of the spring, it was very rainy and wet, so that spring work was much delayed. Several frosts, which killed the fruit, especially small fruits, so that there was very few apples or peaches in our vicinity.

On 15th of 6th Month I went up again to see the County Infirmary and called in to see Nathan. I found him enjoying pretty good health and he still appears satisfied. We generally hear from him every five weeks. We furnish his clothes all the time.

On the 16th I went out to Quarterly Meeting at Salem. The rains have washed out the roads and bridges; it was tedious getting out there, yet it was satisfactory attendance; large on First Day.

7th Month, we have this summer, a bountiful crop of wheat, oats and other spring crops, which no doubt many feel thankful for to a kind Providence for his many blessings bestowed on us; since Thanksgiving has commenced wheat turns out a heavy yield.

9th Month 2nd went up to Eaton. Called to see Nathan at the Infirmary and found him quite complaining with boils. I took a trunk for him to put his clothes in which seemed to please him very well. I left him under thoughtful consideration and felt thanks for his being in so good [a place] and under so good regulations, and remembering we were doing the best for him we could under the circumstances. We were pleased.

Our Quarterly Meeting in 9th Month about as usual in attendance. Enos Pemberton of West Branch and Elwood Ellis of Jonesboro, Indiana in attendance on First Day. A large company present, quite a large and solemn occasion. Our brother and friend, Alan Reeves, having been very sick for several weeks, peacefully passed away on the 15th of 9th Month in time of our Quarterly Meeting and was buried in time of it, on First Day morning; made a happy close. Aged about 75 years. He had been afflicted for several years with an inward complaint.

Our Yearly Meeting in the 10th Month opened rather small, yet after a few days it increased to about its usual size and progressed in a good degree of harmony and brotherly consideration.

We had quite a time of sickness of the typhoid and malaria fever in our vicinity during the 10th Month. Some seven or eight deaths occurred; it was a very afflicting time with us, and several had to part with dear friends and bid adieu to friends of Earth. It continued for some five or six weeks.

In 12th Month, I attended Whitewater Quarterly Meeting. Pretty satisfactory. Our honored friend, Isaac Sharp of Darlington, England acceptably in attendance with Joel Bean of San Francisco. Our English Friend, it appears, left his home in 1877, on an extensive mission of Gospel love around the world and has been engaged ever since leaving England. Going first to Madagascar and then to Norway, sojourning some time at each place. And afterwards to Sweden, Russia and Germany, visiting the small companies and sojourning with Friends for a time in those countries. He then proceeded on to the south of France.

After staying a while there he took a ship to west Africa, and from those parts went on to Australia and took up his time sojourning at Hoberton, Sydney and New Zealand and other parts, visiting and strengthening many believers, whom he found established in the hope and faith of the dear Redeemer and found many Friends established according to the order of the Gospel as held by our religious Society. Sometime last summer, he left those far-off isles and took ship for the Sandwich Islands. And then came on to San Francisco about the 1st of 10th Month. After staying there a while, he came on east and attended Baltimore Yearly Meeting, after staying up while in Baltimore. His companion, Joel Bean of San Francisco, went on to Philadelphia and New York, staying for a while, then came west, calling on the way at a few places until he arrived at Richmond. After attending Whitewater and Spiceland Quarterly Meetings, they went on to Tennessee staying a while, and went on to Helena in Arkansas, visiting the school and Friends Meeting in that place.

## 1883

This year came in with pretty cool weather; much of the time rain and disagreeable, with great amount of rain and some snow.

2nd Month 10th—This day, I have completed the 72nd year of my age and feel the infirmity of age coming on, so that it seems my time here on earth is nearing its close. I often think if called upon, the preparation has been made. If called upon by the great Judge to appear before him, I believe it would be granted to me in great mercy, not through any righteousness I have done, but through me and of the dear Redeemer, whom I have endeavored to serve from early childhood, notwithstanding weakness and imperfections have attended my pathway. Yet I trust a happy admittance will be made for me.

Our Quarterly Meeting in 3rd Month was attended about as usual for this time of year and was a pretty satisfactory time. Attendance quite large on First Day. Susan Ratliff of Mississinewa, Seth Reece of Cherry Grove, Elizabeth Reynolds, all acceptably in attendance.

Our honored and beloved citizen, Dr. J. S. Weinland died along about the 25th of 4th Month. A worthy Christian man of the United Brethren church. He suffered much from a cancer for several months, yet manifested quiet composure of mind and said his peace was fully made with God, and a happy acceptance would be granted him in the Heavenly Father's kingdom. His funeral was largely attended by the people of this vicinity; a worthy and able physician for more than 30 years in this place, and much respected by all classes of the people.

5th Month, 2nd, our friends Lewis and Martha Ann Taylor returned to us from their sojourn at Denver in Colorado. It seemed pleasant to have their company again after several months' absence.

A young man by the name of Stewart Noble came home with them. He seemed to be quite a talented speaker and engaged as an evangelist worker in the West. He professes very high attainments and don't appear to be a member of any church.

9th of 5th Month, I went up to Eaton on business and went out to County Infirmary and met a kind reception with the superintendent, William Lehman, and his amiable wife and Nathan. I took dinner with them and found Nathan doing pretty well and appeared enjoying good health. Yet there appears some more symptoms of insanity, perhaps as he gets older in years.

On Fifth Day morning, 7th of 6th Month, I left home to visit some dear connections in Iowa and other parts of the West. I took the train at Camden about 10 a.m. and went directly onto Logansport. Delayed a few minutes, took dinner, then went to Chicago, arrived late in the evening. After some delay, I started about 10 p.m. and went on all night and arrived at Burlington, Iowa, early in the morning. After a short delay went on to Mount Pleasant, about 30 miles; after a while took Keokuk train to Salem, about 12 miles. I met brother Samuel at the depot about 12 p.m. and went on directly home with him, about 80 rods. Met a very kind and cordial welcome from his family. Lindley, his son and his wife, and his daughter, Mary Anne, and his youngest son, William A., a young man about 22 years old. All of whom extended to me the most cordial and kindest welcome during my stay with them.

Lindley and his wife, who were lately married, are very kind and interesting young people. I felt much for them and had to hold out the language of encouragement in inviting them to seek first the Kingdom of Heaven and its righteousness, and all other things would be added thereto.

Mary Anne, his daughter, is a very interesting young woman. She was married a few years ago to a wealthy planter in the state of Louisiana by the name of Barnabas Jay, who was born in Hancock County, Georgia and was a member of the Baptist Church. He died in the 2nd Month last of pneumonia. Since then, she had come to Iowa with her child about six months old. Her husband was a very prominent man in the South and was wealthy before the rebellion. She said she had ample means left to live on.

On Seventh Day morning, 9th, went into Salem, and met brother Henry and his son William P. in town. Called on some Friends—Doctor Siviter, an English Friend I had seen many years ago in Indiana Yearly Meeting. Also called on Nanny Osborne, a relative; took dinner with J.R. Brown and wife, and it was a pleasant time with us all.

First Day, 10th, attended Salem meeting at 11 a.m. At 2 p.m. attended the Separate Friends meeting. They are both small. A sad affair this separation appears to be, but no doctrine involved as in some other places.

Second Day, 11th, Samuel went with me up to brother Henry's on Cedar. Met a kind welcome from Henry and Phebe. In the p.m. spend some time over at his son William's.

On Third Day, 12th, a very rainy day spent within doors. The country appears flooded with heavy rains so that is very discouraging to farmers about planting.

Fourth Day, 13th, went over to William's and took dinner; spent the day very pleasantly with them. Fifth Day went to Cedar Creek meeting with Henry. Small yet satisfactory occasion. In the p.m. Henry took me to Salem.

Sixth Day, 15th, Samuel and family with myself went to Obadiah Cook's, about 2 miles below Salem. Stayed all night with them. Very interesting people; they manifested much kindness to me. He lives on his late father's, Nathan Cook's, farm, where I saw the old clock that *his* father Eli Cook owned at Elk and who died there many years ago. It was brought by him from South Carolina in the first settlement of Preble County, Ohio. It showed the changes of the moon and was a curiosity and came from Germany, perhaps more than a hundred years ago.

Seventh Day, 16th, Samuel took me down to Pilot Grove, about 12 miles in Lee County, to John and Sally Denny's. Met a very kind reception from them and their children. It had been more than 30 years since we had met each other. And it was a joyful meeting with us all.

On First Day morning it was a very wet morning. We did not go to Meeting. In the p.m. it cleared away, and we went to Grove and called on Jeremiah Osborne, a relative. Also to J. Burnett's, formerly of Waynesville, Ohio, with whom I had some acquaintance. Spent the time very pleasantly with them; returned to John Denny's in the evening.

Second Day, 18th, visited some at Jacob Griffin's who were distant relatives; spent the day very pleasantly with them. Returned to John Denny's in the evening, where his father and mother stayed with us.

Third Day, 19th, after an early breakfast, I took leave of John and Sally Denny, a solemn parting, never expecting to see each other again in this world. Jacob then took me to Houghton station about 6 miles. I went on the train to Salem 5 miles in the p.m. Visited about town some in a social way. Very satisfactory.

Fourth Day, 20th, attended Salem weekday Meeting, very small. Took dinner at J.R. Brown's and had considerable conversation about the separation in Iowa Yearly Meeting as well as that in Western Yearly Meeting. After hearing what they had to say that if charity had a been exercised on both sides, there was no need of a separation.

Fifth Day, 21st, spent with Samuel's family pleasantly and soundly, it being a dull, gloomy day.

Sixth Day, 22nd, we went over to Alanthan Frazier's (who married William Maddock's daughter, Ella) in the spring wagon about 4 miles and did not find them home. In p.m. we rode out with Samuel and his wool wagon.

Seventh Day, 23rd, attended two Meetings today with Lindley Luria that were appointed for revival work by the committee of Salem. Two meetings they attended was very small, yet a few appeared concerned that there should be more.

First Day, 24th, Samuel took me over to J. Cook's on Big Cedar about 5 miles to the Bible school at West Grove. An indulged meeting place, about 60 in attendance. Afterwards attended the Meeting in the Grove, about double attended the Meeting that were in the school. They seem to exercise in song yet it was a pretty good Meeting. Took dinner at Payton Cook's who married in the Bailes family. Interesting young people. Returned to Samuel's in the evening.

Second Day went up with William Brown to Henry's; a very pleasant day. Third Day, 26th went over to William's; took dinner with them, spent the time very pleasantly with them. In the p.m. Henry took me down to Salem, where I learned Jesse Kenworthy and Mary were in the settlement.

Fourth Day, 27th met Harvey Derbyshire this morning and had an interesting time with him. He once had attended Westfield Quarterly Meeting many years ago as a minister from Canada on a religious visit. He has identified himself with the Separate Friends of this vicinity.

Went with J.R. Brown and wife to their Meeting in which Harvey had considerable to say. Also appeared in supplication. It was a good Meeting. He is in his 85th year and appears pretty lively in his gift. Saw Jesse Kenworthy this p.m., who had been out West and reported the high waters so great that I think it best not to go for Kansas until next week.

Fifth Day, 28th took train for Houghton station 6 miles to J.C. Marshal's, who married Ella, William P. Maddock's daughter. [*Earlier Joseph wrote that Alanthan Frazier had married William Maddock's daughter, Ella—see Sixth Day, 22nd, 1883*]. Spent the time pleasantly with them.

In the p.m. went with Evan Marshall and wife to the School Farm purchased by a donation of Josiah White, late of Philadelphia, deceased. It contains a tract of 1400 acres of land—very rich and productive soil and a large dwelling house. Other buildings have been erected for an orphan asylum agreeably to the donor's wish, and to be under the care of Iowa Yearly Meeting of Friends. I spent the time very pleasantly with the superintendent and matron, John and Susan Fay. It is a prairie land

and broke and ready for cultivation. Took supper with them. They have only at present about 15 children in the home, a small number at present for the accommodations.

I returned to J.C. Marshal's in the evening and had a pleasant time in reading the Bible with these interesting young people.

Sixth Day, 29th parted affectionately with those dear young relatives and went to William Taylor's and was kindly received by him and his beloved wife. Had a pleasant and agreeable time with them. In the p.m. William Taylor took me to Salem. After parting with him, Samuel gave me a letter from home, giving the sad information of the sickness of our friend John Kenworthy.

Seventh Day, 30th stayed at Samuel's; not feeling very well. In the p.m. I walked to town, feel some better. First Day, 7th Month, 1st, Samuel took me up to Cedar Creek Meeting, a pretty satisfactory time. Henry and Phebe as well as William and Tamar were present. I went home with Isaac and Sarah Brown, spent the p.m. with them very agreeably, and returned to Samuel's in the evening.

On Second Day morning, the 2nd of 7th Month, I left for Kansas in company with my beloved nephew, William A. Maddock. I took the train at 9:00 a.m. and went on to Mount Pleasant. After some delay to Fairfield where we called on our relation, David P. Stubbs, who lives here and kindly assisted us in procuring tickets to Kansas. The train would not leave until nine. He took us around to see the many improvements that were going on in their town, which seemed to be an enterprising people.

He then took us to his splendid residence, where we were received with kindness by his amiable wife and daughter, who had only a few days before returned from a female seminary at Toronto in Canada and were enjoying themselves very pleasantly. They treated us with much kindness, and we took supper with them.

At 10 p.m. we parted with our kind relatives and Friends and took the train for Kansas. Went on all night. It was very tedious traveling. Got to Cameron in Missouri about daylight. Then on to Atchison. We took breakfast there and went on to Topeka and changed trains. Then on to Sterling. We arrived there about sunset, went to S. P. Stubbs, where we met with a kind greeting and where several of the connections and Friends came in during the evening, and we enjoyed each other's company. A very consoling and pleasant time

Fourth Day, 4th spent pleasantly with connections and Friends, and it being the Fourth of July so-called, it was a day of much parades with the people shooting crackers and torpedoes so that some were seriously hurt and disabled.

Fifth Day, 5th, I walked around some in the morning; attended the weekday Meeting of Friends here. It was very small—three men and four women.

Sixth Day, 6th, visited around amongst connections and others in town. Took dinner at Sylvanus Stubbs' and spent the time very agreeably with him and his amiable wife. In the evening went over where Joseph H. Stubbs [my brother-in-law] was building his new house. I lodged again with them and their daughter, Mary, about 16 years old.

Seventh Day, 7th walked around some in the morning, receiving a card from home giving accounts of some sickness, particularly the sickness of our aged friend John Kenworthy. In the p.m. Solomon took us out in the country over the Arkansas River and crossed on the bridge. We had an extensive view of the Prairie, of the large crops of wheat harvesting, crops of corn and sugarcane growing and the herds of cattle feeding. It was a delightful sight to behold; it seemed the Garden of Eden. Returned in the evening.

First Day morning, I attended Friends Bible School in Sterling. Afterwards, the Meeting was pretty satisfactory. A young man, son of Abel Bond, the great tract distributor, attended and spoke much. Very interesting and intelligent speaker. Took dinner at J.P. Stubbs with Jesse Brown and others who came from Preble County, Ohio. A pleasant time. In the p.m. I lodged again with Joseph H. Stubbs and family.

Second Day, 9th, after breakfast, I took leave of my dear relatives and Friends, a solemn parting it was. I took the train for Iowa at 7:30 a.m. and went on pretty directly to Florence, Elmira to Topeka, and then Kansas City, arriving there late in the evening. After a short delay, I went on in the night to Camden in Missouri, and arrived at Fairfield in Iowa early in the morning.

Third Day, 10th, went on to Mount Pleasant; after some delay, then off to Salem, arriving at Sands about 1:00 p.m.

Fourth Day 11th, William went with me up to Henry's. In the p.m. we went over to William P.'s, had a very satisfactory visit with them, returned to Henry's and lodged.

Fifth Day, 12th, attended Cedar Creek Meeting; very small. After Meeting the Monthly Meeting was held in the p.m. Henry and Tamar went with me down to Salem. As we passed Cedar Creek burial ground, we stopped and attended the internment of Boyd Williams, the son of

William Williams, a worthy minister amongst Friends who died more than 50 years ago. A very small company present. I learned that he had lived in the vicinity several years, and withdrew from Friends in the time of the Hicks Separation and had of later years manifested an interest in returning to Friends, but his wife objecting, he never returned. Parents cannot confer peace on their children. This evening took a solemn leave of Henry and Tamar. It was a contriting [*sic*] time as it was doubtful whether we all should meet again in this world, particularly Henry and myself. We had during my stay here, had several interesting seasons together.

Sixth Day, 13th, expecting to leave for home tomorrow. Called on J.R. Brown and others with whom I've formed some acquaintance. We bid each other affectionately farewell. I went into the Friends burial ground and looked on the resting place of many who had removed from Ohio that I knew many years ago. A solemn thought to one, reminding us that we have no continuing city here. In the evening before retiring, we had a Bible reading in Samuel's family. A very interesting time it was, and counsel and advice held out that we should prepare to meet each other in that land where parting would be no more. At the close, a prayer was offered up for preservation that we might be prepared to meet again where parting would be no more. It was a precious season and will be remembered by me.

Seventh Day, 14th morning, attended breakfast. I parted with Samuel and family with whom I had been so kindly cared for, by Mary Anne and Louisa, as well as others in the family. The many social seasons we had together is thankfully remembered by me as well as them, no doubt.

Samuel going to Illinois on business, we took the train for Keokuk 42 miles, arriving there about 10:30 a.m. Since no trains were leaving for Illinois until p.m. I went with Samuel on the packet down to Warsaw Woolen Mills, some eight or 10 miles, arriving there in about an hour. Samuel has bought considerable wool from them this season. After dinner we returned back again. It was a pleasant ride. At 3:30 p.m., we took the train for Mount Sterling, in all, 55 miles. It being late in the evening when we arrived, we stayed all night.

First Day morning 15th, we hired a hack to take us to John Stutesman's 12 miles in Schugler County. It was bad roads. We did not get there until it was 11:00 a.m. John and his family being gone to Meeting, we went over to his mother's—Rhoda Stutesman—about half a mile. We met a kind welcome from her and her daughter. Samuel had been there before, and she knew him. I, being a stranger, after she knew me, she appeared much pleased. We are first cousins yet had not seen each other for many years. John came over in the evening and we had a pleasant time together. We went home with him and lodged.

Second Day, 16th, we went over to Rhoda's again after breakfast and spent the day very agreeably with her. It rained much in the p.m. She has a daughter, about 28 years old, quite bewildered in her mind, or rather insane; all in all, a pitiful situation. She is indeed come so by religious excitement. Late in the evening, we visited one of Rhoda's daughters by the name of Davis, very interesting time.

Third Day morning 17th, we parted with our very kind relatives, and John and one of his daughters very kindly went with us to Rushville, 9 miles. After parting with them, I went on to Beardstown and arrived there, about 40 miles, about 1:00 p.m. Procuring tickets, went on for Springfield, 43 miles. After some delay to Pena, 46 miles, then to Paris about 75 miles, arriving there about 2:00 a.m.

Fourth Day morning 18th, after some rest and early breakfast, I took the Leiden to Vermillion, 6 miles. Met a very kind and pleasant welcome from Alisha and Joash Stubbs and their friends. Visited some amongst their children as well as the widow of Jesse Hobson Stubbs, who was killed on the railroad several months ago. Had an interesting time with her and could truly sympathize with her sad bereavement. Jesse was much respected in the community as well as the church of which he was a beloved member. They all feel their loss. Read a card from home giving a satisfactory account.

Fifth Day 19th lodged last night at Joash's. Visited some amongst relatives; went to the Stubbs burial ground, where several of the connections were laid. In the PM was informed that my nephew Harvey Stubbs would not be here until tomorrow. He lives about 20 miles off in Clarkson; the other nephew has removed to Missouri.

Sixth Day 20th spent around satisfactory amongst my relatives, especially Joash Stubbs' family and his daughter, Laurel, an amiable and interesting young woman. At noon Henry arrived and we had a very social and interesting occasion. In the evening I parted with these interesting friends, particularly Alisha and Joash Stubbs family, never expecting to see each other again in this world, a solemn parting. In the evening I went to Paris and lodged.

Seventh Day 21st, early in the morning I went on to Chrisman where Harvey resides, about 14 miles. Met a very kind and social greeting from his amiable wife and daughter. After breakfast, Harvey took me to see Patty, widow of Samuel Stubbs, who lives with her son, Joseph, about 2 miles. They seemed glad to see me and I was glad to see them, and we had a very social and interesting time together. Joseph was very sick. After staying with them I affectionately bid them farewell.

I went back to Chrisman and, my nephew going with me to the depot, procured tickets and bidding him farewell, got on the train about 3:00 p.m. and went on for Indianapolis, about 84 miles. I arrived late in the evening, so I had to stay all night as the evening trains had all left. I put up at the California House for the night.

First Day morning the 22nd, about 5:00 a.m., I got on the train for Richmond. Soon after getting on, I found that I had left my teeth in the room that I lodged in at the hotel. But so it was. I had to pass on and arrived at Richmond at 7:30 a.m. There was no train leaving for Cincinnati till morning. I had to stay. I went to Isaac Corman's and got there just as they were sitting down to breakfast, a kind welcome. Went with Isaac to the 12th Street Meeting. Very good Meeting. Joseph Moore had much to communicate in the p.m. I attended a lecture on temperance at the same place at 3:30 p.m. delivered by A. Hoyt, Secretary of the Women's Indiana Temperance Society. A good lecture. Attendance large. An interesting lecture.

Second Day morning, 23rd, I arose and took the early train at 5:00 a.m. for Camden. Arrived at about 6:30 a.m. Meeting with a conveyance, I went directly for home. Met a kind and pleasant welcome from relatives and friends as well as citizens of the village. And it was indeed pleasant to mingle together after an absence of several weeks and feel thankful to my heavenly Father for his preserving care over me in dangers seen and unseen.

Soon after my return I went up to Eaton and was out at the county infirmary. I found Nathan had good health and appeared to be pretty well satisfied.

In 8th Month, our aged and honored friend, John Kenworthy, died after several weeks of affliction with old age. He had long been a faithful and upright pillar in the church. His funeral was largely attended by the people by whom he was respected; a solemn and interesting Meeting was held on the occasion; aged about 86 years. Jared P. Binford and Amos C. Hill from Walnut Ridge were with us. Had some Meetings and visited several of the families. A satisfactory and solemn occasion and was a timely season amongst us.

Quarterly Meeting in 9th Month, attendance about as usual by friends from Salem; very large on First Day. Thomas Jay of West Branch, Eli Cook and Dillon H. Williams of West Grove, very acceptably with us on First Day evening.

After Quarterly Meeting I went to Camden to take the train for Plainfield in order to attend Western Yearly Meeting. I went to Richmond and stayed there all night. On Second Day I took the train for Indianapolis, arrived there at 10:00 a.m.

Stopped at the California House to see about my teeth that I left there when I returned from the West some two months ago. The landlord denied ever seeing them and appeared not willing to give any satisfaction about them. Learning that the hotel was not a place of any credit, I found there was little or nothing that could be done towards obtaining them.

I went to Plainfield and attended p.m. sitting at Western Yearly Meeting, which was very large and attended by several ministers over the continent including Isaac Sharp of England, who had been all over the world on missions of labor, leaving his home in Great Britain more than five years ago.

On Third Day, I attended the Meeting of the Separate Friends at Sugar Grove who meet in the Yearly Meeting capacity. This is a sorrowful affair, similar to the separations in Indiana and Iowa as well as Kansas Yearly Meeting. It might've been avoided had charity and forbearance been observed that is so desirable in the church as well as other ways. Some 300 or 200 were in attendance. It was a good Meeting, far different from those of Plainfield, which seemed more like Methodist. I took dinner at Jod Newlin's, a distant relative, where some friends from Philadelphia were present.

On Fourth Day attended Meeting at Plainfield, large and quite noisy and unsettled. Took dinner with Levi Lane and was a very satisfactory occasion. In the evening I attended a lecture of Isaac Sharp of England and his travels in New Zealand, Australia and the Sandwich Islands, and they were very interesting. Started for home that evening, arrived home next morning. At Monthly Meeting at Elk, Sarah Coat of West Branch attended; visited several families during her stay.

In 12th Month 15th Jacob Moore of Richmond came down here from our Quarterly Meeting at Salem; had two or three appointed Meetings with us and visited several families during his stay with us. Attended Monthly Meeting the Fifth Day 20th; very acceptably with us and the families, as well as the Meeting he held.

## 1884

Very cold weather at the beginning of this month, particularly in the 1st Month much snow fell, and it was unusually cold. Some of the older inhabitants thought more so than it had been for years, the mercury down several times from 20 to 25° below zero.

In 2nd Month, Joseph Wright and Daniel Hill of New Vienna, Ohio attended our Monthly Meeting; afterwards they had a revival Meeting which continued for some two weeks, meeting generally in the day and evening. Two young women from Richmond by the name of Burson attended towards the last. About 36 Meetings altogether, including our regular Meetings. Attendance through the day rather small. Attendance at night larger. It was pretty cold and stormy some of the time, which caused them to be small. Much interest was manifested by some friends and others in the community. I hope it will be of lasting benefit to some at least.

My brother John Maddock was taken down sick with inflammation of the bowels and other inward complaints. He was very bad; he was sick only for five days. His death was very sudden and unexpected to us all. Yet so it is. We know not the day or hour the Son of Man will call for us; prepared or unprepared, we must go. Some years ago, he had difficulties with some members in society. He became dissatisfied and withdrew from the Meeting and never returned, which was cause of sorrow. Yet near his close he expressed that all was well and that a happy home was prepared for him in the heavenly Father's kingdom, and encouraged his family to so live as to meet him there. He died 3rd of 4th Month 1884, aged 72 years, two months, and four days. A large attendance at his funeral.

In 6th Month, I attended our Quarterly Meeting at Salem. The attendance not large, but it was satisfactory. Joseph A. Binford of Walnut Ridge acceptably with us. Quite large attendance on First Day. 7th and 8th Months were cool and dry weather; wheat and oats crops quite light. Also the corn crop will be light. The last half of 8th Month attended New Garden Quarterly Meeting. Attendance pretty good on Seventh and First Day in the p.m. On First Day, attended at Fountain City formerly Newport. The attendance was also pretty good. Lodged with Thompson Harris, where lived our aged friend, Mary Stubbs, widow of Newton Stubbs, who died many years ago at Elk. She was very sick; not likely to live long in this world. She had long been a worthy member in the church.

In 9th Month our Quarterly Meeting was held here; about as large as usual on Seventh Day, quite large and satisfactory.

10th Month, I attended our Yearly Meeting at Richmond. About as large as usual; many of the sittings of the Meeting for Discipline were seasons of divine labor and a good degree of harmony. Yet some of the Meetings in the morning and evening were more like Methodist than Friends.

The state and presidential elections this fall were times of much excitement amongst the political parties. More so than had been for several years. It seemed at times as though there would be another rebellion, yet after a few weeks it settled down pretty quietly. Yet there appears considerable animosity amongst the different citizens and parties in our country at the present time.

On the 9th of 12th Month, I went up to Eaton; was out at the County Infirmary. I met a kind reception from the Superintendent and his amiable wife. I took dinner with them, and it appears at time of pretty good health with them. Nathan seemed to enjoy pretty good health and seemed to be doing well. About 80 inmates in the home.

## 1885

Considerable cold weather in 1st Month this year. In 2nd Month our nephew and niece, Aaron and Martha Talbert of Minneapolis, Minnesota, called and spent some time with us. They had been visiting amongst the missionary stations kept by Friends in Arkansas, Florida, as well as a few other places. They found in places they were not advancing in education and religious growth as could be desired. Yet some appeared to manifest some interest in the Christian course. They found many subsisting as part of the land had been long in slavery. Some allowances are to be made with both white and black.

I was confined much of the time in 3rd and 4th Months. I did not get out to Meeting much of the time so that it was very tedious. I had to remember that in younger days my interest in attendance was very strong. About this time that I was confined, Harvey and Alice Bergman of Van Wert, Ohio visited us. Had several unusual Meetings with us and visited families and stayed several weeks. Although there was not a very large attendance in the day, yet larger at night. They were pretty satisfactory and left a good impression on Friends as well as many in the community. Much cold weather caused many at a distance from attending. There was William J. Thornberrry and N.C. McLain of Goshen, who had Meetings at the other house for some time, on the same hour, but frequently came to ours at the close of their Meeting. They joined in with the Methodists and the UB [United Brethren] church in partaking of the occasion on First Day evening, and left next morning for their homes. This was very trying to Friends, yet we found that they had before exercised and advocated in the thing. It seemed they were ashamed of their conduct as they left so soon. Soon after this circumstance there was a Meeting of the representatives on this occasion by our Yearly Meeting; some advice was issued.

In the 8th Month this year, R. W. Douglas attended one of our First Day Meetings and lectured on the subject in the p.m. of the sacrament to a pretty good company.

During the latter part of summer and fall, my health became more delicate, and I was confined to my room part of the 11th Month, and altogether on the 12th, having return of Hemorrhage of the Bowels and light strokes of paralysis and neuralgia at times. I was quite confined to my room and was not able to be out at Meeting. I experienced a great perdition in being prevented from attending our Meeting. It was quite cold weather here, much of the time.

## 1886

My poor health and indisposition still continuing through the 1st and 2nd Months, with light strokes of paralysis, caused me to remain indoors much of the time during the latter part of winter. Yet I was able to be up and about the house and did not suffer much pain. My system seemed to be very much paralyzed; my left-hand very much so yet not so but I am able to be up and walk out some and be out at Meeting a few times. I feel it to be a great privilege to enjoy this much from my heavenly Father, for his superintending care over me during my affliction and tedious time of confinement.

The latter part of 5th Month, I seemed to strengthen up some, so that I attended Meeting a few times and visited some of our connections and friends, which was indeed a great satisfaction. There seems to be plentiful summer crop coming on. Our wheat crops since thrashing commenced turned to a good yield, although times are very hard and grain is low.

The latter part of 8th Month, and first of 9th Month we had some light shocks of earthquake in our Southern states, especially so about

Charleston in South Carolina. It was severely felt in places here in the North. It created much alarm in places in the southern cities.

In 9th Month, Quarterly Meeting as usual was held here. Enos Pemberton and Rhoda Thomas of West Branch, Ohio, very acceptably with us. On Seventh Day about a common attendance. Very large on First Day, a satisfactory occasion. There seems to be trouble got up in some of the Yearly Meetings, especially in Ohio and Western, since their Meetings were held. Several ministers have administered the water to [i.e., baptized] their class, particularly in Ohio, as well as on common members. Still reports of shocks of earthquakes in Southern states as well as further north, and hard shocks reported in parts of Europe, particularly Italy.

---

The September 1886 entry in Joseph's diary is the final one, and his health continued to decline over the next two and a half years.

Earlier that year, in the Elk Monthly Minutes for May 1886, we find the following:

> Our Home Mission Committee makes the following suggestion: that James H Roberts. Lorenzo Stubbs, Martha Maddock and Sarah Stubbs be appointed in consideration of the pecuniary misfortune and declining health of our Friend, Joseph Maddock, to open voluntary subscription for the benefit of the family. The subscription to be in money or articles of value. Said Committee is authorized to sell or exchange any supplies of articles donated for the use of the family and report once a year or oftener as occasion may require.

## 1888

And from the Minutes of February 1888:

> A proposition from the Home Mission Committee was received at this time that the monthly meeting, in view of the financial embarrassment of our Friend Joseph Maddock, agree to furnish said Friend with all the necessary Flour and Wood for his support, which is united with by this Meeting and the proposition accepted accordingly. All donations for the above purpose is directed to the care of the Home Mission Committee.

In September 1888, Susan Stubbs reported for the Home Mission Committee that "Joseph Maddock has been furnished 18 and 1/3 cords of wood worth $27.50; also 268 ½ pounds of flour worth $6.71."

## 1889

In February 1889, Jesse Kenworthy was appointed "to have the care of the Meeting Records in room of Joseph Maddock who through infirmity has become incompetent."

Joseph Maddock died May 27, 1889, in Dayton, Ohio, perhaps in a hospital there. Records related to his death are scarce, but the cause of death was listed as paralysis. He was buried in the Friends cemetery near the Elk Monthly Meeting meetinghouse in West Elkton, Ohio. The only obituaries so far located are these two:

*The Eaton Weekly Register*, Eaton, Ohio, June 6, 1889

> Another Elkton pioneer has been called up higher. Joseph Maddock, in his seventy-ninth year. The funeral services were held in the Friends' church Tuesday, attended by a large number of relatives and friends. Interment in Quaker cemetery.

*The Piqua Daily Call*, Piqua, Ohio, Friday, June 07, 1889, "Local Laconics: News Notes About Persons and Things"

> Joseph Maddock, a leading Friend at West Elkton, Preble County, died this week in his 79th year.

# Joseph Maddock's Immediate Family

## His Wife, Mary Stubbs Maddock

Mary Stubbs married Joseph Maddock in 1834 when she was twenty-two years old. She gave birth to three children, two of whom lived. Her first child, Nathan, was born with a mental disability that meant he could not take care of himself, even as an adult. Her third child, Martha Ann Maddock,[1] was born when Nathan was eleven years old.

Caring for Nathan must have taken much of Mary Maddock's time and attention, and it seems her health was never very good, but she was nonetheless an active member in Elk Monthly Meeting. Like her husband, she seemed to enjoy traveling and attending Quaker gatherings of various kinds. In the Women's Minutes, Mary is periodically named a representative to Westfield Quarterly Meeting. Occasionally, she joined Joseph for overnight or several-day trips accompanying their friend, Martha Ann Taylor, when she felt called to travel in ministry. When the Maddock's daughter, Martha Ann, was at Earlham College in 1864–65, Mary made at least two trips by train to Richmond, Indiana, to see her. In his diary, Joseph mentions staying home in 1870 with Nathan (whose "epileptic fits" were occurring more frequently) so that Mary could attend Indiana Yearly Meeting. In 1874, she went with Joseph to a conference of Ministers and Elders in Richmond, Indiana.

Around then, she began to lose her sight in one eye and developed cataracts that left her completely blind. In May 1878, she consulted several doctors about her vision, including local doctors Weinland and Robertson, who sent her to Dr. Corson of Middletown, Ohio, who

1. Possibly named after Martha Ann Taylor, a recorded minister at Elk Monthly Meeting, who seems to have been Mary's close friend.

recommended an optician from Cincinnati, Dr. Joseph Aub. His opinion was that she might benefit from surgery to remove the cataracts. Primitive cataract surgery had been practiced for centuries, but in the late 1800s, new techniques were being developed. In Joseph's diary, he gives the following account of the surgery Dr. Aub performed, which attracted an audience of observing physicians.

> After she returned to Middletown and stayed a few days [with family friend, Eva Christiancy], Dr. Aub of Cincinnati came up on the 10th of 5th Month and performed the operation in less than fifteen minutes, binding up and all, some eight or ten physicians of Middletown being present. She suffered little or no pain in the operation. She was confined after the operation in a dark room [in the Christiancy home] with Dr. Corson attending. Also Dr. Aub of the city came up twice to see her. After staying nearly three weeks, Martha Ann being with her all the time, she concluded with Dr. Corson's consent to return home as she had got along pretty well, or perhaps better than could have reasonably been expected. On the 27th of the month she came home. It seemed to worry her some. But after a few days she got better and seemed to improve some, yet her sight was not very much better, yet she rejoiced to be at home and the comfort it was to mingle amid family society again.

Mary never fully recovered. Over the next four months she became bedridden in a darkened room, and she died September 30, 1878. Her doctors gave the cause of death as heart failure, but they were not sure what had caused it, so Joseph permitted an autopsy, which again, attracted an audience of a half-dozen area doctors along with some medical students. The cause of death was inconclusive, though Joseph wrote that the examination revealed, "there was some frill disease[2] lurking on her system," so serious the doctors agreed she couldn't have lived more than a year longer, and the family was "satisfied" that they had permitted the postmortem.

Below is Mary Maddock's obituary, probably written by Joseph and Martha Ann, which appeared in the October 1878 issue of *The Christian Worker* magazine.

2. Joseph does not explain what "frill disease" is/was, and I can find no nineteenth-century definition of "frill disease." "Frill" nowadays is related to vitreous degeneration, which is "a natural process that occurs with aging in most people. The degeneration of the vitreous gel [in the eye] starts early in life . . . This process is more likely to occur in individuals with myopia, diabetes, *recent eye surgery*, and eye trauma." Ashley Mauldin, "Vitreous Degeneration." (Italics mine.)

MADDOCK—Ninth month 30, 1878, at West Elkton, Ohio, Mary, wife of Joseph Maddock, in the 67th year of her age.

This dear mother in early youth gave her heart to God, and, being of a loving disposition, endeared herself to a large circle of friends, and was a bright example through life of many virtues that adorn the Christian, telling to all around her, "Come, follow me, as I have followed Christ." She manifested a lively interest in the affairs of the church and was a valuable elder in the church for many years. She endured a protracted illness of many months accompanied with great suffering at times, but, through all, not a murmur was heard to escape her lips. Thus passed away a mother in Israel. Although not conscious as she neared the close of life, her family and friends have the comforting assurance that she has received the crown that lieth at the end of the race and was gathered as a shock of corn fully ripe, with the redeemed in the heavenly Father's garner. She was a beloved and valuable member of Elk Monthly Meeting, Ohio.

## His Brother, John Maddock

Joseph Maddock's brother, John Maddock (29 Jan 1812–03 Apr 1884), was a successful businessman, landowner, and respected public figure in Preble County, Ohio. He was also deeply committed to the Quaker testimonies (e.g., equality, integrity, peace) he absorbed from childhood from his family and Elk Monthly Meeting. In the decades before the Civil War, he took an active role in helping fugitives from slavery escape to freedom. His inn/tavern/hotel in West Elkton was a station[3]—and he an "Operator" and "Stationmaster"—on the Underground Railroad through Preble County from the Ohio River to Levi Coffin's home in Newport, Indiana.[4]

In 1894, when Professor Wilbur Siebert was collecting information on the Underground Railroad, he contacted John Maddock's son, Alpheus T. Maddock, who sent him a letter that included childhood memories of living in his parent's house when it was an active UGRR station. Below are excerpts from A. T. Maddock's letter.

The [UGRR] started at Cincinnati and points near it on the Ohio [River], through College Hill, thence to West Elkton,

3. A National Underground Railroad marker is located on the site of the inn/hotel/tavern in West Elkton, Ohio, now a Methodist church parking lot.

4. Now Fountain City, Indiana.

> where Jesse Stubbs, John H. Stubbs, John Maddock (my father) and several others were station keepers. . . .
>
> After the Fugitive Slave Law of 1850 had been passed, a knock was heard at our door late one night. My mother remarked to Father that she believed someone knocked. He got up, opened the door and there on the steps stood a black man, bare-headed, with hat under his arm. It was in winter or in late spring, the weather was very disagreeable and he was scantily clothed. My parents took care of him, clothed him and fed him and forwarded him on the way. When in front of our house that night, [the fugitive] told mother that something within prompted him to ask shelter, etc. [at our house].
>
> It was a penitentiary offense after the Fugitive Slave Law of 1850 to shelter or help a slave. This mother told us children after he left. It was sufficient and closed our mouths till full-grown men before we told it.
>
> . . .
>
> The last fugitive I ever saw was in the summer of 1862. He stopped at my father's on his way to Canada. He was the servant of Senator Crittenden of Kentucky, a bright mulatto and dressed exceedingly well. Most of his life had been spent in Washington, D.C. with the senator. He had but little to say on his first trip. When leaving, said he would call again before many months. In just three months he returned. This time he gave us his full history. Had returned to Kentucky, stolen his mother and two sisters, forwarded them by Waynesville, O. route, and came here on his way back to Canada.

Among the names listed in Siebert's "Directory of the Names of Underground Railroad Operators" for Preble County, Ohio, are John Maddock and John H. Stubbs.[5]

In the January 1855 *Eaton Democrat* newspaper, the following announcement appeared:

> TURNPIKE ELECTION: Notice is hereby given to the stockholders of the Butler & Preble Turnpike Road Company, that there will be an election held at the House of John Maddock in

5. Siebert, *The Underground Railroad: From Slavery to Freedom*. Mistakenly shown as "John W. Stubbs" on Siebert's list, but no such person existed in Preble County, Ohio, at the time. John Maddock Stubbs and John Hobson Stubbs both lived in Preble County and were members of Elk Monthly Meeting. Either could be the "John Stubbs" Siebert referred to, but only John Hobson Stubbs regularly used his middle initial.

> West Elkton, on Monday the 20th day of January, 1855, between the hours of 10 o'clock a.m. and 4 o'clock p.m., for the election of five directors to serve said company for the ensuing year.
>
> JOHN H. STUBBS, President. Dec. 28, 1854

Though it was not unusual for local inhabitants to form turnpike companies[6] to maintain roads through their area, it is an interesting coincidence that two Quakers heavily involved in the UGRR were leaders among "stockholders" of the Butler & Preble Turnpike which ran north from the Butler-Preble County line past the John Maddock "Homestead house"[7] into West Elkton, Ohio, and on north toward Eaton.

In 1857 John Maddock was appointed Postmaster in West Elkton, a position of trust because the postmaster handled money as well as mail. It was a political appointment that often reflected which party was in the White House. Postmasters were paid a percentage of the postage they sold that year.[8]

On federal census forms through the decades, Maddock's occupation is listed as "Carpenter," "Keeps Hotel," and "Farmer." He also owned a significant amount of property in Gratis and Somers Townships, including a corner lot in the village of West Elkton, the site of his inn/tavern/hotel. In his will (made September 12, 1872), he bequeathed the following properties to his wife and children:

- "the Mansion home and all of the lots and parts of lots in West Elkton"
- "the Homestead farm where my son Alpheus T. Maddock resides"

6. Klein, "Turnpikes and Toll Roads."

> Private turnpikes were business corporations that built and maintained a road for the right to collect fees from travelers. . . . Although the states of Pennsylvania, Virginia and Ohio subsidized privately-operated turnpike companies, most turnpikes were financed solely by private stock subscription and structured to pay dividends. . . . as New England historian Edward Kirkland (1948, 45) put it, "the turnpikes did not make money. . . . Organizers and "investors" generally regarded the initial proceeds from sale of stock as a fund from which to build the facility, which would then earn enough in toll receipts to cover operating expenses.

7. In his will, John Maddock left the property on the Butler & Preble Turnpike (now Ohio State Road 503) to his son, Alpheus T. Maddock, and the "Mansion home" in West Elkton to his wife, Martha.

8. Prechtel-Kluskens,"Nineteenth-Century Postmaster and His Duties." "The postmaster was a political patronage job and so the dates of appointment sometimes provide valuable clues to the postmaster's party affiliation."

- "my interest in the Rush Run land"
- "the Cooper Farm in Somers Township"
- "the Wright and Beall Farm in Somers Township"
- "all of my western land situated in Page County, Iowa and in Oregon County, Missouri"

John Maddock appears to have been an active member of Elk Monthly Meeting for most of his life, though not all of it. In 1838, at age twenty-six, he and Martha Stubbs, age twenty, married under the care of the Meeting. Even before that, beginning in 1831 and continuing for over twenty years, John (and his brother, Joseph Maddock) served on, and sometimes clerked, the Friends School Committee which was responsible for enticing Quaker teachers to come and teach a term or two for Friends in West Elkton. In March 1869, the Elk Monthly Meeting minutes record John Maddock's appointment, along with three other men, "to construct a new brick building south of the church" which became the Friends Academy in West Elkton. The building was finished in October, in time for the first students to enroll in the fall.

The following month, the Men's Minutes report a complaint against John Maddock for failing to fulfill a "written contract or engagement." No specifics are given in the minutes, so we can't know if this had anything to do with building the Friends Academy. A committee was named to visit him regarding his "deviation" and reported the following month that they had a "pretty full opportunity" with him. A month or so later at the meeting on February 24, 1870, however, the "Friends appointed on John Maddock's case report they have endeavored to attend to their appointment but have not accomplished anything, and wish to be released, with which this meeting unites and directs the case to the Quarterly Meeting as a difficult case." (Most previous references to the entire incident are X-ed out in the handwritten minutes.) The matter was referred to Westfield Quarterly meeting, but its minutes give no details re the cause of the "difficulty" nor its resolution.

All was well for a time, but again, in March 1877, a complaint was brought against him, this time by Francis Maddock. (There were at least two Francis Maddocks in Elk Monthly Meeting at the time: John's brother and John's nephew.) Once again, details of the complaint are omitted from the minute book. In April, the Preparative Meeting reported that John Maddock "has refused to arbitrate a case of difficulty with a Friend according to our order and is out of unity with Friends." Again, Friends were sent to visit John Maddock but met with no success. In their April report, they recommended the matter be dropped "on account of some irregularities of process." In July 1877, the Men's Minutes of Elk Monthly Meeting record that John Maddock requested *in writing* to be released from membership, and his request was granted.

The following 1884 entry in Joseph Maddock's diary notes the event and its lasting effects, without explanation or details.

> Some years ago, [my brother John Maddock] had difficulties with some members in Society.[9] He became dissatisfied and withdrew from the Meeting and never returned, which was cause of sorrow. Yet near his close, he expressed that all was well and that a happy home was prepared for him in the heavenly Father's kingdom and encouraged his family to so live as to meet him there. He died 3rd of 4th Month 1884, aged 72 years, two months, and four days. A large attendance at his funeral.

## His Son Nathan Maddock

Joseph Maddock and Mary Stubbs were married on March 20, 1834, in West Elkton, Ohio, and their son Nathan was born on December 31, 1834. In his diary, Joseph refers to Nathan as being "of unsound mind since childhood," and later, as "manifesting symptoms of insanity." Caring for Nathan took a great deal of his mother's time and attention, though Joseph was helpful, as was Martha Ann, Nathan's younger sister. Several other Maddock families had children with similar disabilities, and there were relatives nearby to help with Nathan's care when needed.

Given how important education was to Joseph and Mary Maddock, it must have been heartbreaking for them that their son could not attend school. Even before Nathan was born, Joseph had served on the Elk Monthly Meeting School Committee, and he continued to do so until the small Friends school closed in 1858. After that, he was involved with establishing the Friends Academy in West Elkton.

Nathan's disability affected the family's lives in other ways. For instance, unlike Joseph's brother and sister-in-law (John and Martha Maddock), he and Mary seem not to have been involved in Underground

9. i.e., the Society of Friends, as in Elk Monthly Meeting of the Religious Society of Friends.

Railroad work in Preble County.[10] That might be simply because Joseph was conservative and hesitant to break the law against helping fugitives from slavery. But it would be understandable if Nathan's disability made it difficult, dangerous, even impossible, to provide food and shelter for fugitives from slavery.

In his forties, Nathan seemed to worsen, and Joseph writes, he began "offering violence to persons when things did not suit him." After his mother's death in 1778, Nathan grew ever more difficult for his father and sister to care for. In 1881, Joseph's diary entry recounts his and Martha Ann's decision to have Nathan committed to the "infirmary" at Eaton, a decision not made lightly.

> Martha Ann and I, after consulting with relatives and Friends, also with two or three physicians, thought best to take him to an asylum. Probably his situation in the future might be worse. Accordingly, I with Joseph Stubbs went up to Eaton. After looking over the Infirmary buildings and the farm of about 200 acres of land and consulting with an attorney and with the directors of the Infirmary, also consulted the statute clauses of Ohio. It appears his case would be one that would come under the provisions of the aforesaid. The clerk of the board at once made out a permit for him to be taken there. On the 20th of 9th month, I went with him up there and stayed all night with him. In the morning we went over the farm and around some. He appeared willing to stay there and I left him without any trouble after he found his clothes were in the carriage box and they wanted work and help on the farm.

The Preble County Infirmary apparently suited Nathan's simple needs—to know where his belongings were and to know he would have work to do. Nathan's response to being left by his father in a strange place, coupled with a comment in one of his sister's letters home from her year at Earlham College, hint at his emotional distance, even from family. "Tell Nathan I often think of him," she wrote, "and wonder if he ever thinks of me." Over the years, Joseph visited his son periodically and always found him content to be where he was. Nathan lived at the Preble County Infirmary until his death in 1913, outliving his father by twenty-four years.

10. However, Joseph Maddock served on the Elk Monthly Meeting Committee for the Concerns for People of Color from its inception. The committee provided various kinds of help for those in black settlements near West Elkton, including educating children.

Another source of information about Nathan comes from federal census forms. In 1840, the federal census form added two new columns: one for enumerating the "Deaf, Dumb, or Blind," and another column for enumerating the "Insane or Idiotic."[11] Census workers were given a definition of "Idiotic" as "a person the development of whose mental faculties were arrested in infancy or childhood before coming to maturity," which would include, among others, those with Down Syndrome or what we might recognize today as autism. In 1840 and 1850, when he was a child and then a teenager, Nathan was not indicated on federal census forms under the column "Insane or Idiotic." In 1860, 1870, and 1880, however, he was. The 1890 federal census for Preble County, Ohio, is not accessible, but in 1900 and 1910, he was enumerated as an "inmate" at the Preble County Infirmary where the logbook indicates only that Nathan was "weak-minded."

## His Daughter, Martha Ann

Martha Ann ("Mattie") Maddock, daughter of Joseph and Mary Maddock, was born August 30, 1845, in West Elkton, Ohio, a birthright member of Elk Monthly Meeting. Her parents had lost a child between the time Nathan was born and when Martha Ann was born, so she must have been a most welcome child.

Martha Ann's parents placed a high value on education, and even though she was a girl, she could attend school. Quaker girls received the same education as boys in the small Friends school in West Elkton where all students (including girls and children of color) were welcome. Her father served on Elk Monthly Meeting's School Committee beginning when he was in his twenties and continuing for over twenty years, making sure there were Quaker teachers for the children of Friends in West Elkton, now including their daughter.

In 1856 when Martha Ann was eleven years old, her parents sold the farm where they had lived "twenty-two days to a day," and moved to a house her father described as "more conveniently situated in attending our religious Meetings, also in respect to schools." In his diary, Joseph Maddock elaborated on this decision:

11. Becky Little. "The 1840 U.S. Census Was Overly Interested in Americans' Mental Health."

> I think we may say it was our only motive in changing our residence. With daughter growing up we think it will be a help to her being now in her eleventh year, and we being very conveniently situated in respect to a good district school, as well as the Monthly Meeting School,[12] which was generally kept up in the winter and summer. We feel much better satisfied in changing our residence. It seemed almost providential that we made the exchange as we did.

When she was nineteen, her parents sent Martha Ann to the Friends Boarding School (which had been recently renamed Earlham College) in Richmond, Indiana, where she attended sessions from October 1864 March 1865.

After her one year at Earlham, however, Martha Ann returned to the family home in West Elkton. In letters from friends and cousins, curious about why she didn't come back to Earlham, there are veiled references to "secrets" and surprises. For instance, in a letter written in October 1865, her cousin and Earlham classmate, Sallie Davis, suggests that Martha Ann intends to get married "to thy little Brown fellow. Tell him I would love to welcome him as a cousin, which I suppose is the reason of thee not going to School anymore." In the letters we have access to, Martha Ann doesn't give a specific reason for not returning to Earlham, but in the five-month term she was there, she often expressed a longing for home, hearth, and family in her letters home. Simple homesickness may have been the main reason she did not to return. Given some of what she experienced in those five months at Earlham, however, perhaps the outside world was too much—too much pressure, too much drama, too much sadness.

Martha Ann never married. She lived with family for the rest of her life. After her mother died in 1878, and Nathan went to live at the Preble County Infirmary in 1881, she continued living at home with her father. He sold the farm just outside West Elkton where they had lived since Martha Ann was eleven, and they moved into a house he bought in town. In his diary Joseph Maddock mentions that Martha Ann's health had not been good for several years, and that living in town was much easier for them both. She lived with him until his death in May 1889. Sometime after that, she moved to live with her cousin, Alpheus T. Maddock, and his family. The federal census records for 1890

12. In addition to academics, the Meeting School hired Quaker teachers who stressed Quaker values and taught Quaker faith and practice.

were destroyed by fire, so we don't know exactly when she moved, but the 1900 federal census shows Martha Ann Maddock (age fifty-four) living in the household of Alpheus T. Maddock, his wife Lydia (both age fifty-three), their twenty-eight-year-old son, Frederick LeFevre, and their adopted twenty-year-old daughter, Leona Wilson.

Martha Ann lived in her cousin's home until she died in 1920. Though she lived the quiet life of a spinster, Martha Ann Maddock did one extraordinary thing: she wrote many letters and kept most of those she received. Someone (probably Alpheus, who outlived her by twenty years) donated her collection of letters to the Preble County Historical Society.

# Letters To & From Mattie

In the following family letters between Martha Ann "Mattie" Maddock and her parents, Joseph and Mary Maddock, spelling has been corrected and punctuation added, but grammar and word choice for the most part, left as written. This is intentional, to give a sense of who these people were, how they were, how they talked. (If you have trouble reading these letters, try reading them aloud, and in that way, hear the past as spoken by some of those who lived there.) In the back and forth exchange between parent and child, we learn some foibles of each writer, such as Joseph Maddock's concern not to waste paper (a more precious commodity then than now), but filling every bit of the page, and Mattie's use of colloquial phrases of the time such as "better believe . . . " or "I like to ride on the cars[1] the best kind . . . "

Educated twenty-first-century readers may be appalled by the incorrect grammar and incomplete or erratic punctuation, but it should be remembered that these are family letters, not written for publication (or for a grade). The mere fact that Joseph Maddock, Mary Maddock, and Martha Ann Maddock were writing these words in the nineteenth century lifts them into the higher echelon of education in a time when most people had only a rudimentary education.

Fortunately for those interested in genealogy and local history, Martha Ann Maddock wrote many letters, and she kept both sides of her correspondence with her parents from October 1864–March 1865 while she was a student at Earlham College in Richmond, Indiana. Generally, Martha Ann's letters are girlish, chatty, ungrammatical, and repetitious (though her writing improved over the five months' term

1. When Joseph and Mattie refer to "the cars," they mean train cars.

she spent at Earlham). Even when Mattie rambles and struggles to find something to say in her letters, she sometimes finally stumbles into sharing a gem of detail about everyday life in the American Midwest in the nineteenth century.

Such details in Mattie's letters give us a sense of what it was like to be a naïve young Quaker woman in 1864. For instance, when she first traveled to attend Earlham College in October that year, her father took her in a horsedrawn buggy six miles to the nearest train station in Camden, Ohio, where she boarded the crowded train for Richmond, Indiana. When they arrived at the station in Richmond, it was full of Union soldiers. In her first letter home, Mattie struggles for words to tell her experience and express her reaction.

No matter what else changes, no matter which war is being fought in what near or distant place, the first year of college has always been very much the same. In the rest of her first letter home, Martha Ann gives a detailed account of the money she spent on books and supplies, ending with an explanation of why she has so little left from the extra dollar[2] her father gave her for her train ticket. Mattie's closing paragraph in her first letter shows how homesick she already is. The homesickness abates after a few weeks, but never entirely leaves her letters.

Signature of Martha Ann Maddock from the Elk Monthly Meeting Centennial Celebration Guestbook, 1905

2. A dollar in 1864 was equivalent to $20.45 in 2025. "Value of $1," CPI.

# October 1864

## *Earlham College,* 10th Mo 13th 1864

Dear Parents,

I have just eat my dinner and seated myself in the schoolroom for the purpose of dropping a few lines to you to let you know how I am getting along here at Earlham. Well now, to begin I hardly know what to say first—well, I am enjoying pretty good health and hope these lines may find you the same.

Well, of course, you know we got to Camden and got on the cars safe, but let me tell you—if I like to ride on the cars the best kind, but it did not pay us so well the other day. We all had to stand up, the cars were so crowded, (Sallie and I and Jabez and William Kenworthy[1]) till we got to Eaton. Then Sallie and I found seats, but Jabez and Will stood up all the way to Richmond. We got to Richmond, and such a crowd there was, it seemed as though it was crowded as bad, if not worse, than at Yearly Meeting. There was a whole Regiment and part of another of Soldiers, drafted men. They said they were taking their leave. One train was loaded, they said, and as soon we got off, they begin to fill the train we were in. We counted about 60 as they went in. We could not but help noticing them; some were crying, some laughing,

1. Jabez and William Kenworthy and Sallie were Mattie's cousins from West Elkton. Sallie/Sally was a nickname for "Sarah/Sara" so regardless of spelling, these are all the same person, i.e., Mattie's cousin and roommate. In his diary, Joseph Maddock mentions Mattie's roommate, "Sally Jones." The only Sarah Jones from West Elkton of the right age to be Mattie's classmate was the adopted daughter of Tabitha (Stubbs) Jones, widow of William A. Jones. When Tabitha died in 1862, her youngest brother, Jesse Stubbs, was the Executor of her will which stipulated that Sarah receive at least another six months of education. In 1864, it seems that Sarah/Sally may have been living with John and Martha Maddock, Mattie's aunt and uncle.

and some were hollowing at the top of their voices, which made the depot ring. Taking all together, it was a rather affecting sight. Well, enough on this subject.

I have been examined, but I was not examined in anything but Grammar. In that, I got 45 per cent. Still, it's better than I expected. I have been classified and got my books, all but Arithmetic. They use Yellers, but the one John give me is not the kind; it is number 2 and mine is number 1.They did not have enough to supply all, and I am one of them. I won't have but three studies. Them is Arithmetic, Grammar, and Geography. My Grammar was a 1.00[2] and my Geography 1.80, which makes 2.80 for the two. And the Arithmetics are 85 cents. In all I will have to pay 3.65 cts for my books. Besides my paper, penholder and pens, Basin Soap, and that is all I guess. So all I have got cost me 4.30 cts, and I have paid for all but my three books. They will cost 3.65 cts. I thought I would not pay for them till I got my Arithmetic. I guess I will get it this evening, and then I will pay for all of them. Then I won't have but 15 cts left. So you can see how I am fixed. I paid the 55 dol on my schooling to Walter[3] pretty soon after I got here, and he gave me a note for the rest. Father knows how we fixed it at Camden; he give me a dollar in the place of one I gave for my ticket. When we got to Richmond we could not find nobody, and we didn't know what to do. The Earlham Omnibus had been there and was gone, so we engaged with another, for which we had to pay 75 cts apiece to get brought out. It was nearly noon when we got here.

I can hardly tell yet how I like the school, but as far as I seen and been, I like it pretty well, but I think from all appearances I will like it better when I get classified and all my studies arranged right. I am very lonesome and wish I could see my dear old home I have left for a season. Sallie and I sleep together and Mattie M. Cope is my walking mate. I have been walking every day since I have been here till today. Well, my sheet is fast filling up, and I must draw towards a close by requesting you to write soon. Be sure and answer right away, as a letter from home would do me more good than anything else. I

2. Martha Ann did not use dollar signs, i.e., "a 1.00" means one dollar, "1.80" means $1.80, etc. The 2025 equivalent costs for Mattie's 1864 expenses: 75 cts = $15.34; $3.65 = $74.64; $55 = $1,124.70; and 15 cts = $3.07.

3. In other words, Martha Ann paid her tuition to Walter Carpenter, who served as Superintendent/General Business Manager of Earlham College in 1864. Carpenter Hall on the present Earlham College campus was named for Walter Carpenter and his wife Susan Carpenter, who served as matron in the 1860s. It may seem odd that Mattie refers to him by his first name, but the Quaker testimony of equality forbade the use of titles or honorifics which suggest an elevated status (e.g. Mr., Mrs., Reverend, Dr., Professor, etc.).

guess I have told all the news of much importance this time, so I remain as ever, your affectionate daughter.

*Martha Ann*

P.S. I have not wrote to Solomon yet but intend to tomorrow if nothing prevents. Our trunks got here safe when we did. Please write soon and tell us how Grandfather is. I went in and seen him the other morning.

The letters Martha Ann received from her parents were written mostly by Joseph Maddock. The handwriting in the one letter signed by her mother is wide-spaced and shaky, which may suggest Mary Maddock suffered from something like palsy or arthritis. Or, it could be that she simply did not have as much education or practice in writing as Joseph did. It seems pretty clear that, for the most part, the two of them together composed the letters to their daughter.

## West Elkton, 10th Mo 19th

Loving Daughter,

We received thy favor yesterday P.M. We may say that we are all middling well; all of us better of our cold since thee left. Also the rest of [our] connections are about as they were. Only Grandfather, who seems to be going down pretty fast the last two or three days, so that he cannot now hardly get up or down without help. I have been with him nearly every other night since thee left us, and some time throughout the day. It looks like that he could hardly stand it many days. His appetite has left a good deal in the last few days, yet he may last some time, as it seems that old people sometimes linger along for a good while. He has some appearance of fever in the last day or two. He had last Fifth Day a very hard spell, some[what] like a chill, but got over it and seemed considerably better for two or three days. We think it doubtful of his ever being any better. He don't seem to suffer much, only at times, and has mostly rested very well at night, except last night, he did not rest very well.

Mother says she is getting along with her work very well. We have had our sorghum made up—a very poor turn out and very thin at that. Yet it is a pretty fair article of molasses, only about 19 gallons.

Uncle John received a letter from Kezia informing that her youngest child was very sick with flux. Uncle John & Aunt Ellen went out there yesterday.[4]

The Scripture School last First Day was larger; several more attended, and it is likely the attendance will be larger hereafter, and of course, more interesting. Our Meeting was pretty large—[the] women's part crowded. Mary R. [Roberts][5] had considerable to say, and it was a favored and satisfactory time. Jane & Sam'l [Jones][6] went out to Honey Creek and, of course, were not with us. It was 2 M. [illegible] out there a Seventh Day last.

We suppose by this time that thee has commenced and will be engaged in thy studies, so that it will not be as lonesome as it probably has been. We would encourage thee to be diligent in them, and endeavour to improve in all that may be useful in the way of education as well as in piety and virtue. From thy well-wishing parents

Jos & Mary Maddock

As thee spoke of having paid out all thy money we enclose $2.00 (U.L. No 82124 Aug 1st 1862[7]). While Grandfather continues sick, we will write probably every three or four days.

[*Added in pencil*]

P.M. 4 o'clock, Grandfather is quite poorly this afternoon. Marmaduke Stubbs is going to Somerville this evening, so that we send there to mail this so that thee may get it to morrow P.M.

From thy father

J Maddock

4. "Uncle John" = John Maddock Stubbs (Mary's older brother), his wife Eleanor ("Ellen" ), and their daughter, Keziah Stubbs, who married Isaac Commons. They lived in Wayne County, Indiana. Keziah's youngest in 1864 would have been Charles Commons, born in 1863.

5. Elk Monthly Meeting recorded minister, Mary Roberts.

6. Jane (Puckett) Jones, sister of Mary Roberts and Martha Wooten, was a recorded minister who traveled "in the ministry" a great deal. She and her second husband, Samuel N. Jones, lived in West Elkton for about two years.

7. Evidently Joseph enclosed a two-dollar "greenback" bill and copied the serial number. "The greenback was America's first true national paper currency, created by the Legal Tender Act of 1862 to finance the immense costs of the Civil War when gold and silver were too scarce . . . Unlike previous currencies which were essentially IOUs for gold or silver, the greenback was a fiat currency, meaning its value came solely from the public's faith in the U.S. government that issued it." "Greenback: The Ultimate Guide to America's First Paper Money."

In a letter dated just ten days later, Mattie reports a dramatic event significant in local history: the death and funeral of Deborah Ann Moore, young wife of Joseph Moore, recorded Quaker minister, and a respected teacher at the Friends Boarding School/Earlham College.[8] His wife, Deborah (nee Stanton) Moore was also a teacher at the school; she had graduated from the Friends Boarding School in 1858 and been hired to teach there. She and Joseph Moore married in September 1862, and in July 1864, the summer before Mattie arrived at Earlham, Deborah Moore gave birth to a son. She died three months later in October, aged twenty-seven years. Her funeral, held on the Earlham campus, was, in Mattie's words, "a sad and solemn day to many and one that will long be remembered especially by the scholars of Earlham."

## Earlham College, 10th Month, 23rd Day 1864

Dear Parents,

It is First Day afternoon and a beautiful afternoon it is, only is a pretty cold out. I have again seated myself in the school room where Sallie and number of others are writing, for the purpose of dropping you a few lines to let you know how I am enjoying myself by this time. Well I am enjoying myself pretty well, only I have got the headache some. But I got some cold was the cause of it. Sallie has it right bad. We were standing on the ground right smart today, which I expect was the cause of it, as it was rather damp.

Today was a sad and solemn day to many, and one that will long be remembered by many, especially by the scholars of Earlham.

Joseph Moore's wife, Deborah Moore, was buried today. She has been a teacher in the school till this winter. Also, Joseph is a teacher yet and has been here all the time since I have been here till the last week or two.

They were both much respected and beloved by all the scholars, so it has cast quite a gloom over the school in her

8. Joseph Moore "collected natural history objects to supplement his teaching . . . At first, he housed his collection in a cabinet in Earlham Hall and later moved it to a small room. The collection was constantly growing and when Lindley Hall was built in 1887, the lower floor of one wing was designated for the museum." ("Joseph Moore Museum," Earlham College.edu). Today, the Joseph Moore Museum is a separate building on the Earlham College Campus. In his diary entry for 1871, Joseph Maddock mentions Joseph Moore as a speaker at Indiana Yearly Meeting in October that year.

sudden death. Her disease was typhoid fever and is considered contagious out here, as her brother died just before Yearly Meeting, and her other brother is at their house very low. [They] do not think he will live any time with the same fever.

The procession all met at College and the scholars attended. First the hearse and those following after it, about forty in number. Then the Governor and his wife; then the boys there; after the boys, Walter and Susan Carpenter, after which followed the girls. All in the best order I ever saw in my life. Taking it altogether, it was the most solemn and orderly procession I ever saw or attended.

First we all followed the remains to their long and last resting place in the Cemetery that belongs to the College. Then all proceeded back here to hold a meeting [for worship] at her request.

It was a large one, the largest that has been held here for some time. It was so nice, all the scholars observing the best order. David H. Bennett, Enos G. Pray, and Susan Pedrick were present, and a solemn and satisfactory time it proved to be. Not one in the house but what were moved to tears; all seemed to feel the solemnity that prevailed. Susan H. Pedrick and another woman I do not know who is supplicated; then Enos spoke some length of time; then David H. Bennett. It seems to me I never heard one speak as nice in my life as he did today. He spoke very nice to the scholars and teachers till all were melted to tears. He had an appointed meeting[9] at Whitewater [Monthly Meeting] this afternoon at three o'clock. Wonder if he has been down about you yet.

Today has been to me the most solemn and saddest day I ever witnessed in my life, I believe, and it is one that will be long remembered by me.

Well what next? I hardly know what to write. I believe I have not told you about my studies. If you would like to know, well, I am getting along pretty well now. I have got some more books since I wrote to you last, but I can tell you I have paid for all. Yesterday I went in the office and paid for every thing I have got since I have been here. When I went in I had 5.85 and came out with 1.00 left. So I don't owe any body any thing. I haven't got only what I had to have, so now I am clear, as the "saying is" and have just 1.00 cts left. I have all I want first now I believe.

9. Traveling ministers routinely notified the Monthly Meetings they planned to visit and appointed a day and time to hold a Meeting for Worship.

Well, the scholars have been [coming] since I wrote lastly, new ones coming in so that Sallie and I get to walk together and sleep together, so it is all right with us now. If it had not been for Sallie I do not know how I would got along. Well, I see my sheet is fast filling up and I must draw towards a close by requesting you to be sure and write soon and tell me how Grandfather is. I want to hear very much. Mother how is thee getting along with the work? How is Ring and Kit getting along? Mother, don't thee believe I tore my dress yesterday, my delain[10] one. Well, in love I bid you farewell, your affectionate daughter,

*Mattie*

P.S. I forgot to say whether I got your letter, but I did; I got it late Fifth Day evening. [It] wasn't quick coming. We were sorrowed to hear of grandfather being worse, and you cannot imagine how glad I was to hear from home. Please write often and tell me all the news. To Joseph and Mary Maddock from their daughter Martha Ann

Well, it is supper time, and I will have to quit. So no more but remain your loving daughter *Mattie*

## West Elkton, First Day P.M. 10th Mo. 23d, 1864

Beloved Daughter, Martha Ann,

We are at Uncle John's this afternoon, and Grandfather is still quite poorly, yet we think some better than when we wrote last Fourth Day. Though since then, he has had some very poorly spells and seemed like he could not live, but got better. What may be the final sine [*sic*] of his sickness, time will determine. We have had to be here considerable of the time last week, and still have to be with him, as Uncle John is quite unwell the last two or three days with disease of the liver, cold, etc. He is some better this P.M.

Uncle Riley Davis & Jos. came down yesterday. They say all are pretty well at home; talk of going home tomorrow.

Job Smith from Iowa was at Mo. Meeting last Fifth Day. We were not at meeting on account of Grandfather being so poorly. Mary Roberts had [an appointed] meeting at Farmersville on Twin [Creek] today, and Jane was not out today, her child being

10. Delaine/delain was a type of cotton and wool fabric used for women's dresses in the nineteenth century.

sick, so that there was not much speaking, I suppose. Mother was there; I stayed with Grandfather.

Luther Jenkins is quite sick with the congestive fever. Uncle Johns[11] have got home from I. Commons [Isaac Commons, Keziah's husband]. The child not much of any better.

Perhaps thee got our letter that we sent to Sommerville last Fourth Day evening. We put a $2.00 bill greenback in it. Please write pretty soon after thee receives this and inform us how thee is getting along in thy studies. How many pupils & whatever may interest us.

We will still write every few days if Grandfather continues with us. If he should be taken away by death, we should like for thee come home and will probably send for thee. How things may turn we cannot tell; he may linger along for several days, or even weeks. Theodore[12] is up from the city [and] will probably stay several days.

From thy well-wishing parents,

*Jos. Maddock*

We are all well as usual, except some colds. Aunt Martha[13] has sent some things in this for Sara. She says she will write in a few days. Please let Sarah read this.

## Earlham College, 10th Mo 30th 1864

Dear Parents,

Once again I have commenced the well-known task of letter writing. Seated in the quiet schoolroom of Earlham I take up my always willing pen to drop you a few scattered lines in reply to your kind and affectionate letter which I received last evening. I suppose it was put in Sixth Day morning. If it was, I think that is quick coming.

Oh, how glad I was to hear from home and Grandfather. A letter from home is always and shall always be a welcome visitor

11. Joseph Maddock uses a first name plural to indicate an entire family, i.e., Uncle Johns = Uncle John and family.

12. Theodore Maddock, Joseph's nephew and Martha Ann's cousin, who lived in Cincinnati, Ohio.

13. Probably Martha (Stubbs) Maddock, wife of Joseph's brother/Mattie's uncle, John Maddock. For several years in the 1860s Martha Maddock was on the committee that "managed" Earlham College for Indiana Yearly Meeting (later known as the Board of Trustees).

to me; so even if the letters are short, they do me a great deal of good, so please write often.

Well, now to begin. I am very sorry indeed to hear of Grandfather's sickness being worse since I left. It makes me feel bad every time I hear from him, expecting to hear of his death any time. If you think it best, I want to come home if he should drop off. I guess Sallie will come too. They will let me come in the case of sickness and death.

Perchance you would like to know how the school is getting along. Well, pretty well, I guess as far as I know. I do not know exactly the number of students—about 72 girls and 92 boys or more, making 164. But some say there is more than that, so I will not say certain how many there is, unless I knew to a certainty, but somewhere not far from it. All doing pretty well for the first, I guess.

I am getting along pretty well since I am classified. I study Geography, Grammar, Arithmetic, Spelling, and Writing; five studies in all. My teacher in Geography is Anna Niles; in Arithmetic, Calvin Pierson; Grammar, Mahalah Jay, the Governor's wife, a very nice woman, I think. I like our Governess very well, and most of the girls do, I guess, better than the other one, Eliza Smith. It has not come my turn yet to be table waiter, but I expect it will pretty soon. I have had my turn in sweeping; I swept two weeks the schoolroom.

Oh, how I wish some of you would come up and see me (I would ask you to, if it were not for Grandfather's sickness) and hope you will, while I remain here. Well, I was at Meeting today and a good meeting it was. Joseph Moore supplicated,[14] and there was a stranger here (I do not know who it was), a very pleasant-looking man, and they all seem very much taken with him. I like to hear him. He spoke some length of time.

The doorbell just now rang, which is very seldom for it to. Only in urgent cases, which made I and Sallie feel rather bad, for fear it was for us till we could find out. There is a great many calls here for the students, but none for me yet. I heard that Kizzie[15] was going to come down and see me. How I wish she would. I would be glad to see anyone from our settlement the best kind, but do not expect I will soon. For I don't know

14. "Supplicate." Per *The Webster's Dictionary* for 1828: "To entreat for; to seek by earnest prayer; as, to *supplicate* blessings on Christian efforts to spread the gospel."

15. "Kizzie," Keziah (nee Stubbs) Commons, a cousin who lived in Wayne County, Indiana where Earlham College is located.

whether anyone thinks enough of me to come or not. I hope you will come some day and see me.

Tell Ella Stubbs I got her very acceptable letter last Fifth Day evening and was very glad indeed to get a letter from her. And tell her that I will answer it pretty soon. Mother, tell all the girls to write to me, for it does me more good to get a letter than anyone else here, I believe.

We just made Old Dixie and Sorghum Bounce[16] here. Just wait till I come home and I will tell you all about our meal. How are you getting along without me? Well, I must quit for my sheet is full. I remain, as ever, your affectionate daughter,

*Martha A.*

Be sure and write often, and I will do the same. Well, I will say farewell for this time.

*Martha Ann Maddock*

Sallie is going to put in some for Aunt Patsy[17] so I will quit my writing to J and M Maddock.

My crackers are all gone!

## West Elkton, 10th Mo 31st 1864

[*Written in pencil*]

First Day night, 1 o'clock

Martha Ann, Grandfather is no more. He quietly departed this life about half-past eleven o'clock tonight. He was not much different since I wrote last Sixth Day evening. Until Seventh Day night when he was taken worse and had a very restless night, but got better or easier yesterday morning. But it was evident there was a change taking place; he never spoke after nine o'clock and laid in a quiet slumber until his close. The funeral takes place tomorrow morning. Meet at the house at ten o'clock. There will probably be a Meeting held.[18]

16. A "bounce" was a cake made with jam or preserves, or, in this case, sorghum.

17. "Patsy" was a nineteenth-century nickname for "Martha." "Aunt Patsy" refers to Mattie's aunt, Martha Maddock, wife of her uncle, John Maddock, and probably foster parent of Sarah/Sally Jones.

18. Quaker "funerals" often take the form of a silent Meeting for Worship. Those who are led to do so may speak out of the silence.

We did think of sending for thee to come home, but it seems the way we are circumstanced and the uncertainty of the case—also taking thee off from thy studies and having to go and return after night from Camden—we thought it would be better for not to send for thee at this time.

From thy well-wishing Parents

*Jos. & M Maddock*

We are somewhat unwell with colds. But so that we are all about [*sic*]. Please write soon and inform how thee is getting along.

# November 1864

## Earlham College, 11th Mo 1st Da 1864

Dear Father,

Sallie has been writing to Aunt Martha and wanted me to put in some, so I thought I would just drop a few lines. Please excuse my writing with a lead pencil.

The bell has just rung for breakfast, and I will have to be brief. I do not feel very well this morning. My throat is right sore, but I don't think it will be anything serious. I want to come home and see Grandfather. Sallie and I both want to come home. Well, I have not much time and will have to be short. Write and tell all the news.

Tell Mother that my crackers are all gone, and I would like to have some more. I could get them, but wait till I come home.

Well, I have just eaten my breakfast. I did not finish it before. I feel better now, since I have eaten my breakfast, but feel bad still. I think of Grandfather all the time.

Well, I must close by requesting you to write often, and I will do the same. As ever your affectionate daughter,

Martha Ann

[*on a partial sheet of paper*]

P.S. You wanted to know whether I got that 2 dollar bill you sent me. Well, I got it safe. I believe I told you in my other letter that I had paid for all I have got since I came. Father said that Nathan stayed by himself at night while you were at Uncle John's. I think he must be lonesome. He also said that Ring was all right.

I wonder if he would know me if he was to see me. It is getting nearly supper time, and I must quit.

*Martha Ann Maddock*

## West Elkton, 11th Mo 3rd 1864

Loving Daughter, Martha Ann,

We take up the pen to address thee, and may say that we are all about, but complaining of colds. Mother seems to be worse than the rest of us. We were helping Uncle John thrash yesterday and it, of course, did not help our colds, that is mine and Nathan's. Mother is able to be about and does pretty well in the day, but at night is worse. Yet after a few days, by taking some medicine and after a good sleep at night, we hope all to be better and enjoy our accustomed health. The rest of connections and friends are mostly well.

Thomas & Rachel Stubbs' youngest child is very sick and has been for several days quite bad. Little hopes of its recovery yesterday. It has the scarlet fever. Eli Stubbs' youngest child yesterday was very bad with croup.

As we started a letter on Second Day which thee perhaps received the next day, respecting the close of Grandfather's last hours in this world, we may give some account of the funeral, which took place on Third Day. Met at the house at ten o'clock,[1] where a large company of relatives, friends, and neighbors assembled to pay last respects to one who had long been resident in this place. After the internment, the company pretty much all went into the Meeting House, which was nearly full, and a solemn, and we trust, an interesting meeting to all it was. After the setting down of the company, a considerable length of silence, a solemn one to many, our M.R. [Mary Roberts] appeared in supplication; imploring aid from Him who is able to give in time of need, and that we all might be strengthened in coming together in our Zionward journey, as the instance in which we had just witnessed would be ours in few more fleeting days or years at most. After which Jane [Jones] had considerable to communicate to the people; perhaps near one hour she was on her feet. After which the Meeting solemnly concluded. The Meeting held some longer than common.

1. "Met/Meet at the house at X o'clock." Joseph always uses this specific phrase to refer to the way funerals began, i.e. by gathering at the meetinghouse of Elk Monthly Meeting in West Elkton at a given time.

Some of the Fouts on Twin [Creek][2] were with us, also Adam Geeting. Peter & Rachel Thomas at Miltonville were up also. After Meeting we went with them to Uncle John's and took dinner together and spent the afternoon very agreeably with them.

We think now, after all is past, that we should a[3] been better satisfied to a sent for thee to come home and had the privilege to a mingled with us on this solemn occasion, but as it is passed, we cannot recall it.

On First Day night about midnight after Grandfather died, we considered it, and it seemed then like being very stormy and cold. We would have to get someone to go in the morning and return in the evening, so that it would be considerable of trouble. And that thee would be exposed to the cold disagreeable night air, and have to leave thy studies, & Aunt Patsy thought perhaps we had better not send for thee considering the way we were circumstanced at this time. We thought best to give some [thee] reasons why we did not send and that was how we were placed at the time.

Abiah Wilkinson (formerly Stubbs) from Little Miami is now with us. Came a week ago today and has been visiting amongst connections all the time. Was up at L.S. Dick's in Eaton on Second Day. Has not been at our house yet; probably will be this afternoon or evening. Her sister-in-law is with her. They came over in a buggy and talk of going home tomorrow. She wished very much to a seen thee, but, of course, cannot at this time. But desired to be remembered by thee, and her love and best wishes for thy welfare. She seems the same in manners and deportment as she used to, an interesting young woman. They went down to Jos. Stubbs today and Maria went with them.

We were at Meeting today, the first time since last First Day. Was a week Mother was once at Meeting in that time. I was with Grandfather all the time on Meeting days, so that it seemed long since we had the chance to attend.

It has been quite cool today, a strong cold wind. Not many out on account of some sickness in town. Eli & Thos' children who are very bad this morning; but little or no hopes of their

2. The Fouts from Twin Township in Preble County were Joseph's relatives on his biological mother's side. Adam Geeding, mentioned in Siebert's list of UGRR operators/conductors in Gratis Township, Preble County, Ohio, was married to Susan Fouts.

3. Joseph Maddock sometimes writes as he talks, such as when he uses "a" in place of "have." For instance, "we should a" instead of "should have."

recovery. Sam Jones' and Jane's child is quite poorly again with the flux.

I am going to town presently and will, when I get there, add more perhaps. We are expecting to go to market a Seventh Day if the weather is favorable. We have not been since thee left. Mother has some 10 or 12 lb butter to send, and Uncle Wm Kellum wants to send their chickens, some of them. Maria and John were down last Seventh Day but did not sell all their butter. Of course, it was brought home again; it was, they said, a dull market and they did not sell much. Butter did not bring but 45 cts. Some sold at 50. So that it is, as it happens, where we got 50 cts at all times.

Ring is lying by the fire while I write, quite composed, and Puss under the stove.

Will add more when I get to town.

[*in different ink at bottom of page*]

I am at town this P.M. The two children are still very bad and look like they could hardly live till morning. Alpheus started yesterday morning for Providence B. S. Rhode Island.[4] He went to the City first and would probably leave the City last night. Little John has a prospect of teaching our District School this winter. There is some prospect of a winter School at the Meeting House. Wm Kenworthy will likely teach. I have just taken out a letter from Roberts in Colorado stating that they were still in the fort at Colorado City. Benajah had enlisted in the 100-Day Service of volunteers; it was dated 9th mo 1st da.

Patsy has just handed me the slip thee put in Sallie's letter, which is grateful though somewhat unexpected at hearing thee was somewhat unwell. We hope thee will be better and wish thee encouraged to persevere in thy studies. And bear up at the circumstances of Grandfather's death as well as thee can. Mother thinks if she gets over her cold, and the weather gets better, and there is some moon in the evening, she may come up to Earlham next week. But don't look too much for her until thee sees her. From thy well-wishing Parents,

*Jos. & Mary Maddock*

4. Mattie's cousin, Alpheus T. Maddock, son of John and Martha Maddock, had attended Earlham College the year before, but attended the Friends Boarding School in Providence, Rhode Island in 1864–1865.

## Earlham College, 11th Mo 6th 1864

Dear Parents,

Once again I seat myself in the schoolroom to take up my always-willing pen to drop you a few of my scattered thoughts. It is First-Day morning, and I have just recited my scripture lesson. I recite to Teacher Anna Niles in north classroom. Our lesson is in Mark the 3rd chapter, and having a few leisure moments, I thought I would improve them by writing to you.

In the first place, I can inform you that I received your kind letter dated the 3rd last evening just before supper. I and Sallie were just ready to take a walk when someone told me there was a letter for me. You had better believe I made tracks to the schoolroom, and the Governess handed me one. You cannot imagine how quick I tore the seal to peruse its contents. Oh, what a good letter it was to me, the best one I have had since I have been here. But oh, you cannot imagine the sorrow that filled my heart when I received the one giving Grandfather's death. But still it did not come very unexpected to me, as I was looking for such news. But it seemed as though I could hardly realize it to be so. So I thought it must be so and tried to be as calm as I could, but you do not know how badly I felt. I received the letter just after dinner Fourth Day and you may believe that I did not feel in a very good mood for study, so the Governess said she would excuse me and that I need not recite as I felt so bad. So I went to the parlor and stayed till recess, but when Sallie came up to see me, I felt worse than ever, for it made her feel bad too.

Oh, how I would have liked to have been at his funeral. It would a done me more good than anything else. How I wish you would a sent for me as I looked for you to, but I hope and trust he has gone to a better world than this, where pain and death and sickness can never come, where the wicked cease from troubling, and the weary are at rest. I hope if I fulfill my duty here faithfully, that when my time here on earth shall be no more, I may be permitted to meet those loved ones that have gone before me to that land from whence no traveler has ever yet returned. But I will say no more on the subject as it will make you feel so bad. Only I hope when I come home I may be permitted to see where he was laid and shed a few tears of affection over his grave.

I hope Mother is better and will be able to come out and see me this week. It was very pretty moonlight last night. I expect to look for her anyhow, whether she comes or not, for it would do me so much good to see one of you. Be sure and come if thee can, Mother, and do not forget to bring me something.

Well, you know, of course, I was at Meeting today. Joseph Moore preached, and we had a very good meeting. It is very windy indeed this afternoon, and it is beginning to turn cold, so I believe we are going to have winter. I am getting along pretty well with my studies, the best I have since I have been here. Daniel Marmon and Charley Moffitt are also here. I saw them and spoke to them the first day I come, but some of them are quite sick, both boys and girls. There is a girl by the name of Anna Howland from Massachusetts here, only able to be about—cannot study much yet—looks very bad. The nursery[5] is just full now, that is, the girls and two or three more that need to go. I expect you would like to know whether I have been in it or not. I have seen it, and it is a beautiful place, I think.

Oh, I guess I have nearly run short of news, for I fear what I have written will fail to interest you. There the doorbell just rung. I wonder who it is. Nobody that wants me, I don't expect. There has been several of the scholars' friends to see them but none to see me yet. Hope there will before long.

Our friend Luther Gordon was here a Fourth Day and Sara Smith a Third Day night and Enos Pray a Seventh and First Day night at Collection. Sarah Smith and Luther Gordon had considerable to say, which proved a solemn time to all the scholars. So you see that we have plenty of preaching. Enos has been here several times since I have been, and it seems very natural to hear him again. Kizzie has not been down here to see me yet, but I am going to look for her someday. Well, it is nearly evening and I must begin to draw towards a close as my sheet is fast filling up.

Mother, be sure and not forget to bring me some crackers and fetch me some good sweet cakes and apples, and don't forget to bring some pieces like my delain dress, the one that has velvet round the bottom, and my dress-sleeves-lining for I begin to need them as it is cool. I expect that this is mixed up so you will not be able to read it. Put all my letters in my letter box so I can read them when I come home. Well, I guess I had better quit by requesting you to write soon and tell all the news.

*Martha Ann Maddock*

5. I think she means "infirmary."

[*postscript on a separate sheet*]

P.S. Now Mother, be sure and not forget to bring my sleeve-lining and pieces of my dress, so I can mend it. As I cannot wear it till it is mended. Well, it is nearly supper time, and I am glad of it, for I am hungry. Oh, I had forgot to tell you what we had for dinner: roasted beef, cabbage, gravy, potatoes, and bread, and some good potato pie. And sometimes they have Turnips, which I bet is good. I was very sorry to hear my Cousin Abiah Wilkinson had been there to see you and did not get to see me. Oh, I would a liked to have seen her so well. But as I was denied the privilege, I will not think anything about it. Also that Alpheus had gone. I expect he hated to leave home, did he not? Going so far from home. How I wish he could come here.

Well, it is raining now pretty lively, and looks like it would be a rainy night. We have Lecture every Seventh Day night and First Day night, reading of some kind that is good. Well I will quit by requesting you to write often, and I will do the same in return. I have written one Composition and read it last Six Day night. Write and tell me what day Mother will come, so I can send for her if you get this in time. Please excuse all my bad penmanship and mistakes, for I presume they are very numerous.

To Joseph and Mary Maddock from their daughter,

Bring some of Uncle John's good apples and some cake, and I expect I will need some money. Will tell you how much I have, and you can see how I am fixed. I have just 87 cts. So in conclusion, farewell.

## Earlham College, 11th Mo 19th 1864

Dear Parents,

Well, I suppose the time has again rolled round that I must seat myself for the purpose of writing a letter home.

This is Seventh Day afternoon and a beautiful one it is indeed. Nearly all the girls are gone, so it seems quite still to what it is sometimes. Some has gone visiting, and some are gone to town, and some are gone home. But it has not come my turn yet, but I guess it will pretty soon, and then I will be glad.

I received your very kind letter last Third Day evening. All day I looked for one but was disappointed. But in the evening, just as the supper bell rung, and I was going to supper, the Governess came up and says, "Mattie, would thee like to have a letter?" "Yes," says I. "Well, here is one." And you better believe I tore it to peruse its contents, but I was starting down to supper, so I could not get to read it all. I could hardly eat any supper because I wanted to read it so bad.

I had been very anxious to hear how Mother was, as she was quite unwell when she left here in the evening. I felt rather uneasy about her that night so I could hardly sleep, In fact, it made me feel homesick, but I have got over it now. But I felt anxious all the time to hear from her.

Hope she is well or nearly so by this time.

George N. Hunt and William Wildman were here a Fifth Day, and George said he would tell you anything I would send, so I thought as I had not time to write a letter I would just send a few words, which I have no doubt you have heard before this time.

They went out to Enoch Gifford's and stayed all night and were going on down there[6] yesterday. I and Sallie had quite a good time a Fifth Day. Tommy Jones and George Hunt and William Wildman—he is an old student here—he has been here two sessions and knows all about the school. There goes the bell for us to prepare for supper, so I will have to quit, so you will please excuse me now.

Well, I have eaten my supper and just ran out in the playroom taking exercise which makes me feel better. So I will again seat myself for to finish my letter.

Well, what must I tell first? Perchance you would like to know what we had for supper. Well, some good white and brown bread, butter, sorghum, and Dixie as they call it. So I had a pretty good supper. Just to think, there goes the warning bell to prepare for lecture and then the large bell rings, and we all march to the lecture room to hear a lecture. Joseph Moore and William Morgan both had good deal to say so we had a good lecture. I think the best we have had since I have been here. Every Seventh Day night we have lecture, and every First Day night some good readings. So we have something to claim our attention all the time.

I hope you will excuse this poor writing, for my pen is so poor, and I am in a hurry. There goes the bell for Collection to go to bed. We collect in the lecture room to hear a chapter read, from whence we return to our beds. We hear a chapter read at the breakfast table every morning. So I will have to quit for tonight. Please excuse me, so fare well.

6. i.e., to West Elkton, Ohio, where they would see her parents.

*First Day morning, 20th*

I again seat myself to try to finish my letter. I have just recited my scripture lesson and am waiting for the bell to ring for Meeting. There it goes, so I will have to quit again. I hope I shall succeed again after a while if nothing happens. Oh, I had nearly forgotten to tell you what happened here the night after Mother left here. Some person got into the boys' abasement and some says took near 300 dollars' worth they think. I will not try to describe all out and out now but wait till I come home. Anyhow they think whoever done it made a pretty good haul.

Well, what next, will I write? For I fear I will tire your patience, but Mother said I must tell how I was getting along and all the news about the school. But when I come home I can tell more and tell in less time than I can to write it. But I expect you are getting tired of my writing, and I had better quit. Our Friend Persus Gardner from New York was here a Fourth Day night and had a meeting with the inmates of the college held near two hours. She supplicated and bore quite a lengthy testimony. She spoke very nice to the scholars and teachers. We had a very good Meeting. This room was full. There were several present from Richmond. Benjamin Fulghum was present and spoke some. Speaks as loud as ever.

Oh, I must not forget to tell you that I received a letter from Sylvanus and Nancy Stubbs last Fifth Day evening. Stating that they were well; also Uncle Joseph [Mary Maddock's brother] was well. It was dated the 13th of this month. Cousin Nancy wrote it nearly all herself, and I expect to answer it pretty soon. She said that Sylvanus was studying and preparing himself to commence school pretty soon.[7] She also said that they received a letter a few days ago from Solomon stating that he was quite sick or had been, but was better. And was going to get a furlough or discharge and come as soon as he was able. She said that they had met with quite a loss for them. Sylvanus had some good hay his father had given him, and he and uncle valued it at 60 or 75 dollars—burned to ashes a few weeks ago. I believe that is all the news of much importance. She wrote a sheet full. I thought I would send it home to let you see it, but I guess I will not, as I may answer it before I go home. So therefore I will not send it, but I will when I come home. Well, it is hardly two weeks till the time comes, and it will soon roll

7. Sylvanus received a medical discharge from the Union Army in January 1864 because of a serious disease. Before enlisting he had been a teacher, so here he must have been preparing to teach where they lived in Colorado.

round. It seems like it hasn't been a week since Mother and Ella were here.

I have been pretty closely occupied in my studies since she was here, so time goes pretty fast now to me. I was examined in all of my studies and got pretty good per cent for me. I got 100 per cts in some of my questions. But the average was in Geography 27 2/3; in Grammar 86; in Arithmetic 46 2/3; and in spelling 96. Only missed 4 words out of a 100. If I had had them right, I would a got 100 pr cts.

Sallie says I got through very well for the first—better right smart than some of the rest did. And I think now that I can get along pretty well, but it is going to take up my time closer than it ever has yet. But I guess I had better quit or you will get tired of my nonsense. And I am getting tired as I have been busy ever since dinner. Well, I will write again before I come home, and you must too. Write and tell me when I must come and all about it the next time. So no more, but remain your affectionate daughter,

*Martha Ann*

Please excuse all mistakes and bad writing this time. Write soon and tell all the news.

*Martha Ann Maddock*

## West Elkton, 11th Mo 25 1864

[*First sheet—written in Mary Maddock's widely spaced, shaky handwriting*]

Dear daughter, Martha Ann,

I have taken pen in hand to address thee and may inform that we are all middling well. We received thy welcome letter in due time. Glad thee was getting along so well. We shall expect thee home next week. Come on Sixth Day morning, and we will meet thee at Camden.

Our dear friend, Ann Marmon, and her companions, Jonathan and Mary Roberts of Whitewater Mo. Meeting, attended our Mo. Meeting yesterday and are now engaged in visiting families in the western part of our settlement. Will likely be in our section tomorrow.

Elihu Stubbs and Susanna[8] with their son were received into membership with Friends yesterday.

John F. Stubbs is going to commence his school next Second Day; Wm. Kenworthy also will begin his at the same time.[9]

I have not been anywhere but to Meeting twice since my return from Earlham. I was very poorly for several days after I got home. We got Ann Reeves[10] to stay the next day and all last week. I have got along pretty well this week. Am rather tired this evening. I have been on the go all day. Nearly five o'clock so farewell from loving mother. Write before thee comes.

Mary Maddock

[*Second sheet—in Joseph Maddock's small, finer handwriting*]

*First Day morning, 11th Mo 27th*

Remembered Martha Ann,

We had intended to a sent this letter by Uncle Johns to Hamilton yesterday morning as they were expecting to attend market, but on account of the appearance of a stormy night they did not go. We thought but to add some more.

We are all pretty well at present and hope these may find thee in the enjoyment of the same inestimable blessing. Our friend Ann Marmon and companions are still visiting families. A Fifth Day P.M. visited in Elkton, including Aunt Katy Green and Hannah Horner. Perhaps will visit some others not members. Her concern is to visit such who are in practice of attending our Meeting on Sixth Day. Visited in the southwest part of settlement yesterday in our part. Took dinner with us; visited Uncle Wm. Kellums, also H.A. Bennetts besides members; also Wm. Coopers. The visit to Bennetts was a satisfactory visit both to visitors and those visited. The girls seems much interested. Uncle Wm. expressed also much satisfaction in the visit as well as Wm. Coopers. I believe it is a satisfactory visit to all and will be remembered in days yet to come particularly by many of the young people.

8. Elihu Stubbs, brother of Martha Maddock (wife of John Maddock). Elihu and his wife Susanna (Gifford) Stubbs, were disowned by Elk Monthly Meeting in 1856 when they were married by a Justice of the Peace instead of in the Meeting. In 1864, they had one child, William Riley Stubbs, born 1862.

9. Individual Quakers with some education offered classes in the village. John F. Stubbs and David Kenworthy were some of Mattie's cousins.

10. Ann Reeves appears to have been a paid caretaker, someone able to come stay with the Maddocks and care for Mary and Nathan as needed.

She is about half-through the visit. Will probably visit several others that are in the practice of attending Meeting in prosecuting [*sic*] the visit.

Aunt Patsy read a letter to me from Alpheus stating that he had arrived safe and well at Providence. He left [here] a Fourth Day evening and arrived there on Sixth Day evening. It cost him, he said, about $30. The rules were more close and stringent than they are at Earlham, he said.

Joseph D. Hoagg is expected to be here and have an appointed meeting on Third Day next and to attend meeting a Fourth Day at Salem. He is likely in Cincinnati today and will come on the train tomorrow morning to Somerville where some of us will meet him. Will have this letter mailed there. From thy well-wishing father,

Jos Maddock

As thee is expecting to come home the last of this week. Please not to come till Sixth Day morning, and we some of us will meet thee there. As the evening trains are late, and nights are now very dark. Of course thee will come to Camden.

## Earlham College, 11th mo 27th 1864

Dearest Parents,

Once again, dear parents, I seat myself this dreary and cloudy afternoon to write home. It rained last night and this morning. Therefore it is rather a cloudy and foggy-looking day, more so than I have seen, I believe, since I have been here. I do not feel much in the mode for writing, and you need not expect to get a very interesting letter from me this time. So I hope you will excuse me if it is not. Now for the news.

You know, of course, that I went to Meeting today. Oh, how I wish you could have been here. Levi Jessup was here from Richmond and spoke some length of time, and then supplicated, which was a satisfactory time to all present. Zaccheus Test also spoke some, so altogether we had a good meeting.

Well, it has been just a week since I have written home, and it has been longer than that since I heard from home. I wonder what is the reason you do not write better? It will be two weeks next Third Day since I received the last. So you might know how anxious I am to hear from home. Sallie and I looked all day yesterday for someone up, as we did not receive any letter. We looked some for cousin Wil but were disappointed in not hearing or seeing anyone. It is too bad, I think.

Well, something about my coming home. I was in such a fix, I did not know what to do hardly, so I asked the Matron how I must do. The way I had thought of doing was this: not to go till Sixth Day morning. The train I would go on leaves about half-past six o'clock, so I would have to get up and start before day and without my breakfast, and I not being very well to go by myself, and carry my things, and walk to the depot, would be too much for me. So the matron and Sallie told me the best way I could do would be to go a Fifth Day evening on the six o'clock train. They are going to break school at recess and give all the scholars their suppers that want it, and plenty of time to get ready, and they will also take me over, so I will not have to walk. All the scholars that are going home are going then, and there will not be any going in the morning, so you can see how it is. And another thing is having to go alone. There will be no company in the morning, but in the evening there will be plenty. I will have company part-way if not all the way to Camden, and I am afraid if there is no one with me, I will miss the right train. I do not know what you think of it. But the matron says it will not be as bad for you to come after me as it would be for me to go in the morning. As I am not very well, she does not wish for me to go so early in the morning by myself.

Well, I guess I will have to draw towards a close as my sheet is nearly filled up, and I do not feel much in the mode for writing this evening. I can tell you more news in less time when I come home. I am sorry to be so much trouble. But I would rather come in the evening and have company than to come in the morning and do like I will have to. So therefore I will come on the six o'clock train on Fifth Day evening, which will get to Camden about 7 or quarter-past seven.

So I will conclude by requesting you to write soon, and believe me, as ever your affectionate daughter,

*Mattie*

## West Elkton, 11th Mo. 28th 1864

Beloved Daughter, Martha Ann,

I take up the pen to write a few lines. Grandfather [Joseph's father, Nathan Maddock] is very poorly indeed, it seems as though he cannot survive many hours. Yet we have thought so ever since yesterday morning, and still he is with us. Has had every hour, or less sometimes, spells of smothering or shortness of breath, so that he suffers much for a few minutes, then gets easier and rests pretty well for a while, mostly goes to sleep. We have been here the most of the time this week with him, both day and night. I came yesterday morning and stayed until this morning; Mother went home last evening and seen to things and come back again. We went home this morning and stayed till after dinner and will likely stay tonight as it looks like he would hardly live till morning. Yet he may continue with us for several days. He has weakened away very much in the last two days, and has not taken any nourishment of consequence since last Second Day.

We are well, with the exception of colds. Being up considerable with Grandfather at night, we feel some worn out. We have been mostly every other night this week with him.

We got thy letter a Third Day evening and were glad to hear from thee.

Old James Morris died yesterday and is to be buried tomorrow. Meet at the house at 10 o'clock.

We received a letter from Uncle Robert[11] a few days ago, dated the 25th of 8th mo., stating that the Indians had been very troublesome near them. Had murdered several of the whites about sixty miles from them, so that they had become alarmed, had left their farm and went to Colorado City[12] and were staying there, and sleeping in the fort at night. Their wheat being all out in shock, they still talked of coming in this fall and expected to start about this time. Henry Hutchins and Amos Gennells were with them and some other of their neighbors.

Nathan stays by himself at night while we are staying with Grandfather and seems willing to do so. Ring and Puss are getting along pretty well. They feel somewhat lonesome perhaps. Ella's Pup went home with Maria one evening and has not returned.

From thy well-wishing parents

*Jos. & Mary Maddock*

11. Robert Harvey Stubbs, Mary Maddock's brother, who had moved with his wife and family to Colorado.

12. "Colorado City Fort *(1864–1868), Colorado Springs.* A civilian log stockade built around the Anway Hotel for protection against Indian raids. The CO Cavalry also briefly occupied the post in 1864. Also known as Fort Colorado." See North American Forts.com. Now called "Old Colorado City" and part of Colorado Springs, El Paso County, Colorado.

A letter received from Sylvanus states that they had had accounts from Solomon[13] that he was well and at the Hospital and still was ward master.[14]

## West Elkton, 11th Mo 29th P.M.

We have just got thy letter stating that thee expects to come a Fifth Day evening.

Please come then, and I will meet thee at Camden, and pay no attention to the letter we just sent to thee which thee will probably get this evening. We send this to Somerville in the morning.

Respectfully from thy father,

*Jos. Maddock*

13. Sylvanus and Solomon Stubbs were Mary Maddock's nephews, sons of her brother, Joseph Harvey Stubbs, who along with his wife Keziah was disowned by Elk Monthly Meeting in 1844 for "joining the Separatists," i.e., Indiana Yearly Meeting of Anti-Slavery Friends. Joseph H. and Keziah were founding members of Elk Monthly Meeting of Anti-Slavery Friends and were active workers on the UGRR through Preble County in the decades before the Civil War. Though they were Quakers, two of their sons, Solomon and Sylvanus Stubbs, enlisted near the beginning of the Civil War. Sylvanus was a twenty-year-old teacher when he enlisted in 1862, and he served until January 25, 1864 when he was mustered out because of "Disease." Solomon enlisted when he was seventeen and served from July 25, 1861 through the end of the war; he mustered out June 11, 1865 with a rank of sergeant. The reference to Solomon "at the Hospital" and that he was "still ward master" suggests he served in a noncombatant role. After the Civil War, the entire Joseph H. Stubbs family moved West to settle in Kansas.

14. Re "ward master." "It will be seen here that two duties are specially assigned to the ward-master. First, the care of the effects of patients. Second, the care of the hospital furniture and utensils." Woodward, *Hospital Steward's Manual.*

# December 1864

## At Home, 12th Mo 11th 1864

Martha Ann, we again take up the pen to write. We are all in good health together with connections, friends & neighbors, as far as we know with some little exceptions. Mary Jones, wife of David Kenworthy, is no more. She quietly passed away from this state of probation [*sic*] on Sixth Day morning last about 6 o'clock. Was buried yesterday. Met at the home at 12. A large and satisfactory Meeting was held on the occasion before the interment. A solemn and interesting season to many it was, no doubt.

This is First Day P.M. We were at Meeting today. It was small as to attendance, silent, but satisfactory. It is very cold this afternoon. The mercury this morning was 18 above zero; in two or three hours it fell to 7 and has been there so far through the day. And it looks like it will be very cold tonight. Some 2 inches of snow on the ground, very windy and cold, it was, a going to Meeting, so that we felt it very sensible. But returning fared better, as the wind was on our backs.

Rachel Maddock's little girl is quite poorly with cold and the effects of diphtheria yet, likely, not dangerous. Some others are complaining of colds, etc.

Wm J. Kenworthy's school is progressing pretty well as far as we know. There was about 15 boys and some 18 or 20 girls came to Meeting last Fifth Day. His school helps out our week day Meeting very much, and the scholars mostly behave very commendably. The school for the colored children is also commenced. It began a Second Day and is attended by about a dozen pupils. And it looks like it might be an interesting school for them and will no doubt be so, if they will be diligent in their attendance, as they have, no doubt, a good Teacher (Angelina Harris) who feels an interest in imparting instruction to them.

Well, we were at market last Third Day. We had 7 lb butter, some 3 or 4 bus [bushels] corn, and Uncle Wm. Kellum sent 13 of his chickens. We got 50 cts for 3 lb of butter and 45 cts for 3 more and 1 at 40 cts. Uncle Johns were down too, and Maria got 50 cts for 1 or 2 lb and 45 cts for the balance. They had some 25 lbs. Chickens were from 25 to 40 cts a piece.

We started about 1 o'clock and got down there about 5, so that we got a good stand and sold out pretty soon, and got home about 12 [noon]. It was very pleasant and nice going down. We had a light shower of rain on us as we went down, otherwise very pleasant. We saw A. Anderson and M. Mitchell, as well as some others of our patrons, who appeared glad to see us in market. I also saw Brother Thomson, the stationed minister in Hamilton M.E. church, and he spoke well of Mary Roberts' Meeting with them on First Day last. We understand since, that it was largely attended; a very still meeting, and solemn and interesting occasion, no doubt but it was to all. Mary has a Meeting today at Collinville on the [turn]pike between Seven-Mile and Somerville.

Well, about little John's school. It is getting along very well as far as we know. Some 20 to 25 pupils in attendance. We have not had any more letters from Uncle Roberts[1] since thee left home. We are very anxious to hear.

We understand from Aunt Anna[2] that after thee got off of the Cars,[3] that some Friend met thee and took thy carpet sack which we suppose was Walter,[4] and that thee got out to Earlham without having to walk or to carry thy things, which we were glad to hear, as we feared that thee would be very tired in walking out and carrying thy things. Aunt Anna got home yesterday and said L. Hunt's wife was better and seemed like she might be about again some.

It is now after night and is very cold. The mercury is nearly down to zero and will be several degrees below by morning. Puss is snoozing away very comfortably on the chair before the fire. We turned it out a while ago, and it came to the door and begged so hard, we let it in again. Ring is at the stable enjoying

1. The Stubbs relatives who had moved to Colorado.
2. Joseph Maddock's older half-sister, Anna (nee Mendenhall) Stubbs.
3. Passenger "car" of train from Camden, Ohio, to Richmond, Indiana.
4. Walter Carpenter, General Manager of Earlham College.

himself pretty well, no doubt. Him and Puss have been in all the afternoon.

I am expecting to go up to Eaton in a few days to attend to some business, pay taxes, etc., and may not mail this letter to thee until I go. Yet if it keeps so cold, I may not get to go for several days, and if I should not go, it may be mailed at Elkton.

We often think of thee and miss thy company in the family circle since thy sojourn at Earlham for the purpose of getting a competent education. Yet we do not regret it as thee seemed to be so well-satisfied and was improving in thy several studies, so that we would encourage thee to energy and perseverance in thy pursuit of a competent knowledge of the several branches of educational studies that thee is endeavoring to acquire. Youth is the season to attend to this duty. As the wise poet said, "It is education forms the common mind, just as the twig is bent, the tree is inclined." How many are the privileges of getting a good education, and a guarded one too, to what it was when we received what little we got. May thee, as well as all others in the younger walks of life in the present day, be thankful for these great privileges and blessings bestowed on them by an All-wise and bountiful Providence. Many parents manifest a commendable liberality in supporting and encouraging of Seminaries of learning in our Western Land, so that there is but little or no excuse for the youth in getting a competent share of education in some school or other. A good education is to be preferred before anything else of a temporal nature. It qualifies the faculties, expands the mind, so that man may enjoy the works of nature, the sciences, and arts and feel his dependence on the Great Author of his existence and prepare him to fill up the many and various duties of life for which he was placed here by his Creator to perform both social and religious.

*12th Mo 12th Evening*

It was not quite as cold as we expected it would be this morning about 2 degrees below zero and was pretty cold till near noon. This afternoon and evening more moderate, yet it will be quite cool tonight. The mercury stood at 10 till since noon, and it has been up to 12 or 14; there has not been very much wind, and it seems more pleasant.

We are still all of us pretty well, this evening. It was so cold this morning that the new clock stopped, and we brought it in here and set it up by the old one, so that they both together make quite a ticking.

It was so cold this morning that I did not go to Eaton. I think some of going tomorrow, if it is not too cold, and if I should go, I shall mail this letter there. As we perhaps have written all that we think of, and that would interest thee, also that our sheet is nearly full, we close and remain as ever, thy well-wishing parents,

Jos. & Mary Maddock

We hardly know whether we shall go to Quarterly Meeting[5] or not, if it keeps so cold. If it should moderate, and we can get someone to stay,[6] we may go. If no one can be had to stay, perhaps one of us may go. I have been writing a letter for Uncle Jos. H. Stubbs which I want to start tomorrow. Also I think of writing to Uncle Sam'l Stubbs[7] in Illinois yet tonight.

Please write occasionally, and we will endeavor to do the same. We shall look for one from thee sure tomorrow.

## Earlham College, 12th Day, 12th Month 1864

Dearest Parents,

The time has again rolled around, and I must seat myself for the purpose of writing home.

This is First Day afternoon and a cold one it is. The coldest one we have had this month, as at least the mercury is the lowest it has been and is still going down and getting colder. The Governess has just told us if we could not keep comfortable in the schoolroom that we might go to the Parlor and Lecture room or other places where it is more comfortable than here in the schoolroom. I am writing with my shawl on, and then I can hardly write I am so cold.

The ground is covered with snow, or has been, and I can tell you it seems like winter, but I suppose it would seem still more so if I were at home and had to be out more than I am here.

The Governess told us that we did know anything about the cold here like we would at home. But it is winter enough

5. In Salem, Union County, Indiana. By 1864, Westfield Quarterly Meeting included only Elk Monthly Meeting in Preble County, Ohio, and Salem Monthly Meeting in Union County, Indiana. It alternated between the two locations, meeting on the third Saturday of the third, sixth and twelfth months.

6. i.e., Stay with Mattie's mentally-challenged older brother, Nathan.

7. Samuel and Martha (nee Miller) Stubbs of Preble County moved West in 1850.

for us here. The boys have had a fine time skating. They gave them leave to go to the river yesterday and skate. Better believe, they turned out with their skates for the river and had a fine time of it, which you know was quite a treat to them after having to stay so close. But the girls did not have such fun. Some few went to the bridge and had quite a time skating, but it was too cold for them. One [of] the girls got her feet wet and paid dear for her fun as she was quite sick last night and today. Well, I guess I have said enough on that subject and will turn to something else more interesting.

Would you like to know how I got along as I came out? Well, Father knew, of course, that I got in the cars at Camden. All of us, Enos and Danny in one car and I and Aunt Anna in another. Well, I done very well till I got to Richmond. There I begin to think about getting off. As you know, I had a pretty good load. My carpet sack was pretty heavy.

When I got to Richmond I saw the depot was crowded like it always is, but before I got off, I saw Walter Carpenter standing on the platform, and he, of course, knew I was coming that morning. He was looking out for me, he said, and when he saw me, came and took some of them [i.e., her bags], so you know that was quite a relief to me.

The cars were so crowded that I had to do the best I could in getting a seat. I stood up till I got to Barnett's Station. Then I found a seat little-better than standing. I gave my seat to Aunt Anna as I knew I could stand up better than her. I never saw Enos or Danny after we got on at Camden, till I got to Richmond. Then I just said farewell to Enos through the window was all. I and Aunt Anna then separated after coming together thus far, and she went to Franklin Hunt's, and Walter told me the Omnibus was there for all that wanted to ride out. So I got in and was ready once more for Earlham. I was the only girl to go out there. There were several boys, some of them my classmates, but they put their baggage what they had in, and all walked out. I arrived here a little before noon, feeling pretty tired, and had the headache some. Sallie had not arrived when I got here and not till afternoon, and missed her dinner. Said she had a good visit with Melvina. And then she wanted to know all about home and everything else she could think of, which kept me busy for a while. After I had answered all her questions or tried to, she said that she almost wished that she had went home.

The health of the students is pretty good. Still there is some sickness amongst the boys and girls too. I have had a pretty bad cold. The worst one I have had in a long time. I suppose it was the cold I took going home and coming back.

Sallie was vaccinated, and it has took, and she is right sick with it, but is better today. I have been pretty much hurried in my studies. My time has been pretty closely taken up and will be the rest of the session. You must excuse me for my poor writing and all mistakes, as I do not feel much in the mode for writing. I looked all the week for a letter but was disappointed. Please write immediately on the receipt of this, if it is worth answering. If not, write anyhow and tell me all that has transpired since I left, and everything you think will be interesting to me. For anything from home does me good. The Governess says letters from home to the students helps them. And that they need their encouragement and their sympathy and prayers to help them, which is a great one to some.

Mother, please send my guard in a letter to me if it is not too much trouble. I will mail a catalogue to Father soon.

*Mattie*

*First Day evening.*

Sallie is right sick this evening with her arm. I feel sorry for her, and do all I can for her. The mercury is two degrees above zero. Tell Ann to write and I will answer right away. Better believe, it is winter. Well, I guess I had better quit or you will tire of my nonsense. We have just had some reading by Charles Coffin.

[*on separate sheet*]

Sallie received a letter from Cousin Alpheus last Sixth Day, a long one it was. Stating he was well and doing well, but it was not as good a school as Earlham.

There has been a great deal of sickness amongst the friends of the scholars. Several of them have been sent for, on account of sickness. Ettie Berson from Laporte, Indiana, that voted for Wallandingham,[8] got a dispatch[9] in a short time after she got here that her brother was at the point of death. She started

8. Probably Clement Vallandigham, an Ohio State Representative who opposed the Civil War. "A prominent leader of the anti-war 'Peace Democrats' (or Copperheads), Vallandigham was arrested on May 5, 1863, and charged with 'publicly expressing . . . his sympathies with those in arms against the Government of the United States.' Upon his conviction, the Lincoln administration banished him to the Confederacy." "Representative Clement Vallandigham of Ohio," U. S. House of Representatives.gov.

9. "Dispatch" seems to refer to students being called home because of illness in the family.

and got there just half an hour before he died. And one of my classmates, Ella Ladd, was sent for for her sister's sickness. And two or three of the boys. They say that there was never as many dispatches come here in two or three sessions before as in this half-session. Well, I guess I had better quit as it is nearly suppertime, and I have a composition to write yet tonight. Tell Ella I would have written to her but have not time. But will as soon as I can. How is Uncle Billie getting along. I want Father to be sure and come out here after a while and see me. Come New Year's and bring me a New Year's gift. So now in conclusion, I remain as ever, your loving daughter,

*Mattie*

Be sure and write as soon as convenient.

## Earlham College, 12th Mo 20th 1864

Dearest Parents,

Third Day evening, 8 o'clock. I have just seated myself to drop you a few scattered lines in reply to your very kind and welcome letter which came to hand last Fourth Day evening, and I should have answered sooner, but had hardly time, and I wrote a letter to Ella, so I suppose you would hear from me. I also sent a catalogue of Earlham to Father at the same time, which I suppose you have received before this time. So I thought as I had a little leisure time, I could not improve them any better than to write a few lines home to let you know that I am still in the land of the living.

There goes the bell for Collection to read a chapter and then retire to bed. Oh, I am so glad. I feel like going to bed. So I will have to quit for tonight. So farewell.

Fourth Day morning. Half-past five. I seat myself again to finish my letter. I have not much time to write so I must cut my letter short. I am enjoying pretty good health except the cold which still hangs on. Arithmetic was getting so hard, and I did not stand a very good examination, so of course, I had to drop back where I could do more good. I am in the first part now. but in doing that, I had to drop Grammar. So I think now the way my studies are arranged, I will get along better than I have ever done yet.

Is Father coming up to see me pretty soon? I wish he would. School is just half out today. It will be ten weeks tomorrow since

I left home to come to Earlham. The Committee[10] and number of others were here yesterday, but nobody to see me. How I wish there had been. Sallie and I expect to look for some of you up the last of this week or next, whether you come or not. Come at Christmas and bring me a Christmas gift. Mother, I have plenty of crackers, but the rest are gone.

EARLHAM COLLEGE.

This Institution was established by the Society of Friends of Indiana Yearly Meeting, and is managed by that body under the following

COMMITTEE.

ABRAHAM M. TAYLOR.................Cincinnati, Ohio.
SOLOMON MACY.........................Spiceland, Indiana.
TIMOTHY NICHOLSON.................Richmond, Indiana.
JOSEPH DICKINSON.....................Richmond, Indiana.
DANIEL HILL...............................New Garden, Indiana.
JONATHAN BALDWIN..................Greens Fork, Indiana.
MARY PARKER............................New Garden, Indiana.
ANNA S. RITCHIE.........................New Paris, Ohio.
MARY JESSUP...............................Richmond, Indiana.
MIRIAM A. MAXWELL..................Richmond, Indiana.
MARTHA MADDOCK......................West Elkton, Ohio.
RACHEL WHITE.............................Milton, Indiana.

List of Committee Members, 1863 Earlham College catalog

Well, it is nearly breakfast time, so I will have to draw towards a close by requesting you to write soon, if you deem this worth of an answer. If not, write anyhow and tell me all the news.

Now Father, I want thee to be sure and come to see me. I will write again when I have more time and tell you how I get along. I remain as ever your well-wishing daughter,

Mattie

10. In the early days of Earlham College, the "Committee" (later called "Trustees") was the group of Friends managing the college for Indiana Yearly Meeting. From 1861-1865, the Committee included Mattie's "Aunt Patsy," i.e., Martha (nee Stubbs) Maddock, wife of John Maddock.

P.S. The doorbell is ringing. It never rings this early in the morning. The girls are anxious to know. Ettie Berson's brother is dead. I wrote a long letter to Nancy and Sylvanus the other day. What was the matter with Daniel Kenworthy's wife[11]? I did not know she was sick. What a number of deaths there has been since I left. There must be a change. I got a picture the other day. Whose do you think it was?

## West Elkton, 12th Mo 20th 1864

Remembered Daughter, Martha Ann,

We again take up the pen to address thee. We are all this morning favored with good health, one of the greatest of blessings conferred on us by an All-wise Providence, and one of which we may and ought to be thankful for.

Well, we have been out at Quarterly Meeting[12] and only returned yesterday in the afternoon between 2 & 3 o'clock. We started a Sixth Day morning about 6, and soon after it commenced a drizzly rain, sometimes quite showers, so that it was as disagreeable a day to be out as any I ever saw, but we went on. The probability of Four Mile [Creek] being up, we went around by Oxford some 2 or 3 miles further, but were favored to reach Salem [near present-day Liberty, Indiana], and met a large number of ministers. Five of them had come without any knowledge of each other (viz) Daniel Williams, Nathan Douglas, David H. Bennett, Eli Newlin & John D. Elliott of Goshen, O. in Alum Creek Quarter. All were very acceptably with us, besides[13] Ann Marmon and companion who [was] visiting families at Salem.

Daniel Williams, Nathan Douglass & David Bennett had considerable to say both on Seventh Day and First Day. Daniel had a meeting with the children in the P.M., a first. Little boys

11. Joseph wrote to her that David Kenworthy's wife had died, but census records show that David was married to Martha (nee Stubbs) Kenworthy (1816–1884). Here, Mattie refers to *Daniel* Kenworthy's wife, Mary Jane (nee Roberts) Kenworthy, whose gravestone in Fairmound Cemetery, West Elkton, Ohio, shows her birth and death dates as 1832–1864.

12. i.e., in Union County, Indiana. Joseph and Mary left about six a.m. Friday to attend Westfield Quarterly Meeting on Saturday at Salem Monthly Meeting, roughly twenty miles from West Elkton. Today, it's a half-hour drive by car, but by horse and buggy, especially in bad weather, it would be about an eight-hour trip. They returned to West Elkton on Tuesday, arriving midafternoon.

13. The sentence construction makes it unclear how Joseph Maddock "rated" Ann Marmon. In his diary, though, he had good things to say about her visit to West Elkton, so "besides" here probably means "as well as" and goes with all the other ministers who "were acceptably with us."

& girls, young men and women, all of the young people. It was at 9 o'clock, not very large, but quite an acceptable number. One apartment nearly filled with young people and some of the older ones. It was a satisfactory opportunity and will be remembered by them no doubt in days to come. Eli Newlin attended, spoke some, and the meeting concluded which was near dark. John D. Elliott did not open his mouth in the time of Quarterly Meeting. There was so many others spoke that there seemed not time for all to relieve their minds. It was although a remarkable and rather an unusual time, as we think we never attended Quarterly Meeting under more discouraging prospect than when we left home, yet since our return we may say that we have been made to rejoice and say that "It was good for to a been there."

As we came home yesterday, Four Mile was up pretty full, but [we] were favored to cross without any difficulty. The water was up nearly to the bed of the Rockaway. About 24 Friends attended Q.M. from Elk [Monthly Meeting]. It was rather larger than common in 12th mo. Sam'l and Mary Roberts, nor Jane Jones, did not attend. James was quite sick with something like diphtheria. Jane's child was quite sick also.[14]

J.D. Elliott has an appointed meeting with us today at usual hour. As we did not hear him speak we cannot say much about him. He is a pleasant-countenanced Friend. As there was not a chance for all at Q.M. to relieve their minds, perhaps our Friend may feel like taking the harp from off the willows today with us.

Ann Reeves stayed with Nathan while we went to Q.M. Ella came and stayed at night so that they got along very well, and Ann went home First Day morning, as we expected to come home that evening. But it was later before Meeting closed, so that we could not a started before 3, so that we considered to stay till next morning, and Nathan stayed all night by himself First Day night. It was well enough that we did not start home that evening as the waters were up more than they were yesterday, and the night was very dark. We sent word home so that Nathan did not say anything against staying by himself. As he stayed several nights while Grandfather was sick, he has become more used to staying by himself.[15]

Little John's school is progressing pretty well as far as we know. Also Wm. J. Kenworthy is going on satisfactory; there is near 40 in attendance. Also the school for colored children is

14. James Roberts was the sixteen-year-old son of Mary and Samuel Roberts; Jane Jones' youngest child at the time was seven-year-old Emma Jones.

15. Nathan turned thirty years old on December 31, 1864.

doing pretty well as far as we know. We have been away several days. We are not as well posted as would a been perhaps, as if we had a been at home.

We got thy letter of date last First Day, was a week a Third Day evening. I was up at Eaton that day and mailed ours to thee whilst there, which thee perhaps received next day.

As it is near Meeting time we shall close for the present. Perhaps add some more after Meeting and remain as ever thy well-wishing Parents,

Jos. & Mary Maddock

Please write as usual.

P.M. We have just returned from Meeting which was pretty largely attended, and our friend J.D. Elliott appeared in supplication, then spoke at some length, perhaps near an hour. We trust a favored meeting to many. It was Jane spoke a few words, then Martha Ann Taylor, and Mary Roberts appeared in supplication. The Meeting then closed. He is one of our little, old-fashioned, humble ministers and appeared much interested for Friends here, and well-satisfied in being with us. He leaves for Springborough this evening. Mother put in thy guard.

## West Elkton, 12th Mo 25th 1864

Remembered Martha Ann,

We again take up the pen to address thee this evening and am thankful to say that we are in the enjoyment of pretty good health. Mother has been complaining some from a geothering [*sic*] or swelled jaw occasioned from her old teeth. Such spells as she frequently has at times. Is better now, [but] may have another such spell, as she has had when she takes cold. Other friends and neighbors are all well as far as we know with some exceptions.

Well, we were at Meeting today. A middling-large attendance, and Jane had considerable to communicate, also appeared in supplication.

James & Delilah Roberts are still quite unwell with the diphtheria or sore throat. Their Mother is also somewhat unwell with something of the same. Rachel Maddock's little girl is some better, yet not very well.

Well, we have had pretty good sleighing for two or three days past, so that we hear the bells tinkling along in the evening nearly all the time. I was down at Hamilton a Sixth Day morning in the sled. It was quite good sledding. I went to take our friend Peter Osborn and companion to the cars[16] in order to get to Salem, as they can go from there in two hours as they wished to be there and have a meeting at 10 o'clock yesterday morning. As the roads we thought it would be extremely rough, and it would be very cold, so that we thought it the best way for them to go. We started about 5 o'clock and got down there a little after 8. The cars would start about 9, so that they got there at 11, and then they would have time to give notice in the P.M.

Our Friend [i.e., Peter Osborn] was at Monthly Meeting with us a Fifth Day. They came in pretty soon after Meeting had set. As strangers had considerable to communicate to us. He appears to be one of our best ministers and speaks in a feeling manner. He lives at Springfield, O. in Center Quarter in Clinton Co. He expected to be at Whitewater [Monthly Meeting in Richmond, Indiana] today and a few other meetings, and then it would slow up his extensive visit to all the meetings in Indiana state. Also, he said he should be with you at Earlham. We think you will all like to hear him speak, and we hope the visit will be profitably received by all the students in the College.

We received thy acceptable letter on Fifth Day after Meeting. Were glad to hear how thou wast getting along, also that thee was well, and would likely get along better with thy studies as thee would fall back in another class. We wrote a pretty lengthy letter after we got home from Quarterly meeting, which thee perhaps got about the same time we received thine.

Well, I think it will not be in my power to come up to Earlham this week, as we have our wheat to haul off, some corn to gather & also that Grandfather's old place is to be offered for sale on Seventh Day next, and I want to be at the sale. But sometime next week, if life and health permits, I think I shall come. Perhaps be at meeting on Fifth Day, as I should like to attend it and stay all night amongst you or somebody else.

It has been very cold, about 4 inches of snow. Mercury down about 2 degrees below zero last Sixth Day morning, the morning I went to Hamilton. Well, I guess we looked frosty for certain when we got there, yet we did not suffer much with cold, as we were wrapped up with shawls & quilts, and had heated stones to [our] feet. I think I suffered more coming home as the wind raised, and I did not wrap up as I did in the morning. There was a

16. i.e., train.

great many out in sleighs with bells on horses, which made Billy raise his head pretty high some times.

Please tell Walter that when I come up I shall pay the balance of thy tuition if he says anything about it, or thee may tell him of it anyhow. I might send it in this letter but don't like to risk so much, as the department[17] is not accountable for money mailed.

As we have written pretty freely about times and other news amongst us, we don't know that it is worthwhile to add much more that would interest thee.

Ring and Puss are getting along very well and are privileged to be with us frequently these few days as it has been very cold, and form a part of the family circle with us. We have commenced feeding Mooly and Fanny since the cold weather set in, and milk in the stable, which is much pleasanter than out-of-doors.

We have not heard anything from Solomon or any of those that went from Elkton since thee was home. Neither have heard anything from Uncle Roberts nor from Uncle Jos. H. Stubbs. We mailed the Y.M. minutes to Uncle J.H.S. last week. We have not got any more Nos. of the Morning Dew[18] since thee was at home.

When I was up at Eaton week-before-last, I got another watch at Chambers Jewelry Store. I think I have a pretty good one now; at least it runs well. It ought to be a good one—it cost $20.00.

Well, this page is filling up, and perhaps we shall not mail this in time to go in the morning. We may add more tomorrow. It is nearly bedtime. We shall close for the present and remain as ever, thy well-wishing Parents,

*Jos. & Mary Maddock*

17. Re the department "not accountable for money mailed" probably refers to the postal service.

18. In the mid-nineteenth century, a series of periodicals related to the Temperance movement written by British lecturer and author, Clara Lucas Balfour, were widely circulated in England. Eventually individual issues were collected and published as a book with the title, *The Juvenile Abstainer.* In 1853, the book was republished as *Morning Dew Drops*, with this inside title page: "Morning Dew Drops. With an Introduction by Mrs. H. B. Stowe. By Clara Lucas BALFOUR." In addition to the introduction by American abolitionist, Harriet Beecher Stowe, the book mentions Quakers in its summary of denominations supporting the early Temperance movement. It is conceivable that by 1864 when Joseph Maddock mentions to Mattie they "have not got any more Nos. of the Morning Dew" since she was home, American Quakers had adapted portions of the book for use in tract form, and that the Maddock family in West Elkton, Ohio, had a subscription.

Daniel Kenworthy's wife was confined [and] left a babe. Sarah Lane has the babe. Daniel and his children went to his Father's, it being Mary Jane's request for them to do so, and for Sarah Lane to take her babe.[19]

Uncle Wm. Kellums are about as common. They, of course, are always complaining as it is a natural consequence of old people when in the decline of life to feel the infirmities of old age coming on. Ann Marmon visited them, and they expressed much satisfaction in being thus noticed. Please write as usual, and we will do the same. We may not write next week if I come up to Earlham.

[*in penciled scrawl*]

*12th Mo 26th*

All well as usual. Very warm and they say snow nearly all gone. Looks like thawing out.

Theodore is up from the City.[20] Is not very busy at City now, as it is the holidays. So nothing more. As ever, thy well-wishing Parents.

J & M Maddock

19. It sounds like Joseph is saying that Daniel Kenworthy's wife, Mary Jane (nee Roberts) Kenworthy, died giving birth to a child in December 1864. Apparently she knew she was dying and requested that Daniel take their three children (ten-year-old John; six-year-old Emma, and four-year-old Margaret) to live with him (perhaps at his father's home?) and give the newborn baby to Sarah Lane, who was forty-five-years-old and had three children of her own, including a twenty-five-year-old daughter living at home. We don't know the reason Mary chose Sarah Lane, but within two years, Daniel had married Sarah's daughter, Mary Jane Lane, who thus might have became the baby's step-mother. But I find no record of a child born in December 1864 to Daniel Kenworthy and his first wife, Mary Jane Roberts, or anyone else.

20. Cincinnati, Ohio.

# January 1865

## Earlham College, 1st Mo 1st, 1865, New Year's

Dearest Parents,

One again I seat myself in the quiet schoolroom of Earlham for the purpose of answering your kind and welcomed letter, which I had the pleasure to receive last Fourth Day evening. And you cannot imagine how glad I was to hear from my old dear home once more, but was rather sorry to hear of Mother being sick. Hope it will prove nothing serious, as she has often had such spells. Hope she will get better soon.

Well, today is New Year's, the first day of the year 1865. But it is not much like a year ago today. It was so cold then and plenty of snow on the ground; so it is now, but not quite so cold as then, but cold enough to suit us. The sun is shining very bright and I think after a while it will be a beautiful day, or at least it seems like it would. There goes the bell for Collection to go to Meeting. Well, I must quit for the present. Just before we go to Meeting, each girl repeats a passage of scripture every First and Fifth Day morning which I think is a very nice practice.

Afternoon. I have just eat my dinner and seated myself again to try to finish my letter. We had a very good Meeting indeed. Zaccheus Test supplicated. How I wish you were here.

Our Friend Peter Osborn that Father spoke of in his letter was here last First Day evening and Second Day evening at Collection, but Second Day evening he had a regular meeting. The students seemed to be very much taken with him and liked to hear him.

John Davis also, from Salem, was here with us First Day evening. I just spoke to him was all. Joseph Wright was here a Fourth Day night, and Luke Woodard was here at Meeting Fifth Day so you can see that we have plenty of preaching to claim our attention.

Well, to something more interesting. This is a beautiful day indeed. I am getting along very well now since I have fallen back in a lower class where I can get along better than I did before. Still I have enough to keep me busy. I have five studies. I got two letters last Fourth Day evening and you cannot imagine how I felt. Who do you think they were from? One was from home, the other from Becca and Mattie Reynolds. Becca wrote a long one, a sheet full. Better believe I was glad to hear so much at once from my old dear home and how the young folks were enjoying themselves, as I used to be one amongst them. But the time came for us to separate for a season. I often think of home and wonder if you think of me as often as I think of you. I have been so busy since vacation, so that time goes off faster than I think sometimes. Oh, I long for the time to come when I can return to my home and enjoy your company in the family circle. I often think of the many happy hours I have spent in days that are past and my dear associates and friends I have left for a season, but I hope soon, if life and health permits, to return to my dear home. Father said when he was up to Eaton he got a new watch. I think it time; the other one done so poor. Puss and Ring are doing very well, are they? Puss as fat as ever. I expect I won't know them when I come home again, hardly, nor they me. I was very glad to hear from Uncle Billies and that they were well. Tell them I often think of them and wish I could be there this pleasant afternoon but cannot. I often think of the many pleasant hours I have spent with them. How are they getting along this cold weather?

I wrote a long letter to Sylvanus and Nancy just after vacation and have received no answer yet, but I look for one all the time. I like to hear from Solomon and Uncle Josephs. I also wrote one to Amanda[1] the other day. Tell Ella it is nearly time she was answering my letter. Tell Elnora if she will write first, like Mattie and Jennie, I will answer it, as I would be so glad to get a letter from her to hear what she has to say.

Well, I declare I must quit as my sheet is fast filling up, and I want to write another one yet this evening. Well, Father, thee is

1. Samuel and Martha C. (nee Miller) Stubbs had moved their family West from Preble County, Ohio in 1850. In 1865, they lived in Illinois. Their daughter, Amanda, was two years younger than Mattie.

coming up to see us this week, is thee? We are going to look any how. We looked some last week but were

[*written sideways across the first page of the letter, across the script*]

disappointed. There were so many boxes come for some of the girls. Nearly every girl got something but I and Sallie. I just wish you could be here and see the things that are sent here. I never knew what it was to get anything till I came here, and now I know what it is. It made I and Sallie feel bad yesterday when so many things rolled in but none for us. But we hope ours are to come yet. Sallie says send a New Year's gift to both. Bring plenty to keep us the rest of the session.

Well, Mother, send me some new handkerchiefs as I need them so bad. If thee has not time to hem them, I can do it if thee will send me some thread to do it. Please send some more needles. I lost some of mine. Small-like, and anything else thee thinks I need. I do not know as I need anything, without thee will send me more towels, and I can hem them well enough. Sallie says bring all thee can, Father. If thee comes Fifth Day morning, thee will have to make good use of time to get here to Meeting. Stay all night here. I hope I will get to be with thee more than I did with Mother.

[*on separate sheet*]

I guess I will have to finish on another piece. Sallie says tell Aunt Patsy to be sure to send those things Tommy left there for her. and to send a white spool of thread, number between 24 and 36, not finer than 36. Mother, please send me some more ruffle and a belt. That is all. Some more good Mince pie if thee has it. If not, some other that is good. Anything here is good.

Father, come Fifth Day sure, and be at Meeting, but I can tell thee that thee will have to make good use of time. So no more, but will close by requesting you to write soon. If thee comes up, I will not look for a letter.

Tell Ella to send some of their good black apples as she wished in her letter. So no more, but I remain as ever, your affectionate daughter,

*Mattie*

P.S. Mother, please send me some scraps of cloth, like some [old] clothes such as to make pin cushions, lamp mat, something for me to work at on Seventh Days. If I had some yarn I would knit a tidy. Well, I will quit and not ask for anything or thee will tire of me.

*Martha Ann*

## Joseph Maddock's 1865 Diary Entry re His Visit to Earlham

1st Month, the 5th, I left home early this morning to visit Earlham College, Martha Ann wishing for some of us to come up again (her mother being up some time ago). I got on the morning train at Camden and arrived at Richmond in about an hour and walked out to the College about a mile. I arrived just before Meeting set. It was an interesting occasion to see so many young people collecting at their usual weekday Meeting and the comely order and sittings that pervaded this large and beautifully open young people. A pleasing sight indeed. The Meeting was held in silence except a short supplication by one of the teachers, after which the meeting was loud, the scholars leaving in relation as when they took their seats.

We afterwards went down to the parlor where Martha Ann and Sally Jones came in to see me and appeared glad that I had arrived in time to attend Meeting. We pretty soon went down to dinner where the same order was observed as at Meeting in taking their seats. I spent the afternoon walking about the premises and heard one or two classes recite. I spent some time in the evening in social intercourse with the superintendent, very agreeably, respecting the school. In the evening before returning to rest, we all collected in the reading room. After a suitable praise, the superintendent read the 12th Chapter of Numbers, which after a solemn praise, we all retired to rest.

In the morning at breakfast, after all had eaten, the 4th Chapter of Acts was read. All returned to their different apartments in their usual order as before. After returning to the parlor and spending a few minutes with Martha Ann and Sally, we took leave of each other and I started for home.

After spending a day and night in the interesting institution of learning I was glad of having the privilege of spending time talking with the superintendent as well as teachers on the committee appointed to the charge of the Yearly Meeting for the improvement of the pupils, manifest both in literary learning as well as religious instruction. It was time well spent by me and will be remembered in days to come. There is about 175 pupils in attendance: 100 boys and 75 girls. The largest attendance since the school was opened.

## West Elkton, 1st Mo, 10th 1865

Martha Ann,

We take up the pen to address thee. We are all pretty well. This is a very stormy day. It has been snowing pretty freely this afternoon, and there is considerable snow fallen today, and it is going to be a very stormy night.

Well, after I left thee and Sarah at Earlham, I went on to the depot, and the Chicago train arrived in about half an hour, so that we started a little after 9. Arrived at Camden at half past 10. Nathan came pretty soon with the spring wagon, and we got home near 1 o'clock.

Well, I thought it paid pretty well to visit Earlham and have no cause to regret it. I was satisfied in attending Meeting. The comely order and decorum of the girls was beautiful and becoming their sex, especially on these solemn occasions. If the boys could be encouraged to imitate the same exemplary order with the girls, your Meetings would be seasons of favor with Him who still deigns to be with his devoted worshippers wherever they meet.

Sampson and Sara Ann Reeves are here on a visit from Grant Co, Indiana. Perhaps thee remembers them. They stayed with us last night and are interesting visitors. They have a little girl about as large as Betty's little girl, and is as full of life and monkeyshines as any little girl can well be. Her name is Cyrena Ann. They came on the cars. Got in here last Fifth Day and will probably start for home this day week

Mary H. [nee Haisley] Brown, Jos. Wife, is quite sick and has been for several days. She has the smallpox without doubt and is said to be very bad with it. Is some better today. The doctors say that today would be probably the turning point; as she was some easier, we hope she may recover again. Another day or two will decide. Jos. had something of the same, but it was light, and there was no mistrust of its being the smallpox till Mary was taken down, and Dr. Dunham being called in, he pronounced it at once smallpox. There has no one taken it but Mary, even in Jos. family. It is thought that it hardly will spread any further than in their family. Jos. don't know any chance of getting it or catching it, as is said. He had been to Hamilton at Market [illegible] some but never heard anything about it till he was taken down sick, or Mary was taken sick. However, we hope it will spread no further.

We were expecting a letter from thee today, but none had come this evening.

I may be at Eaton tomorrow. If I should go, I shall probably mail this there.

So nothing further at present. We remain affectionately, thy well-wishing Parents,

*Jos. & Mary Maddock*

As I was up last week and told all the news I could think of, I shall be brief for the present. Please write weekly as usual. We would like to hear how thee is getting along with thy cold hoarseness, etc.

Well, I am at Eaton Fourth Day P.M. We are still well as usual. We are up here about Grandfather's will. Mary Brown was some better this morning. It was good sleighing up here. I will mail this letter here. Nothing further. I close and remain thy well-wishing Parent,

*Jos. Maddock*

## Earlham College, 1st Mo 15th 1865

Dearest Parents,

Once more the time has rolled around to seat myself to write home. This is First Day afternoon and a beautiful one it is. Only it is rather too cold to be pleasant. I have not been out for several days as I had some cold and did not want any more, so I have stayed pretty close the last few days.

I expect you are getting uneasy about me, as Father said in his letter that you expected a letter from me last Third or Fourth Day, so I suppose the week passed away without receiving any as I did not write any. Well, I must give an excuse I suppose for not writing.

I told Father that I would not write till he wrote, which he said he would do the first of last week. So I keep putting it off until I thought I could do no better than to sit down and write and be done with it.

Father knows I had pretty smart cold when he was here. Before that I had had a very bad cold and hoarseness. But I got more cold some way and felt rather unwell that day. I recited in my classes, but it was as much as I could do. But I kept along pretty well till Seventh Day evening. I felt quite sick, so I did not eat anything, but felt better towards Lecture time. I went to Lecture but I did not feel very good. Went to bed at the usual hour feeling pretty bad. About three o'clock I was sick as I have ever been lately at my stomach. Next morning I arose, feeling some better than I did the evening before, but not very well. Ate nothing. Nearly scripture time I was taken with such pain in my stomach the worst I believe I ever had in my life. The doctor said my blood was out of order, he thought, was the cause of it. I took some medicine for it and felt some better toward Meeting time, but the nurse would not let me go to Meeting for fear I would be taken again. It was the first Meeting I had missed. I did not feel much like writing so I did not and have not had time since until now, so I hope you will excuse me this time, and I will promise to do better in the future and not be so negligent.

Sallie is enjoying herself fine. And she is as lively and mischievous as she can be. I can hardly write for her, she is pestering me so. I should feel very lonely and homesick without her. We are like sisters since we came here. She has been so kind to me when I am sick.

The health of the students is pretty good with some exception of cold and sore throat among some of them. Our school is progressing finely. I am getting along in my studies pretty well and well-satisfied.

But alas, our school is fast towards a close. Then we will have to separate, some of us probably never to meet again in this world. We have become much attached to each other.

Well, I have written one letter today and my hand feels somewhat tired. I wrote to Elenora and commenced one to Cousin Hannah but did not finish it, but think I will tonight.

I am glad Father had such a good visit up here. How I wish Mother could be here at Meeting and see what she thinks of it.

Well, it is nearly suppertime and I must be brief and go get ready for supper. Just listen—there goes the old bell. I am getting tired of hearing the bells ring so much.

I was sorry to hear of Mary Brown's sickness. Hope it will spread no further. Does Jane Jones preach as long as ever? There goes the bell for Collection, so I will have to quit for the present.

Well, Reading is over. Timothy Harrison of Richmond read for us tonight. Oh, Mother, I had like to forgot to tell thee I wore my new dress today for the first time. The girls say that they never saw as nice goods. Sallie says she expects to have one like it. It fits pretty well, only that tuck will have to come out. I like it very well. It is pretty delaine I think.

Well, I must close as my time is about up. Hoping this may find you and relations well. Please write as soon as you get this. Write every week and I will do the same. I will try to do better after this. So no more, but remain as ever your affectionate daughter

Mattie

Tell Ella to answer my letter and Jennie and Mattie Reynolds. Write and tell me sure when Maria is coming up so I will know when to look for her. I have got my album nearly filled. Oh, how glad I am, Mother, because thee put uncles and aunts in. I wish thee had sent yours. Please do not forget to send them by Maria. Now don't forget it. I had a nice photograph given to me the other day. I received your kind letter last Fourth Day, the same day it was mailed. Quick coming. I and Sallie are going to get our pictures when we go to town. So no more. As ever yours,

Mattie

## Earlham College, 1st Mo 21st, 1865

Dearest Parents

Once again I seat myself to the well-known task of letter writing.

In the first place, I can inform you that I am enjoying pretty good health. Hoping that when these few scattered lines reach their destined spot, they may find you and the rest of relations and friends well.

This is Seventh Day afternoon, and a dreary and rainy one it is. So it makes a body feel homesick and lonesome, or at least, it has made me feel so. I had nothing particular to be at, so to pass the time off, I thought I could not put it to any better use than to sit down and write my thoughts home. This afternoon my thoughts have been wafted back, as it were, on the gentle breezes of morning to the many happy days and hours I spent with my friends whilst at home. But I hope that the day is not far distant when I may be permitted to return to my dear old home I have left for a short season.

Often have I looked back to the many days I have spent that are past and gone, I have been made to feel very thankful since I have been here, towards you, my dear parents, for sending me here and all the privileges and blessings you have bestowed upon me, a disobedient daughter as I have often been. I have often thought of the privilege you had in your younger days to what I now enjoy & feel very thankful to you for your blessings to me. I want you to pray for me that I may not be led away by the sinful vices of this world, but that I may be kept in the right way so that when the summons come for me to leave this troubled scene on earth, that I may be prepared to enter one of those mansions prepared for all those that love and serve Him here on earth. To which so many loved ones that have gone before to that happy land from whence no traveler has ever yet returned.

To something else. I am getting along fine in my studies. Examination is going off now; it commenced yesterday. I was examined in two of my studies yesterday: Geography and Spelling. But do not know what per cent I will get, as I have not received my papers yet. But I think I will get better per cent than I have ever got yet. But I may be mistaken. Only I will wait till I get them. I get along fine in Arithmetic now.

Sallie is all right, only today she has the headache right bad and is right sick this evening. There were another dispatch the other day for some of the students, for Miles and Mary Trueblood that live at Raysville. But what for, I do not know.

The mail just come, but nothing for me. Oh dear! I looked for one from home and from somewhere else besides but was disappointed in receiving any. Well, just to listen. There goes the bell for Collection for supper, so I must quit till after supper.

Supper is over and I feel as gay ad happy as the next one, better believe. But poor Sallie, she is sick and did not go down to supper. She is in the parlor on the sofa; she says she don't feel any better. I feel sorry for her.

Well, Father, I have got my shoe at last, but I never got it till last week.

William Morgan is going to lecture for us tonight and a good lecture I expect it will be, for they say he is so good.

Well, I have about run out of news I guess, so I had better quit, I guess, as I fear what I have written will fail to interest you. So I will dry up my nonsense.

I remain as ever your loving daughter,

Write soon as you get this and tell all the news, as anything from home is always a welcomed visitor by me. I am anxious to hear from home since Aunt was up and told us about the smallpox and of Mary H. Brown situation, which must be a very bad one indeed. I expect it creates a good deal of excitement, does it now. So no more, but remain as ever, your daughter

*Mattie*

There goes the bell for lecture.

*Mattie and Sallie*

[*In pencil*]

*P.S. First Day afternoon the 22nd.* I am well and happy, but Sallie is right sick. She was right sick last night and had very high fever. Did not rest very well but is some better this afternoon.

I guess I will have to have some more money. I expect you think I don't do anything but spend money. I have not got my shoes, yet but will next week. There was a girl got a pair yesterday and give five dollars,[2] she said. They were the cheapest she could find that were good. I have had to get several notions,[3] and I want to get my picture when I go to town. So I haven't much change, only the $5 bill thee gave me when thee was up. It will take it every bit to get my shoes. Send it by Cousin Wil, please. Well, I will close by requesting you to write soon. As ever your daughter,

*Martha Ann Maddock*

Sallie is better this evening. Mother, please send me some white thread to knit a collar. 36, 40, or 50. That is all, I guess.

*Mattie*

## West Elkton, 1st Mo 22nd 1865

Often Remembered Martha Ann,

We again take up the pen to address thee. We are all pretty well with the exception of colds, etc. The rest of connections and friends are mostly well. Our beloved and much-respected Friend, Mary Brown, died of that awful disease the smallpox on Third Day evening last. It was one of the most trying scenes that we ever witnessed amongst us. No one visited her in the time of the last sickness but Arnuel and Lydia Lane. On account of

2. Five dollars in 1865 was equivalent to $98.48 in 2025.

3. "Notions" refers to sewing implements and accessories like needles, thread, buttons, etc.

the fear of taking the disease no one went near, and none but Dr. Weinland, A. Lane, and W. Coggeshall and Jos. Brown [her husband] of men friends attended the funeral. Mary Weinland, Aunt Mary in Town & Angelina Harris, were several of the women that attended at the grave. The Doctors advised strongly against anyone attending. The interment took place a Fourth Day P.M. We did not hear of her death until late that evening. It was one of the most trying and solemn scenes that ever transpired amongst us. That one so much respected and esteemed as a sister beloved, that we could not be privileged to pay the common and last Christian respect to her here on earth, but so it was, and so it had to be. Yet no doubt the relatives and friends have the consoling evidence that the dear departed one was permitted to enter one of those mansions prepared for the righteous, where the sickness ceases from troubling and the weary are at rest with the dear Redeemer.

We were at Meeting today and dear Mary Roberts alluded to our late beloved friend, Mary, who but a short time since was permitted to assemble with us, but now was no more. It was a solemn and good Meeting in which many hearts could respond to the language "Be ye also ready as ye know not the time when the Son of Man cometh." Martha Ann Taylor appeared in supplication and Jane spoke some near the close. Many felt for the beloved relatives and family, and many tears of sympathy and condolence were shed in the Meeting for the bereaved ones. After which the Meeting closed under feeling, better felt, we trust, than expressed.

The family are still quite sick, some of them, but not thought to be dangerous Jos. mother [Mary nee Randall Brown] is quite bad with the disease and not able to be up. The children have not been so bad. We hope they all will now be better and that the disease will spread no further. They have got a colored woman to come and stay with them from down near Germantown. We hope they will be taken care of better than they were in time of Mary's sickness.

We have had quite winter weather for the past week. Yesterday it commenced thawing and has been getting warmer, so that the snow is fast melting away, though there is some little appearance of its freezing up again this evening. It has been fine sleighing for more than a week past. Many went out in their sleighs at Meeting today. We were out at Delilah Stubbs [wife of William Stubbs] last Sixth Day on a visit; we went in the sled and it was fine going. When I was up at Eaton, we broke the sled but got home, and it was several days before we got it mended again.

We were also last Sixth Day was a week at Sam'l Jones on a visit, and last First Day at Marmaduke's. Elizabeth is quite poorly this winter. Not out much.

We butchered our meat hog last Second Day. Ann helped mother some. And Nathan and I went to Hamilton a Third Day with 2 hogs to market. We started about 4 o'clock and had a pretty cold trip. We got a small stove at Hamilton for the parlor and have got it fixed up so that it warms up the room in a short time to what a fire in the chimney does.

We received thy letter last week the next day after it was mailed. Aunt Patsy going up to Earlham, we did not think it worthwhile to write, as she could tell more than we could if we should a written at that time.

Luther Jenkins is still confined at home with a relapse of the fever he had some time ago. He has been up about the house several times but took a relapse and is very poorly at this time. Some think he will soon not be any better. Old Dr. Alexander is attending on him. One or two of the girls is quite sick with the typhoid fever at this time, it is said.

Mahlon Denney's wife is quite poorly and very much confined to her room. Some think she will hardly likely live longer than spring.

Ira Stubbs is quite confined to his room. Has, it is thought, the typhoid fever. Has not been in the store for several days. So that it seems there is considerable complaint amongst us.

Wm J. Kenworthy's school has not been so large for the last week or two as it was some time ago on account of sickness. There is still quite a good school, some 30 or 35 in attendance.

J.L. Stubbs' school is doing very well, not so large as some others, but he is getting along very satisfactory, we think, with it.

As thy time, we understand from Aunt Patsy, will from this time until the close of the school be very much taken up in thy studies and in reviewing them, that probably we must not look for a communication every week from thee. She says she thinks the school is getting along much better than it has for some two or three years past. And we hope it is. I thought when I was up there it certainly was a great chance to acquire a good education, both in literary learning as well as religious instructions in scriptures, etc.

Well, it is now after night, and we take up the pen to finish up our letter. We received a letter from Uncle Henry in Iowa about a week ago stating they were all pretty well. As well as Uncle Lands. They said it was pretty cold weather in Iowa.

As our sheet is fast filling up, we must close. We often think of thee since thee left us to sojourn at Earlham for the purpose of acquiring a competent share of school education and other branches of learning connected with it, and desire thy preservation in the path of self-denial, that in pursuit thou mayest be kept out of unprofitable company, which we hope is the case, as I was favorably impressed when I was privileged to mingle with you in attending the Meeting and seeing the beautiful order and decorum that was conducted in the large family at Earlham. That all was working well, and that nothing but a good feeling toward each other prevailed, and that thee, in days yet to come, would have to look back to the many privileges enjoyed amongst the many pupils, as well as Teachers, interested in the acquiring of a religious and guarded education at Earlham.

We remain as ever, thy well-wishing parents,

Jos. & Mary Maddock

Please write as often as thee conveniently can, at least every two weeks.

*Second Day morning, 1st Mo 23*

We are all pretty well. There was quite a snow fell last night. Is still snowing.

Jos. & Esther talk of moving from this locale, perhaps day-after-tomorrow. Will move some things today and tomorrow.

## West Elkton, First Day evening, 1st Mo 29th 1865

Beloved Martha Ann,

We again sit down this evening to write thee a few lines. We are all pretty well except colds. The rest of connections, friends & neighbors, all middling well. Some exceptions of cold, etc. Jos. Browns are getting along pretty well, so that they are nearly well. The two youngest children did not have the smallpox, or if they had it was very light. and it has not spread any, and it will not likely spread any further.

It has been very cold the past week so that we have done but little as to work, only got wood, sit by fire, and burn up wood. It has been fine sleighing. We were not out much till yesterday and today.

Last Fifth Day was Monthly Meeting, a very cold day and meeting small. A committee was appointed to visit the families, also some that are in the practice of attending our meetings, if way should open for it. The committee met yesterday morning at Jehu Kenworthy's, a very cold morning, indeed it was, but proceeded on visiting Jones Elihu Roberts and took dinner at S. Roberts. And after a sitting with them, we were at L. Connoroes, Walter Roberts about to visit. It was about 10 o'clock before we started. All satisfactory [*illegible*] we trust to all, both visitors and visited. The committee are Jane Jones, Delilah Stubbs, Martha Kenworthy, Martha Ann Taylor & Mother [i.e., Mary Maddock] of women friends. Elisha Stubbs, Jesse Kenworthy & myself of men friends & of us when together. We were at Lorenzo Stubbs & Wm Reynolds this P.M. Won't, it is likely, visit any more for a few days.

A letter was received a few days ago that Hannah Green was very sick at Ridge Farm, Illinois. Marmaduke & her with their children had started to come here to see their relatives and friends. They came to Marmaduke's brother Jacob's, near Ridge Farm to visit them on the way. Hannah was taken down whilst there with the typhoid fever, and they wrote here that she was very bad and but little or no hopes of her recovery. Thomas Taylor started out there last Fourth Day evening. And last evening Thomas & Marmaduke with the children came back, informing that Hannah was no more. We did not learn when she died, but her corpse was sent by express to Camden. Last evening, we understand, when they got to Camden, the corpse had not arrived which was a sad disappointment to them. It may be a day or two before it arrives. There is likely some mistake or neglect on the part of the Express Agent, or it would a been here when they arrived.

We understand from letter received from Jacob Green since Thomas started, that her remains would be brought in here for burial, and it will take place it is likely in a day or two. It is very trying on her parents, as they anticipated meeting their only daughter once more. But it seems it was not to be so in this troublesome world by an All-wise Providence, but her relatives and friends have the consoling belief that the dear departed one has entered one of those mansions prepared for the righteous in the realm of everlasting bliss.

Meeting today middling large, people out mostly in sleighs. Jane spoke considerable, though not too lengthy, as at some other times. Delilah & Elisha came home with us from Meeting. After dinner, we went over to L.S. & W. R.[4] as stated above.

We received thy letter of last First Day a Fifth Day after Meeting. Were sorry to hear of the misfortune of thee spraining thy ankle. Hope it will get well soon.

As our sheet is nearly full, we must close and remain as ever, thy well-wishing Parents,

Jos. & Mary Maddock

*1st Mo 30th*

All well. I send this by N. Hornaday to some office on Railroad. I enclose $2.00 U.S. No.71708, Aug 1st 1862.[5]

Please write soon whether thee gets this bill.

## Earlham College, 1st Mo 29th 1865

Dearest Parents,

Once again I seat myself for the purpose of writing home again. I have just eaten my dinner and been out on the walk. It is as slick as glass, so we can hardly walk along. I was out this morning and the girl that was with me, Ellen Wright, fell down twice, and a jolly time we had indeed.

Sallie is writing, too; so are several others. We have some splendid times this winter. It is slick as it can be on the walk. It is nice skating now. The boys have five times. They gave them all leave to go to the river yesterday to skate, and a splendid time they had, which was quite a treat. Well, I have not much time write, so I will have to be brief.

I don't know as I have much news to communicate this time, as news is rather scarce.

I wrote a long letter to Samuel and Ella today, so you will hear all the news anyhow. I also wrote a long letter, nearly two sheets full, to Cousin Hannah Stubbs. Oh, how glad I would be to get a letter from her.

Sallie is as full of mischief as she can be. I can hardly write for her [bothering me]. She says tell the folks she is all right and as gay as ever. I am getting along very well in my studies.

4. Lorenzo Stubbs and William Reynolds.

5. Serial number and date of "greenback" two dollar bill.

I received your very kind letter last Third Day and was glad indeed to get a letter from home. But ere I tore the seal to peruse its contents, quite a gloom was cast over our minds in reading of the distressing death of our friend Mary Brown. What an affecting sense indeed. Well, a touching scene, it must have been, at her burial.

Well, the bell is ringing for Collection so I must quit. I don't believe anyone has as hard times to write as I do, for there is sure something to hinder me.

*Third Day evening the 31st*

Dear parents,

As I did not get to finish my letter the other day, I now seat myself for the purpose of finishing it. I received your very welcomed letter of the 29th this evening and was very glad to hear that the smallpox had spread no further, and that Joseph Brown's more nearly well. You said that you were sorry to hear I had sprained my ankle. I can inform you it is about well. But I never had my ankle to hurt me so in my life. I could hardly walk for a few days, but it is well now.

Father, I think thee and Mother put in the time visiting since I left, but I suppose you don't have much to do this cold weather. I was sorry to hear of Hannah Green's death. It must go hard with her father and mother for their only daughter to be taken off so far from home. Thee said thee wanted to know if that bill arrived safe. Well, it came all safe.

I have the promise to go to town Seventh Day if it is a nice day. I am still getting very well in my studies. Well, the school is fast drawing towards a close.

One thing I must tell you is that the Mumps is in school. Teacher Calvin Pierson has had them right bad, only able to be down. Two of the girls has them now. One is right bad with them. I suppose I stand a chance for them. Oh, what shall I do? Sallie says tell you and the rest she is as gay and happy as a bird. Well, I must quit for it is nearly study hour. Yes, there goes the bell, so I must quit till after study hour. Study hour is over, and I feel rather tired studying, so I shall not try to write much more. I am pretty well. So no more at present, but remain as ever, your affectionate cousin [*sic*],

Mattie, daughter

There was a dispatch this evening came for one of my classmates, Curtis Goss of Gosport, Indiana. It seems there is hardly a day or week passes without a dispatch or bad news. This is 3 dispatches for him since he has been here. He has a hard time. I pity him. Sallie says tell the folks she is still a kicking and breathing. Well, I must close. Excuse all mistakes and bad writing as I have written in a hurry like common. Write soon for you have more time than I have. I will write as often as convenient.

Your well-wishing daughter

# February 1865

## Earlham College, 2nd Mo 5th 1865

Dearest Parents,

First Day afternoon. I seat myself this beautiful afternoon to drop a few scattered lines home. Sallie is writing home too. I don't know as I have much news that will interest you, but thought I would scratch a few lines anyhow. News is scarce out here. I won't have any time through the week as we are very busy in our studies. We are reviewing now for the examination at the close.

Well, Mother, thee is coming out at the close is thee? When will thee come? What day?

You need not be surprised if you hear in the next letter that I have got the mumps. They are spreading. There is one girl has them right bad. Teacher Calvin is nearly well. He has had a pretty hard time of it.

I have got the headache some today and do not feel very well, but you need not be uneasy. I wish I was at home, but it will not be long till it is out, and then I will be glad to return home to join the family circle around the old familiar fireside. Tell Nathan I often think of him and wonder if he ever thinks of me. I expect it would please him if he could see near 100 boys out playing foot ball of an evening. It is fun, I think. The girls often stand on their walk and look at them. Cousin Maria has not been to see me yet. I suppose she is waiting till the close. Wish she would come before then. I believe I will write her a note and tell her to come.

Father, I have forgotten whether I told thee in my other letter about that 2 $ bill thee sent me. If not, I will say it came all safe and sound and was acceptably received, thee may be sure.

There was another dispatch last Sixth Day came for one of my schoolmates. It seems there is hardly a week passes, there was three last week. It seems to me that there a good deal of sickness prevails in the country round about. For I think there must have been a good deal at home since I was home last. But I was glad to hear by the last letter that friends and relations were pretty well.

Have not been to town yet but will go this week if the weather is fit. Mother, tell Elenora I want her to answer my letter, as I would like to get a letter from her or anyone else, so it is from home. Sallie has got her letter done to Aunt, and here I am scratching away. If paper is scarce down with you, it is here too. For it is the highest up here. Father takes the least he can find, I believe, so I will do the same this time as I have not much to write. There goes the supper bell, so I must quit till after supper. Supper is over and a jolly time it was. Nearly all the scholars will have to report for laughing at the table. Father knows how they laughed the evening he was here.

There the bell is ringing for Collection for Reading, so I suppose I must go for a short time. Reading is over and a interesting time it was. Governor Jay read for us. Well, I must close for I don't feel like writing any more. My head aches and one side of my face is swelled, so you can guess what the matter is. As ever your affectionate daughter,

*Mattie*

## West Elkton, 2nd Mo. 5th 1865

Loving Daughter, Martha Ann,

We take up the pen again to address thee this evening. We are all enjoying pretty good health, only some colds. The rest of connections and friends are all pretty well, as far as we know. With some exceptions of colds. They are all getting along pretty well at Jos. Browns, we understand. We here know of no further spreading of the smallpox. Hope it will not spread any further. They have not been out from home any yet, or at least, not at Meeting.

The funeral of Hannah Green took place last Third Day. The remains did not arrive till a Second Day evening. Lewis Taylor went up on the morning train and found them at

Richmond, and they had laid there since Seventh Day night. Met at the house at 2 o'clock. A very large company attended, as large as we ever have seen. We then proceeded to the graveyard and after interment, a large and solemn Meeting was held. People mostly coming in. Women's apartment[1] was about full; men's nearly so. It was a satisfactory and solemn season. Jane appeared in supplication and afterwards spoke at some length. The Meeting held over an hour, then concluded under a very solemn feeling near 4 o'clock.

The committee have not been out on their visit since last First Day on account of the funeral taking place the first of the week. And since then Jane and her children have been quite unwell, so that she could not leave very well, so that we shall not, it is likely now, turn out until the last of the week. We were at Meeting today. It was rather small for First Day. But a considerable number were in attendance. Jane not being present on account of one their children being unwell. Mary [Roberts] spoke some, perhaps near half an hour. Very impressively too. to the young people, in particular. We trust it was a time of favor; hope it will be remembered.

We are writing after night, a very pleasant evening indeed. Will freeze pretty hard tonight. We have been alone this P.M., reading, etc. Ring and Puss are lying very composed before the fire, as it is cool out tonight.

Eli Kenworthy has returned home from his trip or sojourn down south. He is quite sick since his return, was not up this morning before they started to Meeting, it is said.

We received thy letter mailed last Fourth Day. We did not take it out till Sixth Day as we were not looking for one this week as none had come a Third or Fourth Day. We were glad to hear that thee had got well of the sprain. We thought if thee had not got any shoes, perhaps if thee could do without them till school closes, thee had better not get any as they are so much higher in Richmond than here. We thought of sending thee a pair if William had a went up to Earlham. We can get them here for $2.75 to $3.50, pretty good shoes. But if thee has got some, it is all right. There will be but little or no passing now till school closes. It is nearly bedtime, and our half sheet is nearly full. We close and remain as ever, thy well-wishing parents,

*Jos. & Mary Maddock*

1. Quaker meetinghouses could be separated by a sliding partition to accommodate women's business meeting on one side and men's on the other. These separate sections or compartments were referred to as "apartments." The partition was removed during Meeting for Worship.

[*on a scrap of paper, written in pencil*]

*Third Day evening, 2nd mo 7th*

All well as usual. We omitted to mail our letter yesterday, have just now thine of date last First Day [i.e. her letter dated last Sunday]. Sorry to learn of the mumps spreading in the school. Hope they will not spread much. If thee should take them endeavor to be as patient as thee can. They are not dangerous but are very tedious sometimes. Hope thee will get along pretty well, as they seem to care for all very diligently. I expected to have gone to Eaton today and mailed this, but as it is very cold this P.M. I shall mail it here. Please write as usual. From thy well-wishing father,

Jos. Maddock

We have been in house pretty much all day. Made some spils [*sic*] and think of making some molasses when sugar making begins.

## Earlham College, 2nd Mo 12th 1865

Dear Parents,

This beautiful First Day afternoon finds me seated in the quiet schoolroom of Earlham to write a few lines home in reply to your very welcome letter which I received a Sixth Day evening just before supper. One of the girls came down in the basement wanting to know who wanted a letter, and I, of course, wanted one, and lo behold, there were two rolled out for me, one from home. So the next thing I done was to tear their seals and peruse the contents. I was very glad to hear from home as it had been near two weeks since I last heard. Glad to hear that connections and friends were well, and that there were no more cases of smallpox.

Paper must be precious and scarce, is it not? For when Father does write, he just picks up some scrap he comes across and writes it full and calls it a sheet. He said Ring and Puss were lying very composed by the fire. I expect they help to fill up my place, do they not, this winter during my sojourn at Earlham. Oh, just to think in 3 more short weeks our school will close, and then we that met as strangers will separate as dear schoolmates. Some of us probably never to meet again in this troubled world.

Before I forget it, I must tell you that I went to town yesterday. Well, I suppose you will ask the question what did I get. I got a pair of shoes, very good ones, the best ones I have had lately.

But you will think they ought to be good when I tell you how much they cost: they only cost $4.25[2]. I like them very well. I needed a pair pretty bad, at examination especially. So I thought I had better get them so I could have them at the close of school. It's all right, is it, for me to get them? And I got a very good picture. All the girls say they think it is such a good one. The Governess wants it, but I guess I will keep it and let Mother have it if she wants it, as it is a good one. And I bought a nice one. David H. Bennett's for .25. They have any amount of them to sell at a quarter a piece. That was all besides a few other notions. It was a beautiful day, and a good time I had indeed. There was good many of the students went—girls and boys. There were good many got their pictures taken too. Just let me tell you. I heard the doorbell ring and said I wished that was for me, so sure enough, the Superintendent come and called me in the parlor. and who do you think it was? You may guess.

I received three letters last week, which is the most I have ever got since I have been here. One from home, and one from Cousin Mary Lib, and the other from Cousin Amanda Stubbs dated 2nd Mo 5th. She wrote a sheet full stating that they were all enjoying pretty good health and that she was somewhat surprised to hear I was here going to school. She said she had also been going to school, but the school was broke up by the man[3] going to war. She also said that Joseph was going to start the next and that seemed pretty hard to see him go. She said she had a splendid time keeping house while Uncle and Aunt were gone to Ohio.

Sallie says tell you to please give us a call in your visiting families. I was sorry to hear that Eli Kenworthy was back from his trip down south and was quite sick. Hope it will prove nothing serious. Well, as I am out of news, and my letter is nearly full, I will lean towards a close as I want to write to Cousin Amanda. So no more, but remain as ever your daughter,

*Mattie*

P.S. Tell Cousin Libby I will answer her letter pretty soon but have not time now. I saw Mattie Pray this morning and had a nice talk with her. She is going to graduate next summer. Said they were all well, and she sends her love to Aunt Anna Stubbs. She supplicated today in Meeting and Zaccheus Test and teacher

2. $4.25 in 1865 was equivalent to $83.71 in 2025.

3. i.e., The teacher left to go to the war. Amanda says her eighteen-year-old brother, Joseph Stubbs, was next to go to war.

Joseph Moore spoke some to the students. I think we have such good Meetings. Well, I will have to quit as it is nearly supper time. Mother, I would be glad to get another from thee as the other one thee wrote done me so much good. Now Mother, write again before thee comes up for the examination. Tell Elena I will write her another letter if she don't answer mine pretty soon. I will quit by requesting you to write soon, and often think of me at night and pray for me that I may not be led away from the true faith of virtue. Your daughter,

*Martha Ann*

## West Elkton, 2nd Mo. 14th 1865

Loving Daughter, Martha Ann,

We take up the pen to address thee as usual. We are all in pretty good health, some colds amongst us. The rest of connections and friends only middling well. Uncle John Stubbs[4] is and has been quite unwell the last few days. Has been complaining with cold for the last two weeks, and has got down nearly bedfast. Has something like a return of his old complaint (Dispepsia). Was taken last week with a pleurisy pain, some neuralgia affliction. Is a little better this morning, though it seems like he might have a tedious time, and is indeed quite poorly, though perhaps not dangerously bad. Has been up about half the time through the day. Rests middling well at night. The Doctor has visited two or three times. Little Emma Talbert is quite unwell with something of a white swelling of a scrofulous nature. She has been confined to her bed for two weeks past. There is considerable of complaint of colds in the last week. Some quite unwell. Hetzler's children have been quite sick but are some better now. Minerva Jenkins is no more. She died a week ago this evening. She was taken very bad, continued so long as she lived. Anna & Luther are getting better, they think they will get well again as they seem to be mending. They have had a tedious time. Luther has been sick for more than three months. They have old Dr. Alexander attending on them, and of course, it may be a tedious time with them.

4. John Maddock Stubbs, brother of Mary Maddock (Joseph's wife and Mattie's mother).

Jabez and Valerie Kenworthy have moved down here. Are at his mother's. Eli Kenworthy has got about well again and was at Meeting last First Day.

Were at Meeting a First Day, rather small. Mary R. [Roberts] or Jane [Jones] were not out.[5] Of course not much communication. Martha Ann T. [Taylor] spoke some. Jane was out last Fifth Day, spoke at considerable length, and Meeting held longer than usual for a weekday Meeting. Perhaps the scholars thought so. The committee[6] were out at two or three places a First Day P.M. Don't know when we will be out again as some are complaining of colds, etc.

It has been very cold for two or three days past, so that we have done but little out-of-doors. We were out some yesterday and today cutting wood. It seems like being pleasant this P.M., thawing some. As we having nothing very interesting to write, we shall close for the present. And remain thy well-wishing parents,

Jos & Mary Maddock

Mother thinks of being out at the close and examination of the school if nothing interferes. Perhaps she will write further about it next week.

*P.M. At town.* Just read thy letter of last First Day. We suppose thee has not got the mumps or forgot to say any anything about it. I have just received [a letter] from West Creek from Sylvanus stating that him and wife would be here in about 4 weeks from the time he wrote, the 6th of this mo. They were well and he said his father and mother were gone to Laban Haworth's. Please write as usual next week. As ever thy well-wishing father,

Jos Maddock

## West Elkton, Fifth Day morning, 6 o'clock, 2nd Mo. 16th 1865

Beloved daughter Martha Ann, we have the sorrowful tiding to inform thee of the very sudden death of Uncle John Stubbs who died about two hours ago. He has been complaining of

5. i.e., were not there at Meeting.

6. The Elk Monthly Meeting visitation committee previously mentioned by Joseph, on which he and Mary served.

cold for about two weeks, but we did not think him so dangerous until yesterday morning. Since then he has been very bad. Seemed to suffer much to his last. His lungs were very much diseased, which caused his sudden death.

We would like for thee to come home if thee can. Any how at all, come. Wm. Blanchard is going up on this morning train to let T. Commons know, and thee may come with him on tomorrow's morning train, as the funeral will not take place until tomorrow P.M. Meet at the house at perhaps 2 o'clock. Mother thinks thee had better bring thy carpet sack full of clothes so that thee will not have so many to bring home when the school closes. We expect for thee to return a Second Day and attend the close. From thy father

*Jos. Maddock*

We wrote pretty full about Uncle John being quite unwell a Second Day, but perhaps thee will not get it tomorrow. John [Ferrell Stubbs] went out for Maria yesterday P.M. They will return this morning. It will indeed be sad news when they get to see their dear father a lifeless corpse.

## Earlham College, 2nd Mo 21st 1865

Dear Father,

I seat myself in haste to pen a few lines home to let you know how I am and how I got out from the depot. You need not be surprised when I tell you that I walked out. When I arrived at Richmond, I saw no one and begin to think what I would do. I waited nearly a hour and no one came. So I thought I would try it anyhow. Aunt Patsy sent her bonnet out by me to Sara Cadwallader, so of course, I went there first and left it there, and concluded to try walking the rest of the way out here. So I came to Main Street and started in full speed for College. I felt rather tired then, as I had been waiting so long, so I took it easy, walked slow.

I arrived here about noon I expect, for they were eating dinner when I got here. So I expect you will think that I missed my dinner, but I did not. I got it after all and felt like eating too, better believe, after walking so far. I felt pretty tired and I did not feel much like studying all the afternoon but am well and happy today.

The Superintendent had been there but was gone I suppose, for he did not know certain that I would come yesterday. This is beautiful weather. Indeed I think it seems like Indian Summer. It is so pleasant to go out and breathe the fresh air after being in the house all day studying. I wonder how Father is by this time; no worse, I trust.

Maria White, one of my schoolmates, had the mumps when I went home. Hettie Goss also has them. I guess they will keep them here till the close. There is another girl taking them, they say. I suppose it will be my turn next, think it won't.

I received a letter today from Albert, dated the 12th and mailed the 18th of this month, stating that there were all pretty well except the baby which had a very sore mouth. He also said that Sylvanus, Nancy, and he was coming in to *Old Preble* in three or four weeks. Maria White, (Thomas White's daughter that lives in Hendricks County not very far from here) that I told you about at first. She has the typhoid fever now, very bad indeed, and has been ever since about 10 o'clock last night. Not likely last till morning. In, out of her head. She did not know her father and mother when they come. Her sister is also here. Well, I have had a ramble this evening and feel much better.

We can hear Maria scream all over the house nearly. She suffers very much indeed. She is worse now they say. Oh, does not it seem bad?

The school is dismissed on Fourth Day, so wait till Fifth Day morning or come Fourth Day night. I would rather wait till Fifth Day as the scholars are nearly all going then, so I and Sallie would like to go when the rest does. But any way you say.

They don't think Maria will last many hours as she is growing worse very fast.

Well, I guess I have written all that will interest you, and more too, I presume, so I will close by requesting you to write and tell how Father is.

I remain as ever your daughter,

*Martha Ann*

(Excuse me for writing with a lead pencil.) Mother, please bring me a collar when thee comes. Don't forget it, please. That is all. I want to come home worse than I did before. So no more at present.

*Martha A*

## West Elkton, 2nd Mo 22nd 1865

Martha Ann, we take up the pen to address a few lines to thee. We are about as we were when thee left us a Second Day morning. Only I feel some better. I have been up yesterday and today pretty much all the time. Was out yesterday three times through the day, to the stable and about the yard some. It was a fine day to be out. This morning it is quite dull out and rained some the latter part of the night and this morning, but now about 11 o'clock, it seems like that it may break away and be pleasant this P.M. I have not rested very well the two last nights. Through the night don't seem to suffer any, only in my leg below my knee. It pains me pretty smartly at times when I lay down, or it has sometimes when I walk out pained me for a little while. I expect I shall have a tedious time of getting entirely well again.

Nothing further. I remain thy well-wishing Father,

*Jos. Maddock*

Mother thinks of coming out to Earlham next week, if I got no worse and am still getting better. And will come a Second Day morning. If she should not come, will likely send word by Bennetts' girls or some others that may go up.

*Jos. Maddock*

Still about as I was this morning. About 2 o clock P.M. Have not laid down today. Only a few minutes this morning.

# Appendix A: Traveling Quaker Ministers Mentioned in Joseph Maddock's Diary

All Joseph Maddock's life (1811–1889), the Quaker meetings he attended were "unprogrammed," i.e., Friends met in silence unless someone was powerfully moved to speak out of the silence. An individual whose gift for vocal ministry was apparent, was recognized, noted, and "recorded" as a Minister of the Gospel by their Meeting. None of them were paid.

Between 1827 and 1883, eight ministers were recorded by Elk Monthly Meeting: Jonathan Osbun, Martha Wooten, Enos G. Pray, Mary Roberts, Elwood Osbun, Martha A. Taylor, Rachel H. Maddock, and Carrie Taylor.

The first paid minister at Elk Monthly Meeting was Hiram S. Wollem, who was hired in 1898, nine years after Joseph Maddock died.

In his diary, Joseph Maddock faithfully records the names of traveling ministers, including some who were, or who became, quite well-known, that he heard speak at Orthodox Quaker meetings including Elk Monthly Meeting (EMM), Westfield Quarterly Meeting (WQM), General Meeting for Worship (GMW), and Indiana Yearly Meeting (IYM). He often refers to these ministers as "our Friend (name) . . ." and gives a brief assessment of their ministry in his diary entry.

| DIARY YEAR | MEETING | TRAVELING or VISITING MINISTER (Listed by year of diary entry) |
|---|---|---|
| 1842 | IYM | Charles Osborn |
| 1845 | EMM | Enos Pray (Recorded minister, EMM) |
| 1850 | WQM | Benjamin Seaborn and Robert Lindsey from England |
| 1851–52 | EMM | Naome Coffin of Whitewater MM |
| 1853–54 | EMM | Eli Newlin of Bloomfield MM, Indiana |
| 1856 | WQM | Thomas Jay of West Branch MM |
| | EMM | Nathan Stacy of Wabash MM |
| 1859 | EMM | Mary Roberts (Recorded minister, EMM) |
| | EMM | John Miles of Milford MM |
| | EMM | Hannah Pierson and husband, Thomas, of Lockport, New York |
| 1860 | EMM | Joseph Doane and wife of Center, Ohio |
| | IYM | Joel Bean of Red Cedar, Iowa |
| 1861 | IYM | John Hodgkin from England |
| 1862 | EMM | Thomas Jay of West Branch |
| | IYM | Joshua Douglas from Maine |
| | EMM | Arneat Black of Greenwood Monthly Meeting, Indiana |
| 1864 | EMM | Ann Marmon, a young Minister of Whitewater MM |
| | WQM | Daniel Williams; Nathan Douglas of the State of Maine; David H. Bennett of the State of New York; John Elliott of Ohio; and Eli Newlin |
| 1865 | EMM | Jane Jones from Honey Creek MM |
| | EMM | William Beard of Salem MM |
| | EMM | Owen Edgerton of Whitewater MM |
| | IYM | English Friends, Joseph B. Bealthwait [*sic*][1] and Joseph Craftsfield |
| | IYM | John Henry Douglas of Center, Ohio |

1. i.e., Joseph Bevan Braithwaite.

| DIARY YEAR | MEETING | TRAVELING or VISITING MINISTER (Listed by year of diary entry) |
|---|---|---|
| 1866 | WQM | Milton Winstow of Back Creek MM |
| | WQM | Wright Book from Vermillion, Illinois and Charles Fleoffers of Richmond, Indiana |
| | WQM | Elwood Ashburn from Iowa and Mary N. Hadley of Springfield, Ohio |
| 1867 | Miami QM | Irone Jay of Indiana and Zeri Hough of New Garden MM |
| | WQM | Elkanah Beard from Cherry Grove and John Jessups of Dover |
| | WQM | Thomas Jay of West Branch |
| | EMM | Charles Swain of Eaton, Ohio, a Minister of the Methodist Church |
| | EMM | John L. Fall, a Minister of the Wesleyan congregation of New Paris, Ohio |
| | EMM | Martha Ann Taylor (Recorded minister, EMM) |
| | EMM | Martha Watkins of Goshen, Ohio, and Nathan Ogleby, a Minister of the Methodists in Middletown |
| 1868 | EMM | Allen Jay, a Minister of Greenfield MM, Indiana |
| | EMM | Stephen H. Leas of New Garden MM |
| | EMM | Warvel L. Francis, a United Brethren Minister, and D. Lancaster, Methodist |
| | WQM | Levi Jeppart from Richmond; Rufus King of Walnut Ridge MM; and Vienna Johnson of Cherry Grove MM |
| | EMM | Jesse L. Hartley, a Minister of Gilead MM, Ohio; Levi Francis, a United Brethren Minister |
| | WQM | William Brown of Salem MM |
| | WQM | Jesse Johnson from Cherry Grove MM, Indiana |
| | WQM | Miles Mendenhall of Springfield and Priscilla Hedgecock of Ripe Creek, Indiana |
| 1869 | WQM | William Laughton of Raysville, Indiana |
| | WQM | Thomas Hannate of Miami and Thomas Miller of Springsboro |

| DIARY YEAR | MEETING | TRAVELING or VISITING MINISTER (Listed by year of diary entry) |
|---|---|---|
| | WQM | Thomas Jay of West Branch MM |
| 1870 | WQM | Miles Mendenhall of Springfield, Indiana |
| | WQM | Joseph Pemberton of West Branch MM; also Enos Pemberton |
| | GMW | Robert W. Douglas and Daniel Hill |
| | WQM | Hazel D. Green and Gershom Purdue of Fairfield, Ohio |
| 1871 | WQM | Isaac Roberts of Richmond; Mordecai M. Gilbert of Hopewell MM; Ruth Johnson of Cherry Grove MM; A.M. Kenworthy |
| | WQM | Joseph and Enos Pemberton of West Branch MM |
| | IYM | Enos Pray; William Roberts; Jane Jones; Elijah Hodson of New Garden MM; Joseph Moore and Susannah B. Pedwick |
| | WQM | Owen West of Fairfield, Ohio and Levi Jessup |
| 1872 | WQM | David J. McMillan and Robert Hodson from Bridgeport and Plainfield, Indiana |
| | WQM | Sarah Ann Linton of Center, Ohio; William Gilbert and Rebecca Talbert |
| | EMM | Enos Pemberton of West Branch |
| | WQM | Joseph Wright; William West; Joseph and Enos Pemberton; Rebecca Talbert |
| 1873 | WQM | John Jessup of Dover, Indiana; Jared Binford of Carthage, Indiana |
| | WQM | Thomas Miller of Springsborough; John Jessups of Dover; William West; J. Daniels; Amos Kenworthy; Rebecca Talbert |
| | WQM | Mahlon Hocket of Walnut Ridge, Indiana; Jesse Pierson of Union |
| | WQM | John Allen of Deerbrush, Indiana |
| 1874 | EMM | Lewis Francis of U.B. [United Brethren] and John L. Fall of the Wesleyan Methodists |
| | EMM | William Allen of Richmond, Indiana, "a Colored Man and member" |

| DIARY YEAR | MEETING | TRAVELING or VISITING MINISTER (Listed by year of diary entry) |
|---|---|---|
| | WQM | Joseph Hobson of Gilead, Ohio; Jaret P. Binford of Carthage, Indiana |
| | EMM | Rachel H. Maddock (Recorded minister, EMM) |
| | EMM | Elwood Osborne from Iowa |
| | WQM | William Allen of Oak Ridge, Indiana |
| | EMM | N. McLain and E. Burris, two young men from Indiana, David L. Coppock of West Branch |
| 1875 | EMM | Harris Howard, "a Unionist of Cincinnati" |
| | WQM | Benjamin and Louisa Fulghum of Milford; Hazel D. Green of Fairfield |
| | WQM | William West of Caesar's Creek |
| | IYM | Rufus King, "an honored and beloved young Friend" |
| | EMM | Noah C. McLain, "a young colored man and acknowledged Minister" |
| 1877 | WQM | Isaac Jay; the Mills of Cherry Grove; Noah C. McLain |
| | EMM | David Tatum, Minister of Cleveland, Ohio; and his wife a Minister |
| | IYM | Stanley Humphrey and wife and Walter Robinson from England; Robert W. Douglas of Center Quarterly Meeting |
| 1878 | EMM | Noah C. McLain |
| | WQM | Stanley Humphrey and wife from England; Noah C. McLain |
| 1879 | WQM | Samuel Pitts of Dover; David Jay Coppock of New Garden, Indiana; "young friend" Rhoda J. Thomas of West Branch, Ohio |
| | EMM | "young friend" Helen C. Balkwill of England; Anna S. Ritchie of Whitewater |
| | WBQM[2] | C. F. Coffin of Richmond |
| | EMM | Anna S. Ritchie, and her husband, Samuel Ritchie |

2. WQBM, West Branch Quarterly Meeting, Orthodox.

| DIARY YEAR | MEETING | TRAVELING or VISITING MINISTER (Listed by year of diary entry) |
|---|---|---|
| | WQM | Thomas Jay and William West; Enos Pemberton |
| | IYM | Stanley Humphrey from England |
| | WQM | Samuel Pitts; James P. Hayworth of Illinois |
| 1880 | WQM | John Jessups of Dover; Isaiah Jay of Indiana |
| | IYM | Sarah B. Satterwaite and Mary White from England |
| 1881 | EMM | Myron T. Hartley of Michigan; Rebecca E. Talbert of Spiceland, Indiana |
| | WQM | Thomas Miller of Springborough |
| | WQM | Thomas Jay and Enos Pemberton of West Branch; William G. Hubbard of Columbus, Ohio |
| | EMM | Mary C. Moon, the Minister of Oak Ridge, Indiana |
| | EMM | John Jessup and Samuel Pitts of Dover, Indiana; William S. Wooten of Danville, Indiana |
| 1882 | WQM | Enos Pemberton of West Branch; Elwood Ellis of Jonesboro, Indiana |
| | WWQM[3] | Isaac Sharp of Darlington, England; Joel Bean of San Francisco |
| 1883 | WQM | Susan Ratliff of Mississinewa; Seth Reece of Cherry Grove; Elizabeth Reynolds |
| | EMM | Stewart Noble from Colorado ("talented speaker," evangelist" and "don't appear to be a member of any church" |
| | — | Harvey Derbyshire, "had attended Westfield Quarterly Meeting many years ago as a minister from Canada" |
| | EMM | Jared P. Binford and Amos C. Hill from Walnut Ridge |
| | WQM | Thomas Jay of West Branch; Eli Cook and Dillon H. Williams of West Grove |
| | WYM[4] | Isaac Sharp of England |
| | EMM | Sarah Coat of West Branch |

3. Whitewater Quarterly Meeting, Orthodox, in Richmond, Indiana.
4. Western Yearly Meeting, Orthodox.

| DIARY YEAR | MEETING | TRAVELING or VISITING MINISTER (Listed by year of diary entry) |
|---|---|---|
| | WQM | Jacob Moore of Richmond |
| 1884 | EMM | Joseph Wright and Daniel Hill of New Vienna, Ohio |
| | WQM | Joseph A. Binford of Walnut Ridge |
| 1885 | EMM | Harvey and Alice Bergman of Van Wert, Ohio; William J. Thornberrry and N.C. McLain of Goshen |
| | EMM | R. W. Douglas |
| 1886 | WQM | Enos Pemberton and Rhoda Thomas of West Branch, Ohio |

# Appendix B: More on Wrightsborough's Joseph Maddock: "The Quaker Migration to the South" by Ralph Hayes

## Edited by Sarah Shaw Tatoun

*This account from Ralph Hayes, a Maddock descendant whom many of us 'cousins' are grateful to for the bulk of our information, gives a very good picture of Quaker migrations South, following the fate of one couple, Joseph and Rachel (Dennis) Maddock. I have cut out some sections which had to do mainly with Joseph and his family so that the story would be of general interest to those with Southern Quaker ancestry, but the whole story of Joseph's long life is fascinating and should be known by all his descendants.* —S.S.T.

About 1740 Josef Maddock married Rachel Dennis, daughter of Samuel and Ruth (Tindall) Dennis, at Haddonfield, New Jersey. It appears that the young couple settled in Chester County, Pennsylvania, and the records show that for a time Joseph was a magistrate in that county. On 3 May 1746, Rachel Maddock was received as a member of Newark Monthly Meeting.

By this time many of the Pennsylvania Quakers, hungry for new lands, and losing their influence in the seacoast areas due to the influx of large members of people of other convictions, had begun to move south and west down the mountain valleys into North Carolina. Cane Creek Quaker Meeting was established in 1751 in Orange County (now

Alamance County), North Carolina, and the New Garden Meeting was established in 1754 in Guilford County. In the twenty-year period 1750–1770, Quaker settlements were established in numerous areas in both North and South Carolina.

The way was hazardous and hard. There were few roads and towns, no maps to show the way. And since the horses and wagons were loaded with all the worldly goods the settlers owned, most of the settlers and their families walked every step of the way. In addition, the Indians were a constant menace, and hundreds of settlers lost their lives to the Indians. But the lure of new lands for the taking was irresistible, and soon thousands of families were trekking southward and westward.

Preparations were made. Since only the family's most useful and valued possessions could be carried with them no doubt many of the family's possessions had to be sold. Goodbyes were said, and with one long, last look at their old home, the family set out on the long, difficult journey southward that fall of 1754, little knowing the hardships and sorrows that lay ahead. Their certificate from Newark MM was dated 3 Sep 1754 so they left after that. It is very probable that a number of families made the trip as a group including four of Rachel's brothers: John, Jacob, Isaac, and Abraham.

An examination of an early map makes it easy to determine by what route the little group traveled southward, for any good map of that area showed clearly that from the earliest colonial days a road of sorts extended southward from Wilmington, Delaware, through Baltimore, Maryland; Alexandria, Fredericksburg, Richmond, and Petersburg, Virginia; and then through Warrenton, North Carolina to Hillsboro in Orange County. Part of this route was over the Occaneechi Path, long used by the Indians to trade at the Indian village of Occaneechi. That village on the Roanoke River was long gone by the time our travelers came down the road. Present day Interstate Route #95 follows the course of this old road almost exactly all through Maryland and Virginia.

The records of Cane Creek Monthly Meeting, which was located fourteen miles south of the present-day town of Graham in Orange County (now Alamance County), show that on 2 November 1754 Joseph and Rachel Maddock and their daughters, Deborah and Mary, were received into membership by a certificate of transfer from Newark Monthly Meeting in Pennsylvania.

The family settled some ten or fifteen miles northeast of Cane Creek on the Eno River, near the present-day town of Hillsboro, North

Caroliina, and there Joseph built a grist mill. A mill was a valuable addition to a settlement, since it meant that the settlers could readily have their grain ground into meal and flour, and there is little doubt that Maddock's mill soon prospered.

Joseph and Rachel and their family settled down to life in North Carolina. The family prospered and life was good. The family was well-respected, and Joseph became a well-known citizen of the community.

During these years Joseph Maddock became close friends with two other influential citizens of the community, Hermon Husband and Jonathan Sell. All three were active Quakers. Husband was also a man of considerable property, and a contemporary writer describes him "as a man of superior mind, grave in deportment, somewhat taciturn, wary in conversation, but when excited, forcible and fluent in argument." He served as a member of the North Carolina Assembly in 1769 and 1770. About 1763, trouble started in Cane Creek Monthly Meeting which was to considerably change the lives of each of these three friends.

In 1762 Rachel Wright, a member of Cane Creek Meeting, committed some forbidden act and was disowned.[1] As was then customary, she submitted a paper confessing and condemning her act and requested reinstatement. This was apparently accepted, but when in 1763 she asked for a certificate of transfer to Fredericksburg, South Carolina, she was accused of insincerity in her confession, and the certificate was refused. This caused a considerable squabble among the membership of the meeting. Hermon Husband so loudly and publicly condemned the actions of the Meeting that on 7 January 1764 he was disowned by Cane Creek Meeting, and he was never again to become a Quaker.

A group of Husband's supporters, led by Joseph Maddock and Jonathan Sell, presented a paper to the Meeting expressing dissatisfaction with the disowning of Husband, whereupon the whole matter was referred to the next higher authoritative body, Western Quarterly Meeting. The Quarterly Meeting, in February 1764 decreed the suspension from membership

1. NOTE from MDH: Rachel Wright was a recorded minister in the Meeting, married to a recorded minister, and she had played an important part in the founding of Cane Creek MM. In 1761, her fifteen-year-old daughter was disowned when a young man in the Meeting bragged that he had carnal relations with her and several other girls. Though Rachel's daughter denied it emphatically, she was disowned. Rachel's "forbidden act" was in speaking sharply to defend her daughter and protest her disownment. For this, Rachel herself was disowned. She "produced a certificate" apologizing for her behavior, but apparently some in the meeting did not believe she was truly remorseful. See Roberta Tuller, "Cane Creek Dispute."

of Maddock, Sell, and the other dissidents. Maddock, Sell, and the other members of their group then appealed to the highest authority available to them. The Yearly Meeting decided that the Western Quarterly Meeting had been in error; Rachel Wright received her certificate; and Joseph Maddock and his fellow dissidents were restored to membership. However, Hermon Husband had apparently made too many enemies among his Quaker brethren, and he was not restored to membership. Officially the matter was closed, and Joseph Maddock and Jonathan Sell continued to be active members in the church. However, the wounds were not healed, and there continued to be dissension, and this no doubt contributed to the eventual exodus of Maddock, Sell, and others.

When the people of North Carolina began to rebel against British taxes, a group called the "Regulators" called an historic meeting at Maddock's Mill in 1766. They advertised their rallies to be at Maddock's Mill because there was no liquor there. This must have been too much for Joseph and his peace-loving Quakers. On 1 Sep 1767 [Quaker] Joseph Stubbs presented to the Georgia governor a petition of "sundry families at present residents in Orange County in the Provence of North Carolina but lately from Pennsylvania, setting forth that they were desirous to remove into and become settlers in this province, and praying that a reserve of land for that purpose might be made for a certain time." As a result of this petition, 12,000 acres [in Georgia] were reserved for them. On 18 Feb 1768 another 12,000 acres were reserved. Under the system of granting land then in force, the head of a family was authorized two hundred acres and fifty acres for his wife and fifty acres for each child. In late 1767 or early 1768, Joseph and about seventy Quaker families and peace-minded neighbors moved further along the Occaneechi Path to Georgia to get away from the political intrigue in North Carolina. On 25 July 1768 [Joseph] petitioned for two hundred acres to build a gristmill on the north fork of Briar Creek called Sweetwater [near what would become Wrightsborough, Georgia]. The petition was approved but not granted until 2 April 1771.

Joseph was a founder of Wrightsborough, Georgia, about thirty-five miles from Augusta, on the border of what became the Ceded Lands. He served as a commissioner for the sale of the Ceded Lands tracts to prospective settlers. On 3 July 1770 he and Jonathan Sell received a grant of five hundred acres on the north fork of Briar Creek called Sweetwater Creek above Joseph's two hundred acres about ten or eleven miles southeast of Wrightsborough village, although still in Wrightsborough Township, as a trust for the Quakers. The land was used as a communal cow pen. A deed for another piece of land in this area mentioned it as being bordered for a mile by Maddock land. Joseph also bought lot number 66 in Wrightsborough town on 3 July 1770. The town was located on Town Creek, Wrightsborough Township (now called Middle Creek), and the Township included all of the present McDuffie County, and portions of Warren and Columbia Counties in Georgia.

The settlement grew faster than expected and on 6 December 1768 Joseph Maddock and Jonathan Sell presented another petition to the Governor that was approved on 7 February 1769, namely: that more land be allocated, a road be built, the land be surveyed, and warrants be issued.

On twenty-two different occasions between 1768 and 1774 various petitions, orders, and other matters affecting the town and township of Wrightsborough were noted in the minutes of the Governor and Council. Perhaps the most serious matters considered were the Indian depredations, because marauding bands continually stole [the settlers'] horses and cattle, with practically no protection given to the Quakers by the government. In fact, in 1769 there was such a total loss of stock that they could barely plant and cultivate any crops at all. From fear of the Indians, some twenty-five heads of families left the settlement in 1771, but of these, thirteen soon returned. By 1772 [the settlers'] situation was so desperate that they proposed enlisting two companies of militia from their own number, but this offer was not accepted. During all of that period of five years, the government appropriated only one hundred pounds for their protection, plus fifty pounds for a fort built in 1774.

The Quakers had great trouble during and after the Revolutionary War.[2] Many of the settlers were declared traitors and their property confiscated. The Quakers were exempt from banishment and confiscation but were taxed an extra 25% in place of serving in the militia. It is not known if Joseph was a Loyalist[3] during the war or just a pacifist as were the Quakers generally.

2. Officially, the Revolutionary War lasted from 1775–1783, but the years before and after were unsettled and disruptive.

3. NOTE from MDH: Much that follows this statement calls it into question. Documents exist that show Joseph Maddock openly supporting the Loyalist side. In 1774, he was one of the signers of "A Protest of Declaration of Dissent of the Inhabitants of St. Paul's Parish, against any Resolutions expressive of Disloyalty to our Most Gracious King, and the Lords and Commons of Great Britain." See "Revolutionary Documents," Georgia Historical Collections.

> On 12 October 1774, just after the Boston Tea Party, Joseph and others (many Quakers) signed a petition in support of the British king. In their petition they expressed dissent with a resolution in South Carolina supporting the people of Boston and outlined four reasons for their support of the government of Great Britain: 1) resolutions against the King and Parliament were illegal, 2) grievances can be resolved legally through their representative in the Assembly, 3) since they had no dealing in destroying the tea, they should not partake of the consequences either, and 4) they could not expect any assistance from the forces of Great Britain against an Indian war if they supported the Boston people. They felt that their area would be laid waste by an Indian attack if British forces did not help them.[4]

By 1779 the settlers in Wrightsborough were having a very difficult time. As if the war was not enough, the colony was plagued by lawless bands of raiders who looted, burned, and killed everything in their path. By 1780 Wrightsborough was laid waste. In March 1781 Joseph's plantation and mill on Sweetwater Creek were burned by the raiders. Since he had been a Magistrate, Deputy Governor, and Clerk of Wrightsborough Monthly Meeting, priceless records were destroyed. In 1775 part of Joseph's property was sold by the Marshal of Savannah, and Joseph went bankrupt. In 1782 a group including some Quakers was ordered to serve as soldiers for two years. This created a real dilemma since their lands would be seized if they did not serve and [they would be] dismissed from the church if they did. As a result of the Revolution, twenty members were dealt with by the Wrightsborough Monthly Meeting for military activities, of whom fifteen were disowned.

> Joseph Maddock had particular reason to fear the wrath of the rebels. He had done all that he could to support Royal Governor Wright and the King's cause. In July 1775, he declined to take the seat to which he had been elected at the Whig's Second Georgia Provincial Congress. The following month, Maddock joined some forty prominent frontiersmen in signing a petition opposed to Georgia meetings that supported the Boston Tea Party. When that petition was refused by the Whigs, Joseph and a few other Wrightsborough Quakers joined the hundreds of backcountry Georgians who signed new protests that were published in the Georgia *Gazette*. In November, he travelled to Savannah to present Governor Wright with an officially sanctioned letter

4. Ralph Hayes. "Notes on Joseph Maddock."

> from his Monthly Meeting of their non-involvement with the rebels. When a British agent arrived in Wrightsborough in early 1779, Joseph Maddock helped him to find guides to South Carolina, to recruit a regiment of Loyalists there. The British army briefly occupied nearby Augusta shortly afterwards and the Quaker leader was part of a delegation of Friends sent to meet with the commanding officer. For these activities, Maddock was soon arrested by the rebels, interrogated, and imprisoned at Charlestown, South Carolina, for several months.[5]

In the summer of 1780, all of Georgia and most of South Carolina was restored to royal rule. However, by the following year, the tide of war had again shifted as rebel guerrillas, led in part by former Wrightsborough Quaker, Josiah Dunn, were operating on the Georgia frontier, killing and plundering persons who had supported the King's cause; those who had not militarily supported the American cause; and, in some instances, those who simply had property worth stealing. By the end of May 1781, thirty-five persons on the frontier were reported to have been killed by these raiders, including eleven settlers who were murdered in their own beds.

Joseph sought refuge in British-occupied Ebenezer, Georgia, in the autumn of 1781, bringing with him [as refugees]some one-fourth of the Wrightsborough Quakers. At nearby Savannah, Sir James Wright had been restored as Royal Governor, and he provided the Friends with financial aid.

With Wright's assistance, Maddock and his followers also applied through Daniel Silsby to the London Meeting for (Friends) Sufferings for aid. In these papers, the story of the Wrightsborough Quaker community is told from its beginnings in Pennsylvania *circa* 1754. Also described in detail are the hardships the community suffered during the Revolution, particularly those that involved Joseph Maddock.

However, Joseph's troubles were not over. He and his fellow Quakers continued to suffer from the same food shortages, severe weather, and diseases that were afflicting other refugees. On 1 May 1782, they petitioned Governor Wright to allow them to return to Wrightsborough to take their chances with the rebels. Despite their claim that the violence had abated, their request was turned down. [When]Savannah was evacuated by the British army on 11 July 1782, the Quaker refugees returned to Wrightsborough. Shortly afterwards, Daniel Silsby informed them that they would be allowed to draw up to five hundred pounds upon the account of the London Friends.

5. Hayes. "Notes on Joseph Maddock."

By 1784 the Quakers tried to resume their lives as before, but so many non-Quakers had moved into the colony bringing with them slaves, that Quakers could no longer do as they wished. Unable to compete with slave labor and unhappy with the conditions, the Quakers began a general exodus from Wrightsborough about 1803 that was completed by 1805. Joseph remained in Wrightsborough throughout this period and lost almost everything. He died a poor man on 9 April 1794. Rachel did not die until 18 Aug 1823, but it is not known if she remained in Wrightsborough or migrated with one of her sons or daughters to Ohio or Indiana.[6]

6. NOTE from MDH: The information given here re the deaths of Joseph Maddock and Rachel (Denis) Maddock is erroneous, though it still exists in all the sources Ralph Hayes may have found. There is no known record *per se* of Joseph Maddock's death, but his will was probated in December 1796. At least one source indicates that Joseph Maddock (1720–1796) married a second time, i.e., to Mary Watson in 1784, which would have to have been after Rachel died. See Engstrom, NCpedia.

There is also no known record in Quaker minutes of Rachel (nee Dennis) Maddock's death, nor of her admittance to Quaker meetings in Ohio or Indiana. There is mention of her in Wrightsborough MM minutes in 1774, when a certificate from Hopewell Monthly Meeting in South Carolina is read informing that Rachel Maddock and a group of other Friends from Wrightsborough had arrived there in a group in July 1774. A Rachel Maddock is mentioned in the minutes of 1797 as representing Wrightsborough MM at the Newberry Quarterly Meeting in July. But that could refer to her daughter-in-law, Rachel (nee Jones) Maddock (wife of son Samuel Maddock), who moved to Preble County in 1805 with her husband, elderly father, and two sons. She died August 18, 1823 in Preble County, Ohio.

# Bibliography

Balfour, Clara Lucas. *Morning Dew Drops.* 1853. Digitized by Google. https://books.google.com/books?id=nSg3Fwmpea4C&pg=PR9&source=gbs_selected_pages&cad=1#v=onepage&q&f=false (accessed December 2025).

Carter, Jimmy. "Author's Q & A" #4. *The Hornet's Nest.* New York: Simon & Schuster, 2003.

Davis, Robert Scott. "Children of Dissent and Revolution: Joseph Maddock and the Wrightsborough, Georgia, Quaker Community." *Quaker History* 99, no. 1 (2010): 1–14. http://www.jstor.org/stable/41947684 (accessed October 2025).

Engstrom, Mary Claire. "Joseph Maddock." *Dictionary of North Carolina Biography*, 1991. NCPedia. https://www.ncpedia.org/biography/maddock-joseph (accessed October 2025).

"Epizooty." Merriam-Webster.com Dictionary, Merriam-Webster, https://www.merriam-webster.com/dictionary/epizooty (accessed November 2025).

"Gratis Township, The First School." *History of Preble County, Ohio, with Illustrations and Biographical Sketches.* H. Z. Williams & Brothers (1881): 198. https://archive.org/details/oh-preble-1881-williams/page/n247/mode/2up (accessed Dec 2025).

"Greenback: The Ultimate Guide to America's First Paper Money." U.S. Law Explained. https://uslawexplained.com/greenback (accessed December 2025).

Hayes, Ralph. "Notes on Joseph Maddock." Roots web. https://freepages.rootsweb.com/~wrightsborough/genealogy/maddock.htm (accessed October 2025).

———. Sarah Shaw Tatoun, Ed. "Quaker Migration to the South." Southern Quakers. Geocities.org. https://geocities.restorativland.org/Heartland/Plains/2064/ (accessed 2023).

"Joseph Moore Museum, About." Earlham College.edu. https://jmm.earlham.edu/about-the-jmm/our-history/ (accessed December 2025).

Klein, Daniel B. and John Majewski. "Turnpikes and Toll Roads in Nineteenth-Century America." Economic History Association. https://eh.net/encyclopedia/turnpikes-and-toll-roads-in-nineteenth-century-america/ (accessed November 2025).

Little, Becky. "The 1840 U.S. Census Was Overly Interested in Americans' Mental Health," updated May 27, 2025. History.com. https://www.history.com/articles/census-change-mental-illness-controversy (accessed November 2025).

Mauldin, Ashley, *et al.* "Vitreous Degeneration. What Is It, Causes, Severity, Treatment, and More." Osmosis.org. https://www.osmosis.org/answers/vitreous-degeneration (accessed December 2025).

"Old Colorado City." NorthAmericanForts.com. https://www.northamericanforts.com/West/co3.html, (accessed 20 Dec 2025).

Prechtel-Kluskens, Claire. "The Nineteenth-Century Postmaster and His Duties." TwelveKey.com. https://twelvekey.com/wp-content/uploads/2014/10/ngsmagazine 2007-01.pdf (accessed December 2025).

"Representative Clement Vallandigham of Ohio." Historical Highlights. United States House of Representatives.gov. https://history.house.gov/Historical-Highlights/1800-1850/Representative-Clement-Vallandigham-of-Ohio/ (accessed December 2025).

"Revolutionary Documents Connected with the History of Richmond County." Georgia Historical Collections. Ancestry.com. https://www.ancestry.com/imageviewer/collections/6706/images/GenRef-Hist-Collection-GA-000617?pId=617 (accessed November 2025).

Siebert, Wilbur. *The Underground Railroad: From Slavery to Freedom*, Appendix E, p. 428. Internet Archive. https://archive.org/details/DKC0090/page/n469/mode/2up?q=Appendix+E (accessed November 2025).

Smith, Lewis. "Whatever Happened to Wrightsboro?" *The McDuffie Progress*, March 12. 2019. https://www.mcduffieprogress.com/opinion/what-ever-happened-to-wrightsboro/article_d1f922ce-4518-11e9-9f37-9f3cefb5fbad.html (accessed October 2025).

"Supplicate." *The 1828 Webster's Dictionary*. https://webstersdictionary1828.com/Dictionary/supplicate (accessed December 2025).

Tuller, Roberta. "Cane Creek Dispute," 2020. An American Family History.com. https://www.anamericanfamilyhistory.com/Quakers/Meeting%20Cane%20Creek%20 Dispute.html (accessed December 2025).

"Value of $1 from 1864 to 2025." CPI Inflation Calculator. https://www.in2013dollars.com/us/inflation/1864?amount=1 (accessed December 2025).

Woodward, Joseph Janvier and Ira M. Rutkow. *The Hospital Steward's Manual: For The Instruction of Hospital Stewards, Ward-Masters, and Attendants, in Their Several Duties*. United States Army Medical Dept, Internet Archive. https://archive.org/details/hospitalstewardoowoodgoog/page/n52/mode/2up?q=ward-master (accessed December 2025).

# Index

www.ingramcontent.com/pod-product-compliance
Lightning Source LLC
LaVergne TN
LVHW050621100826
845148LV00011B/1675

* 9 7 9 8 3 8 5 2 6 9 9 9 0 *